TRAVEL
temptations

SIP

CALIFORNIA

Delicious Destinations,
Secret Hideaways,
Expert Sources

LENA KATZ

travel
Guilford, Connecticut

The prices and rates listed in this guidebook were confirmed at press time. We recommend, however, that you call establishments to obtain current information before traveling.

To buy books in quantity for corporate use
or incentives, call **(800) 962–0973**
or e-mail **premiums@GlobePequot.com.**

Text design by Sheryl P. Kober
Maps © 2009 Morris Book Publishing, LLC

Library of Congress Cataloging-in-Publication Data is available on file.

ISBN 978-0-7627-5076-4

Printed in China

10 9 8 7 6 5 4 3 2 1

CONTENTS

WINERY
ENTRANCE

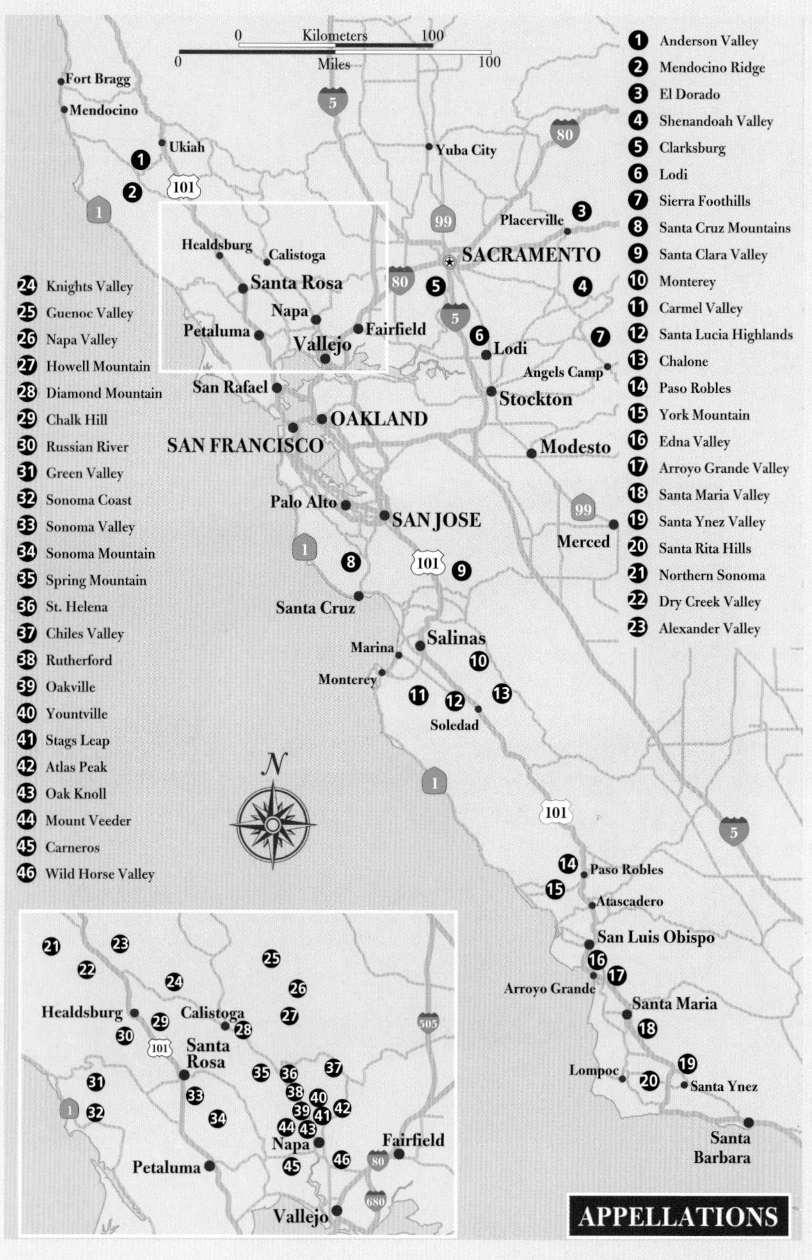
APPELLATIONS
1 Anderson Valley
2 Mendocino Ridge
3 El Dorado
4 Shenandoah Valley
5 Clarksburg
6 Lodi
7 Sierra Foothills
8 Santa Cruz Mountains
9 Santa Clara Valley
10 Monterey
11 Carmel Valley
12 Santa Lucia Highlands
13 Chalone
14 Paso Robles
15 York Mountain
16 Edna Valley
17 Arroyo Grande Valley
18 Santa Maria Valley
19 Santa Ynez Valley
20 Santa Rita Hills
21 Northern Sonoma
22 Dry Creek Valley
23 Alexander Valley
24 Knights Valley
25 Guenoc Valley
26 Napa Valley
27 Howell Mountain
28 Diamond Mountain
29 Chalk Hill
30 Russian River
31 Green Valley
32 Sonoma Coast
33 Sonoma Valley
34 Sonoma Mountain
35 Spring Mountain
36 St. Helena
37 Chiles Valley
38 Rutherford
39 Oakville
40 Yountville
41 Stags Leap
42 Atlas Peak
43 Oak Knoll
44 Mount Veeder
45 Carneros
46 Wild Horse Valley
0 Kilometers 100
0 Miles 100
Fort Bragg
Mendocino
Ukiah
Yuba City
Placerville
SACRAMENTO
Healdsburg
Calistoga
Santa Rosa
Napa
Petaluma
Fairfield
Vallejo
Lodi
Angels Camp
San Rafael
Stockton
OAKLAND
SAN FRANCISCO
Modesto
Palo Alto
SAN JOSE
Merced
Santa Cruz
Salinas
Marina
Monterey
Soledad
N
Paso Robles
Atascadero
San Luis Obispo
Arroyo Grande
Santa Maria
Lompoc
Santa Ynez
Santa Barbara
5
80
101
1
99
505
680

PREFACE

We are fortunate enough to live in a time when "making the most out of life" is encouraged—and experiential travel is an important part of that.

In case you're not familiar with this concept, it means this: Get out of your bubble and give yourself over to the destination and the culture you're visiting, because *that's* how you get the most out of it. Immerse yourself in the customs, food, music, lodgings, fashion, landscape, nature, and personalities in each destination. Give up your normal boundaries and routines. When in Rome, drink Chianti and wear Prada.

Travel is only one of many pieces in the busy, modern lifestyle—and a small one, compared to career and family. Trips often get squeezed into four- to seven-day slots, interspersed throughout the year. Which is fine . . . as long as you don't waste a single hard-earned getaway day.

Whether because of the sped-up pace of life or the human tendency to pigeonhole things, people often look at the world through the "next big thing" paradigm: Santa Barbara is the next Napa. Croatia is the next Ibiza. Cabo is the Vegas of Mexico. And so on. This is the worst attitude a traveler can adopt. Every destination in the world—or at least every one that you'd want to visit—has its own characteristics and specialties. Find what's unique about a destination, and you've found its essence. Everything else falls into place around that.

These are not standard guidebooks—they're destination-focused playbooks that hone in on what's unique about a destination and what it does best. They're equal parts education, inspiration, and aspiration. They're not formulaic. No two interviews are alike. Their purpose is to forearm you with knowledge, get you past any invisible walls or unfriendly zones, and ensure your time is well spent.

I write with the help of a couple hundred people—some of whom are in the "expert galleries," and some who stayed off the record. All of them freely donated their time and wisdom, knowing exactly whom this book would reach. And as far-fetched as it may seem, they were all equally excited to share their best insider knowledge with you. Pick your temptation and pack your bags!

ACKNOWLEDGMENTS

I could not possibly have written this book without massive support from everyone in the California wine industry, as well as the travel/hospitality folks in all eight regions. Many thanks to Shannon Brooks of the CVB and Jim Fiolek of the local vintners association in Santa Barbara (my guinea pig chapter) for endless patience and great picks. Napa . . . seriously, as a county, you amazed me. Special thanks to Paul Wagner, Tim Hanni, Tim Gaiser, and Catherine Seda for sharing your wealth of knowledge and insane Rolodexes. Mark Pope, for giving me Cab picks you hadn't even released to your mailing list yet. Gillian Balance, you're a rock star. Eden Umble, Michael Wangbickler, and all the PR people, thank you for holding it down. Mendocino and the girls at Hype House . . . Chris Taranto, the one-man army behind Paso Robles . . . Pooch and Mark up in Gold Country . . . thanks so much for all the picks, and when are you going to write your own books already? Huge props to Michael Heintz, Kristine Keefer, Jo Diaz, Carrie Head, Tim Zahner, and other coordination superstars, without whom I wouldn't have the juicy stuff. And of course I cannot forget all-star intern Estelle Wagner, my wonderful agent Andrea Somberg, and editors Kaleena Cote and Amy Lyons. Lastly, to all my experts—thanks for giving us your best.

ABOUT THIS BOOK

What's the deal with this book?
This is an experiential travel book for the quick getaway traveler who's only going to a specific spot for three to five days and wants to get the most out of that time. The point is to get right to the best things the destination has to offer, skipping all the confusions and shoulda-woulda-couldas. This is not about traveling on a shoestring, nor is it about the forced march of hitting as many tourist traps as possible. Experiential travel is about feeling a sense of place, having adventures, connecting with people, and feeling like every minute and every penny was well spent.

How's it different from what I can get on the Web?
It's the polar opposite. The Web is information overload, coming from a zillion sources, and you usually don't have a clue as to who or what they are. This book offers specific, personal information that comes from forty to fifty local insiders: winery owners, pro athletes, hotel managers, chefs, and so on. In fact *every* venue, attraction, and activity has been chosen with their help. You can get to know them on the "panel" page at the beginning of each chapter, and many of them are conveniently quoted throughout the venue write-ups.

In addition to pointing out their favorite regional hot spots, our insiders give personal insight into whatever topic they know best. This is exclusive information—you cannot get it on the Web. It's also specifically written to be "evergreen" (meaning current for *at least* five years) and useful in a broad sense.

How is this book organized?
There are eight sections that cover the top eight destinations within California for wine-related activities. Each destination is organized not by geography but *by experience.* The reason for this is that each destination has a few things it does really well, which is what visitors come to experience. You can mix and match, and you'll know what you're in for.

If you prefer to plan your trips according to geography, that's fine. Our "Bird's-eye View" at the front of each section goes over basic geography and then breaks the destination down into what can be reached by car in one day.

If you want to make vacation planning *really* a no-brainer, we've compiled multiday experiential itineraries within each region.

Is there anything this book doesn't cover?
Yes, there is quite a bit this book doesn't cover: chains, most corporate-owned businesses, and anywhere that feels generic. If you've seen it advertised on a billboard, you probably won't read about it here. This book is dedicated to unique venues and signature experiences. Also, you won't find many rock-bottom-budget places, mega-splurges, or family-oriented places. (Note: Family *friendly* is different).

So, do the venue picks cover every place that's good in the destination?
Um, no. Were you seriously planning to hit every place in the destination in five days? Visiting 500 wineries, staying in 50 hotels . . . we think not. This book only covers the best spots, consistent with what the area does best, as determined by people with the best taste. While the overall selection process was terribly difficult, the ones that made the cut definitely earned their spots.

Should I skip places that aren't in the guide?
You should do as you wish—spontaneity is a beautiful thing. However, it's also a gamble. Whatever you choose to do, we'd love to receive any kind of feedback based on the travels you go on and the experiences you become a part of.

SYMBOL KEY

- Admission/tasting fee (where applicable). Always Y/N, because the dollar amount changes.

Hours

- B/L/D + days for restaurants
- AM/PM/OWL + days for nightspots
- Days and notable oddities (AM only, by appt) for wineries and other attractions

Hotel Cost:

$	$100–175
$$	$175–250
$$$	$250–325
$$$$	$325+

Restaurant Cost:

$	Under $20 per person for meal, one drink, tax, tip
$$	$20–45
$$$	$45–70
$$$$	$70 and over

Key:

AT = attitude (the vibe, the service, etc.)

CHEESE = cheesy but likeable anyway

DS = date spot

FO = far out (a drive, and possibly not near anything else, but worth the trip)

GAY = gay friendly

LENA STAMP = Lena Katz's LK stamp of approval

LN = logistical nightmare (terrible parking, horrible traffic, etc.)

SF = Silver Foxes—AKA older clientele

PETS = dog friendly

PU = pickup spot

RR = reservations required (used sparingly)

XP = way expensive

KIDS = very family friendly, kids underfoot

SCENE = dress to impress (everyone on display, famous people, etc.)

SKETCH = a sketchy or super-edgy venue

TH = tourist haven (but in a nice way . . . the places you have to go, just because everyone does)

VEG = vegetarian friendly

FUNDAMENTALS OF TASTING

Tim Gaiser, education chair, the American Chapter of the Court of Master Sommeliers, and adjunct professor, Culinary Institute of America at Greystone

Before you taste

Everyone's senses of smell and taste are unique. When someone describes a wine and uses terms like *raspberries* or *shoe leather,* these are just handles. That's how we relate our experience of the wine. But those characteristics don't exist for everyone in the same way. If you're tasting new releases, the red wines—with the exception of Pinot Noir—are probably too young to drink. Cabernets and Merlots especially will tend to be tannic and astringent.

Accepting the glass

Make sure to hold the glass by the stem, because if you don't, any snobs who are around (and there are always snobs around) will judge you. And while it's not fair, they may think you're completely unsophisticated.

Look

Tilt the glass at a 45-degree angle, over a white background. Is the wine clear? Does it reflect light? Look at the color—both at the center "core" of the glass and at the edge. Look for the color green in a young white wine—it's a sign of chlorophyll in the wine from the unripe portions of the grape.

Swirl once

Look for viscosity by swirling the glass. How do the tears/legs drip down the sides of the glass? Slower, thicker tears are an indicator of higher alcohol content.

Swirl again

This releases the esters—aromatics—that are attached to the alcohol molecules in the wine.

Get the nose

Smell is the most important sense. Current research suggests we can smell 10,000 different things, but we can only taste five. Hold the glass at a 25- to 35-degree angle and take several short sniffs. Most people position it between their nose and upper lip, but some people need it farther away. Above all, don't bring the glass straight up to your nose. It must be at an angle.

Taste

When you taste, you're only confirming what you've smelled and checking the wine for the balance of fruit, acid, and (in red wines) oak/tannins. You're also getting the "mouth feel" and in red wine, seeing if it's smooth and approachable. Sip the wine, swirl it around, swish (don't be ridiculous about swishing or gargling), and swallow or spit. *Then* (important) sip in a little air to coat the inside of your mouth with the wine one more time.

Consider the finish

This is simply the aftertaste—the lingering fruit, minerality, acid, oak, tannin. How long is it? Is it smooth? Is it nice? Typically, the longer the finish, the better the wine.

Think

How does the fruit taste? How does it smell? Is it in balance? Or is it oaky, tannic, or hot?

Ordering Off the Wine List at a Restaurant

Why do restaurants give a taste of wine to the person who ordered it?

To make sure it's okay. Once upon a time, wine was tasted to make sure it wasn't fraudulent or poisoned. Now one tastes the wine to make sure it's not corked or otherwise bad. It is *not* to make sure you like it. If you order the wine, it's assumed that you know and like it. If it was recommended, that's a different situation. Proper wine service dictates that the restaurant should take back a bottle if a diner is unhappy with it.

How can you recognize cork taint?

Cork taint is usually caused by the presence of the chemical compound called TCA. It smells and tastes like wet, moldy cardboard and old books. The level at which individuals can detect TCA varies, even though a few parts per trillion can taint a wine.

YOU AND YOUR BUDS—NEW WORLD TASTING

Tim Hanni, Master of Wine, Certified Wine Educator, founder of WineQuest

From Napa to New York, Tim Hanni is rolling out a new wine tasting paradigm that is more inclusive and interactive than currently accepted. It asks people to evaluate their taste buds and their psychological values, and based on that, comes up with a tasting profile.

Are you a more sensitive or less sensitive taster?

Why you like what you like is greatly influenced by how many taste buds you have or don't have. The range is as follows: sweet, hypersensitive, sensitive, and tolerant. Tolerant tasters actually have fewer taste buds. These people crave intensity and don't mind bitterness and astringency. Sweet tasters are the opposite: They can't stand astringency and crave sweet flavors.

Do you care about wine tasting, and what influences do you care about?

The more aspirational you've become, the more psychological everything becomes. Aspiration could be memories, level of interest, importance placed on educational aspects. Do you like to explore? Do you have a high risk tolerance? Do you have a system you apply: points, trusted sources, and so on? Do you like the educational aspects, or do you just want to see what's out there independent of any of this stuff?

Through simple, self-guided tests available online at budology.com you can learn more about your own tasting profile and what kinds of wine you like before you ever arrive in wine country.

Remember: Where you go on the Budometer is declarative—meaning, you drive the experience. The more honest you are with yourself, the better your chances of finding what you like and having a good experience. There are 6.5 billion points of view on this earth, and no two are the same. So, two people can taste the same wine and have totally different experiences.

APPELLATIONS, OR WHAT'S IN AN AVA?

What is an appellation?
An appellation is a geographical identification that is used to recognize the region where the grapes for wine are grown. The rules that govern appellations are dependent on the country in which the wine was produced. The term *appellation* has historically been used within the United States to refer to politically designated borders (i.e., county lines); however that is becoming less frequent.

What is an American Viticultural Area (AVA)?
An AVA is the U.S. term for an officially recognized appellation of origin. The geographic pedigree of its wine, it is advertised by a tag on its label. An AVA must meet federal and state legal requirements. AVAs have distinct boundaries. AVAs are approved and have these boundaries defined by the Alcohol Tax and Trade Bureau (TTB).

What are sub-AVAs?
An AVA can apply for official recognition of sub-AVAs. Approval depends on whether it can provide empirical evidence (geological, microclimate, and so on) that supports the need for sub-AVA designation.

Information above provided by the Wine Institute. For more information visit www.wineinstitute.org or www.ttb.gov.

Roger Dial, Director, Appellation America

Why do we need AVAs?
Place identity is a huge psychological security zone for all human beings. How much of what you know about anything comes back to knowledge based on a "sense of place."

What's the point of learning anything about appellations?
It helps to discover and distinguish the signature or typical characteristics of wines from a certain place: What distinguishes wines of the Lodi AVA in California from the wines of the Santa Maria Highlands or the Texas High Plains? What should we be looking for? You'll be able to find real connections between the character of a place and the taste profile of its wine.

What came before the AVA?
The United States has a peculiar void historically. The rest of the world grew up knowing wine by its region. We got off on a track in the late 1960s of consumers knowing wines primarily by their variety and corporate name. However, in the late 1960s to the 1970s, there were fewer than 50 wineries; today there are more than 6,000 in North America.

What was the first officially designated AVA?
Augusta, Missouri.

How many AVAs are there now?
As of May 2008 there were 190 officially designated wine-growing regions in the United States.

How is the campaign for a new AVA initiated?
A group of producers or wine-growers stakes out an area of ground and says, "We're different than everywhere else." The ensuing process generally takes two to three years, though these days it's taking even longer. Applicants have to justify why they should be distinguished as a separate wine-growing region.

How do applicants do it?
Justification usually follows a mosaic of some sort of historical experience, geographical and/or microclimate distinctions, and some pretty obvious geographic parameters (from the river to the bottom of the mountain).

Why would applicants want to do this?
Sometimes it's market driven—they just want their own identity. Sometimes it's purely political. Sometimes it's only related to the geological and climate features of a specific area. Sometimes it's because the old political boundaries don't make sense.

How are appellations officially designated?
They must be officially recognized by the TTB.

***TT* Note:** The Great AVA Debate
AVAs are not set in stone, nor are the rules that govern them immutable. Conflicts arise around trademark names, marketing strategies, politics, and the natural competitiveness among neighbors in the same industry. Therefore the TTB has been very slow to officially recognize official AVAs in recent years—and now, it is at a virtual standstill. As Roger Dial puts it, "The TTB is in the middle of various family feuds—and nobody wants to be in the middle of a family feud."

Remember this as you travel through California's many AVAs and sub-AVAs. Winemakers are passionate about their chosen AVAs—and two neighboring AVAs' viewpoints might be diametrically opposed. At the end of the day, there is no one perfect map of AVAs, and no empirical evidence proving that one is better or worse than the rest.

For more information visit www.appellationamerica.com or www.discovercaliforniawine.com

0 Kilometers 10
0 Miles 10
N
LAKE COUNTY
YOLO COUNTY
NAPA COUNTY
SONOMA COUNTY
SOLANO COUNTY
Middletown
Lake Berryessa
Calistoga
Angwin
Deer Park
Napa River
St. Helena
Sonoma Highway
Rutherford
Oakville
Yountville
Kenwood
St. Helena Highway
Glen Ellen
Agua Caliente
Fetters Hot Springs
Boyes Hot Springs
El Verano
SONOMA
NAPA
Adobe Road
Travis Air Force Base
PETALUMA
Stage Gulch Road
Arnold Drive
FAIRFIELD
Jameson Canyon Road
Lakeville Road
Marine World Africa U.S.A
Sears Point Raceway
Sears Point Road
SAN PABLO BAY
VALLEJO
Grizzly Bay
53
175
29
128
16
12
121
221
116
101
37
80
680

NAPA

What can I say about Napa that hasn't been said already? Hmm . . .

How about *a lot*. In less than forty years this county has become a celebrated vacation destination—basically the only wine region in the United States with worldwide name recognition. And just like any no-last-name-required celebrity, it's acquired an epic and rather fearsome reputation that has little to do with reality. Casual visitors, critics, wine connoisseurs, and, yes, travel writers all have helped build this county's reputation as a beautiful yet snooty destination for the wealthy and privileged. "Sigh, boo . . . Napa has gone too commercial," is the refrain. Its wineries are derided as glossy tourist traps, where you pay $40 for a tiny taste and then get booted out the door. It is impossible, people say, to find family-owned wineries or tiny tasting rooms on picturesque little lanes, where a winemaker will talk to you about his latest vintage while pouring a generous taste.

The "experts" who claim this are either blind or crazy (or both), and the tourists are sadly misguided—and all of them need to get off Highway 29, because it's the source of 90 percent of their grief. Famous though it is, Highway 29 is only the tip of the Napa iceberg (or the first sip of the bottle, to use a more appropriate analogy). There are entire sub-appellations of Napa County where you can pretty much throw a rock and hit a family-owned boutique winery (though I wouldn't recommend it). There are dozens of tiny producers who don't have tasting rooms but who will happily arrange private tastings in their living rooms for people who bother to call and ask. Most of the winemakers who work for established brands also have half a dozen side projects of their own or in collaboration with colleagues. For every snobby tasting room employee terrifying the tourists on Highway 29, there are three friendly ones—who definitely know more about their product—up on Stag's Leap, or in Calistoga, or just off one of the small roads connecting Highway 29 with the Silverado Trail. As for the Trail itself, the wineries that border it run the gamut from famous to unknown, landmark to brand-new.

And if you should encounter snobbery along Silverado Trail, on the highway, or perhaps in St. Helena (where I certainly have), take comfort in this: Whatever little psychological games Napa Valley dwellers may play with you, they're perpetrating ten times worse on each other. Land is a scarce commodity, money is all over the place, everyone lives in each other's apron pockets, and as a result, the game of Nosy Neighbors takes on terrifying proportions. No one is wealthy enough to escape "newcomer on the block" status—but since all of Napa is, let's be honest, new money, each new millionaire gets assimilated into the landscape after a few harsh years. Meanwhile, winemakeres who prefer to battle elements other than the City Council move up to the mountain appellations and muck around with heavy machinery to their hearts' content.

The scene here is dynamic and exciting, competitive yet collaborative—and yes, wine is the *only* business (unless you count tourism separately, which I don't). Napa residents regret that a bit, and are prone to confessing that they wish their county was a little more diverse, like its neighbors. However, for better or for worse, Napa County has found its niche. Whether new to the neighborhood or old-time millionaire farmers, its residents are utterly dedicated to creating world-class wines.

A warm Wine Country welcome.

Getting Here

Napa has its own airport, but the only people who use it are those with private planes or helicopters. Regular people fly into San Francisco, Oakland, or Sacramento. The latter two are smaller and more convenient if you can swing it. The drive is just over an hour from Sacramento, an hour from Oakland, and about one and a half hours from San Francisco. Evans shuttle service goes to Oakland and San Francisco and conducts pickups/drop-offs from some hotels.

Weather

It's hot in the valley in summer—as hot as 100°F. November to February is rainy and cold, sometimes carrying over into March. The hottest time of year is July and August, with triple digits regularly. Because of a weather phenomenon known as diurnal swing, temperatures can drop by 30°F to 50°F at night. In winter it's chilly throughout, with a less extreme swing—possibly from 55°F degrees in the afternoon to 40°F at night.

Recommended Transportation

Booking a limo is probably the best way to go, as the drivers know where to go and how to get there. The pedestrian-friendly downtown areas are in St. Helena, Calistoga, downtown Napa, and Yountville. All of them have tasting rooms, shops, and restaurants—but the only way to get to the wineries is by car. Warning: Bike tours are dangerous everywhere except Calistoga, which has its own bike path.

Style

The style in Napa is business casual or resort casual—khakis and oxfords. A few restaurants require a jacket and tie. If you don't want to dress up, you don't have to—especially in the mountains—but in the valley you'll be treated a little more seriously if you are. Remember the extreme temperature fluctuations and always bring a sweater or a wrap.

Historic downtown Calistoga hasn't changed much in the past century.

Fees

Tasting fees generally run $5 to $20, but can get as high as $50 at the wineries known for premium Cabernet. For the most part the fee is waived if you purchase a bottle or more. Some of the small premium boutique wineries have no fee; but it's understood that if you get the private tasting appointment, you have serious intentions to buy. The huge "cattle call" wineries on Highway 29 don't typically require advance reservations—however, for most of the places in this book, it's a good idea to call ahead, especially if you want special tastings or tours.

Bird's-eye View

Highway 29 is the main artery and the place where you run the most risk of getting snob treatment. It cuts through all the towns on the valley floor. The Silverado Trail runs parallel and has good wineries that aren't as touristy or crowded. Traffic is not as heavy on this road. The small, perpendicular roads that connect the main thoroughfares have a rural feel: fields, vineyards, and long gravel driveways that lead to half-hidden vineyards.

The town of Napa is going through a renaissance. Formerly run-down and utilitarian, it's getting a city center and a number of major tourist developments. The focal point is the Napa River.

Yountville, Oakville, and Rutherford are small, expensive towns built around the wine industry. The only one that's also a restaurant/retail/hotel destination is Yountville. St. Helena is farther north. All the wealthy winery owners move here, making it an adorable but snooty little fishbowl. At the far north end of the county is Calistoga: a charming, historic outpost known for its healing mineral springs. It has more in common with Geyserville or Mendocino than with its southern neighbors.

Surrounding the valley floor are the mountain districts: Spring Mountain, Diamond Mountain, Howell Mountain, Atlas Peak, and Mount Veeder. These are rugged hillside lands—appropriate for preplanned day trips but not to spend the night.

Area Key:

NA = Napa Carneros, Stag's Leap

NV = Napa Valley AVAs including Yountville, Oakville, Rutherford

SH = St. Helena

NN = North Napa including Calistoga, Spring Mountain, Diamond Mountain, northern Napa County

The Panel

Gillian Balance, wine director, PlumpJack

Michael Dellar, chief executive officer, Lark Creek

Connie Gore, general manager, Milliken Creek

Violet Grgich, Grgich Hills

Thomas Keller, chef/owner, French Laundry and Bouchon

Mark Pope, owner, Bounty Hunter

David Rasmussen, owner, Eclectic Tours

Mike Reynolds, president, HALL

Sheldon Richards, president, Spring Mountain District Association

Darryl Sattui, owner, V. Sattui and Castello di Amorosa

Kate Stanley, event organizer, Napa Wine Auction

Legendary Napa

Napa is filled with marquee names, dynasties, legacies, landmark estates, visionaries, and yes, the winemakers who won the Paris tasting. If you want to understand what's so great about it, visit the venues in this section. They're not necessarily the ones you see plastered on billboards or the ones with the biggest tasting rooms. The selection process for this chapter considered substance over style—and one insider thumbs-up carried more weight than a million-dollar ad campaign.

WINERIES

Grgich Hills Estate
(NV) 1829 St. Helena Highway, Rutherford, (800) 532-3057, (707) 963-2784, www.grgich.com; Fee: Y; Open: Daily; Key: SCENE, AT

"You're in our cellar. It's very plain and extraordinarily comfortable and homey," is how Violet Grgich describes the tasting room at Grgich Hills. Indeed the plainness (and cellar-ish lighting) inspired many benevolent jokes among Napa wine business people over the years, and its recent update was the talk of the town.

Founder Miljenko (Mike) Grgich is currently the talk of the wine business, period. The Chardonnay he made while working at Chateau Montelena won the award at the Paris Wine Tasting in 1976. That was more than twenty years ago, but a recent slew of wine-related movies and books has stoked public interest to new heights. Grgich left Montelena in 1977 and has since produced world-class European-style wines under his own name. This winery is still family owned, and mid-day often finds eighty-something-year-old Mike Grgich in the tasting room talking to customers. All Grgich vineyards practice organic or biodynamic grape growing; in fact, this is one of the largest biodynamic grape-growing concerns in the country. Wines are known for being well balanced and food friendly. Chardonnay is the most famous varietal, but fans of Zin should check out the estate-grown Miljenko Old Vine Zin, from grapes grown on the Grgich's Calistoga estate. Visit Friday afternoon for barrel tasting.

LENA STAMP: Every three years Mike Grgich releases Violetta, a dessert wine named after his daughter. Now that's a sweet gesture every woman can appreciate.

Rubicon Estate
(NV) 1991 St. Helena Highway, Rutherford, (800) 782-4266, (707) 968-1100, www.rubiconestate.com; Fee: Y; Open: Daily; Key: TH, XP

As famous for its parentage as for its wines, the historic Niebaum-Coppola estate is easily as dramatic as any Coppola film set. It has potential to intimidate; however, excellent service ensures that visitors feel comfortable from the minute they pull into the (complimentary) valet parking station. The entrance to the grand château is

Growing Up Inside a Legend: Violet Grgich, daughter of Miljenko Grgich, founder of the Grgich Hills Estate

Warm, approachable, and often spotted behind a table pouring wine for civilians, Violet Grgich is the opposite of a scary heiress. In fact, she's the ideal person to clear up the myths and misperceptions surrounding Napa County.

TT: How far back does your personal identification/association with being part of a "Napa wine family" go?

VG: Actually, forever. When I was a baby, my dad would take me to the wineries he was working at. I remember my dad's office was in the tower at Mondavi. Tim Mondavi used to make me paper airplanes. When our winery was founded in 1977, I started on the bottling line. "Napa wine family" sounds very dynastic, but it wasn't like that. Wine's not as glamorous as everyone thinks. It's a lot of hard work, and you have to have passion for what you're doing. Napa has always been a land of farmers.

TT: When Grgich Hills was founded, did your family expect it to turn into the success it is today? Did anyone actually sit down and plan it?

VG: When we sat down, an attorney said, "Here's your five-year plan. You can be successful and break even in five years." And my dad said, "You know, I think I can do it before that." And he did. He had spent most of his life without money, and he knew most things you really don't need. So he kept it simple.

TT: What about the winery makes you most proud?

VG: So many things. Our wines are amazing. We have a reputation for quality and consistency. I'm incredibly proud of my father. We have an amazing team, without whom we wouldn't be able to do what we do. We have a lasting legacy that can get passed to the next generation.

TT: How is Napa different now than it was twenty-five years ago?

VG: Well, it has this amazing world-class reputation—and a quantity of world-class restaurants, where we used to have one decent restaurant in the whole valley. We've become a destination for affluent jet-setters, so there's an influx of wealth. Also, there's a new category of winery owners who made their fortune elsewhere, but have come here because they love wine and want to be part of it. [Then] there are

(continued)

a lot of people who have been here forever, working the land, and are now able to invest in it and develop their own wineries.

TT: What are your feelings about Napa's reputation on the world stage?
VG: The reputation that it's one of the best places to grow grapes is certainly true. And its reputation for beauty is true. But some people think that only the rich and famous can visit, and that's certainly not true.

TT: What does the "wine country lifestyle" mean to you?
VG: To me, it's more than a style. It's a way of life. Wine is part of my life; it's the way I grew up, and generations of my ancestors before me. There's a huge emphasis on family and friendship. Wine and food slow you down and put you in the moment so you can actually appreciate the immense joy of being alive.

TT: What do you wish the public knew about Napa?
VG: Napa was founded by ordinary people who had extraordinary passions. All that passion went into their wine. It's a land that was built by poor immigrants, and we're still here, and we welcome everybody from all walks of life.

a great photo op, with fountains in front and a broad stairway leading from the foyer to the top landing. The main tasting room is vibrant and colorful—as much of a gift shop as a wine facility. Two flights are available to taste: the estate wines and the Captain's Reserve. Over in the wine bar—called "Mammarella" after Mamma Coppola—all the estate and reserve wines are available by the glass. Several tables are set up outside for people who want to enjoy a glass in the afternoon sun.

LENA STAMP: The girl in the vintage ad poster above the hall is the young Mammarella—Francis Ford Coppola's mother.

Quintessa
(NV) 1601 Silverado Trail, Rutherford, (707) 967-1601, www.quintessa.com; Fee: Y; Open: By appt.; Key: XP, DS, SF
The tasting room is sophisticated, the staff gracious, the wines elegant . . . but what stands out about this winery is the land itself. From a scenic lookout point halfway up the hillside, a private lake glimmers

bowl-shaped in the midst of 280 acres of vines. The hills curve as gracefully as though an artist had shaped them by hand. It's peaceful and idyllic and commanding all at once. Vineyard manager Valeria Huneeus described the 2005 grape crop as "lingering in a state of bliss . . ." and it's easy to relate.

The "Quintessential" tour experience also visits the wine caves, the gravity-fed winemaking facility, and sometimes the rooftop crush pad. It winds up in the cool, sleek tasting room for a seated tasting experience that includes the current release of Quintessa, plus two or three other wines from the library, single-block releases or barrel-sampled. Canape pairings are by Bouchon, Ad Hoc, and other local restaurants. This winery takes special care of its regular customers and/or repeat visitors: visits are completely customized to allow for more time in the vineyard, or perhaps for a vineyard tasting, or for a special trip to a second lookout point farther up the hill. Though the fee is steep ($65 for tour/tasting/food pairings), this journey into the heart of wine country is worth the money. Leisurely and personalized, it can be the highlight of a day—and one of the most memorable stops of the trip.

LENA STAMP: Though known for its reds, Quintessa does a marvelous "Illumination" Sauvignon Blanc on the DL. It's not available to taste (except occasionally for regular visitors), nor is it officially for sale. But if you ask, it's around.

Quintessa: a winery fit for royalty.

Schramsberg
(NN) 1400 Schramsberg Road, Calistoga, (707) 942-4558, www.schramsberg.com; Fee: Y; Open: By appt.; Key: FO
Jacob Schram was one of the first three winemakers in Napa, along with Jacob Beringer and Charles Krug. He founded Schramsberg in the 1860s, bringing in Chinese immigrants to dig the wine caves at this classic property. It was abandoned for decades, until the current owners bought it in the 1960s. Tours can accommodate between twelve and eighteen people and combine some history with behind-the-scenes wine production glimpses and a fun, laid-back tasting experience. Call a week in advance to get an appointment. This winery is funky by modern Napa standards, but nonetheless iconic.

David Rasmussen says: "Jack and Jamie Davies have produced competition-winning sparkling wine since the 1960s. Hugh Davies's son is now the CEO and winemaker. Their bubbly is a great way to start your day—the best buzz, if you will. Magazines talk about approachable or award worthy, but they never say, 'Wow, I got a great buzz off of that.'"

Chateau Montelena
(NN) 1429 Tubbs Lane, Calistoga, (707) 942-5105, www.montelena.com; Fee: Y; Open: Daily; Key: TH
The Chardonnay that won the Paris tasting in 1976 continues to rank among the world's best, though it's seen several winemakers come and go since then. The château itself becomes more beautiful every year: The stone edges mellow with age, while the blanket of greenery surrounding and adorning it becomes more lush. This is the winery on which the film *Bottle Shock* was based, and there is one last twist to the story: In 2008, right about the time the film came out, French wine conglomerate the Reybier Group put in an offer to buy Chateau Montelena.

Joseph Phelps Vineyards
(SH) 200 Taplin Road, St. Helena, (707) 963-2745, www.jpvwines.com; Fee: Y; Open: By appt.; Key: DS
Any discussion of Phelps needs to begin with the Insignia, which

was the first proprietary Bordeaux-style blend produced in California. It's still famous, but it's far from the only blend. While neighboring wineries tout their "Cab only" status, Phelps's wine portfolio includes everything from ice wine to an interesting proprietary blend called Pastiche (red and white), which features Bordeaux and Rhône grapes. This is a fun place to visit, with gorgeous scenery and an interesting hospitality/education program.

Hall

(SH) 401 St. Helena Highway, St. Helena, (866) 667-4255, www.hallwines.com; Fee: Y; Open: Daily; Key: TH

Even though Napa's status is set, there's still room for newcomers to build a legacy of their own. All it takes is near-unlimited willpower, funding, vision, and patience. Enter Hall, the $115 million wine estate on a historic site just outside of downtown St. Helena. The Frank Gehry–designed visitor center—a two-story glass shell with a woven wood trellis undulating over it—is the focus of everyone's attention, though it's only one piece of a much larger property. The full Hall estate measures 3,300 acres, 500 of which are planted. Its scope exceeds anything the neighborhood has seen in recent years.

"From the moment we saw the property we had two goals," says president Mike Reynolds. "First, we wanted to restore the preexisting resources and celebrate them. Second, we wanted to create something really spectacular that would celebrate wine, art, and architecture."

The original nineteenth-century building—a squat little stone structure in the center of the construction—is under restoration after being obscured beneath several layers of rubble for several decades. Meanwhile all around it, a massive state-of-the-art winemaking facility is being built from the ground up. Art is scattered casually across the property—much of it commissioned by the Halls specifically for the winery. Hall is a work in progress that typifies Napa's constant struggle between those who came before (usually only about ten to twenty years before—how quickly they forget) and newcomers who will do anything to make their mark. At the center of it all, Reynolds (a winemaker first and foremost) begs everyone to remember that outstanding estate Cabernet is really the reason everyone's here in the first place. Their other location is in Rutherford—it has limited hours, by appointment only.

Winemaker to Bottle Washer: Sheldon Richards, President, Spring Mountain District Association

With their diverse microclimates and rugged, sometimes treacherous terrain, the mountains are a world unto themselves, and growing grapes here requires year-round hands-on attention. When done well, though, it results in wines that are not only world-class, but also distinctive enough to demand their own AVA. Diamond Mountain, Atlas Peak, and Spring Mountain are a few to have earned this distinction.

"We're a small community of independent growers, with small vineyards surrounded by nature," says Sheldon Richards. His family's winery, Paloma, is one of many independent mountain wineries to have earned recognition on the world stage. Its 2001 Merlot was ranked number one in the world by *Wine Spectator* in 2003.

A former marketing executive, Richards serves as "everything from winemaker to bottle washer" at Paloma. This is typical of the mountain winemaker profile. Many gave up tremendously successful careers and invested everything in their vineyards. Hardworking, stubborn perfectionists, they thrive on the constant physical challenges of eking a crop from the volcanic soil.

"People say, 'What a romantic life,'" chuckles Richards. "They don't get that in the winter I'm out pruning in the rain and wind. When it's 100 degrees, I'm shoot-thinning and hanging out with rattlesnakes. We spend eleven months growing the grapes and only one making wine."

Nonetheless, he considers himself fortunate for a number of reasons: the privilege of being able to make wine from his fruit instead of selling it to an outside winery; the neighbors who share a common passion; the day-to-day pleasures of amazing food and wine . . . and the fun of sharing it with other people.

"Up here, you don't stand in line and pay," he says. "You pull into someone's garage and taste out of their living room."

But by all means feel free to admire the *Wine Spectator* awards glinting on the mantle.

Pride Mountain Vineyards
(NN) 4026 Spring Mountain Road, St. Helena, (707) 963-4949, www.pridewines.com; Fee: Y; Open: By appt.; Key: FO
One of the most popular places on the mountain to visit, this winery straddles the Napa/Sonoma county line. In fact, the line literally bisects the vineyard. If it's time to crush Napa grapes, the crusher has to be on the Napa side. When vineyard workers start crushing Sonoma grapes, they push the machine over to the Sonoma side. Their wines, particularly the Reserve Napa Cabernet Sauvignon—which is a perennial Robert Parker favorite—have a crazy semicult status. As soon as a release is announced, fans have reserved it down to the last bottle. In spite of—or perhaps because of—its elite reputation and connoisseur following, this winery's very fun and down-to-earth to visit. The tasting fee is a mere $5 as of 2008. The mountain road that leads to it is crazy, but it pales in comparison with the steep, bumpy/twisty private access road—hence the souvenir T-shirts proclaiming, "I survived the drive to Pride."

Way Out on Spring Mountain

Make a day out of this climb up the mountainside, to three unforgettable wineries. Be sure to get a picnic spread at Sunshine Foods before you start; there are no restaurants along the way.

Paloma
(NN) 4013 Spring Mountain Road, St. Helena, (707) 963-7504, www.palomavineyard.com; Fee: Y; Open: By appt.; Key: FO
Paloma has some of the best Merlot in the world—and the owners are proud to be distinguished as "an excellent value for money" as well, which is something of an anomaly among Napa winemakers. When *Wine Spectator* awarded the number-one ranking to the 2001 Merlot, it was the first time a California Merlot had earned a 95 ranking.

Smith Madrone
(NN) 4022 Spring Mountain Road, St. Helena, (707) 963-2283, www.smithmadrone.com; Fee: N; Open: By appt.; Key: FO
Widely known as "the mountain men," the straight-talking, blue jean-wearing, ever-engaging Smith brothers epitomize the mountain winemaker profile. Stu is a Berkeley graduate; Charles is a former teacher and

current World Croquet Federation champion. They've been on the mountain since 1971, and since the beginning, have fulfilled every vineyard and production function themselves rather than hire winemakers or vineyard managers. "When it's raining in the middle of the night, we're out in our slickers and boots making sure the ditches are open," says Stu. It's hard to say how many mountain winemakers have been inspired—and supported—by the Smiths over the past three decades.

The winery makes only three varieties: Riesling, Chardonnay, and Cabernet. The Smith brothers have four considerations in wine making: The wine should give pleasure, have balance, show complexity, and have a sense of uniqueness and place.

"As a philosophy, we try to get whatever Mother Nature has imparted into the grape into the glass. We don't always know what that is, but that's what we try to do," says Stu. He likens wine making to building a house from the ground up every year. "Sometimes two years will be very similar—with just a few changes to the porch, or the trim. Others are as different as a Victorian mansion versus a Frank Gehry. That's the beauty of it."

ATTRACTIONS

Napa Valley Wine Train
(NA) 1275 McKinstry Street, Napa, (800) 427-4124, (707) 253-2111, www.winetrain.com;
Fee: Y; Open: Daily (runs twice); Key: CHEESE, TH, SF, XP
Three-hour excursions combine wine country sightseeing, historic throwback ambience, and a formal food-and-wine experience. The train cars date back as far as 1915; though refurbished, they retain classic design features like high-gloss wood paneling and swagged red velvet curtains. The route runs parallel to Highway 29, starting in downtown Napa, traveling to St. Helena, and passing many famous vineyards and tasting rooms along the way. There are two excursions daily: One starts at 11:30 a.m. and includes a tasting room component as well as lunch; while the 6:30 p.m. excursion features a multicourse dinner and is quite formal—jackets suggested, in fact. Reservations are recommended, but note the twenty-four-hour cancellation policy. A new wine director has done much to improve the wine selections onboard.

Westwood Hills
(NA) First Street at switch to Brown's Valley Road, Napa;
Fee: N; Open: Daily (until sunset); Key: DS
Even though it's right around the corner from downtown Napa, this hike takes you into what feels like the middle of nowhere. A short and easy walk leads through rolling hills and gorgeous scenery—a hidden oasis that heads to a memorable scenic lookout.

Violet Grgich says: "When you get to the top you have this gorgeous view of all of Napa. I lived in Napa for years and never knew it existed until an out-of-towner pointed it out to me."

RESTAURANTS

French Laundry
(NV) 6640 Washington Street, Yountville, (707) 944-2380, www.frenchlaundry.com; $$$$; Open: L, Fri–Sun, D, daily; Key: XP, DS, SF, RR
This is the ultimate haute cuisine experience—unique on the West Coast and renowned throughout the world. Three things define French Laundry: exquisite high-concept food made from the finest and rarest ingredients in the world, wonderful service ("They treat you like you're royalty," comments one satisfied customer), and scarcity. With only ten tables downstairs, five above, and a small private dining room, this is a tough reservation to get. Reservations are accepted a maximum of two months in advance. If you do procure one, dress the part of royalty when you go and prepare for a serious and very grown-up dining experience. There's a choice of two menus: One highlights meat, the other vegetables. There is no a la carte. There are no paintings and no music in the dining room. Voices are hushed, posture straight. Everyone's focusing on the exquisite culinary creations before them—and building a unique memory to take away.

Chef Thomas Keller's Local Wine Picks

- Sloan and Colgin have great red wines.
- Vine Cliff on the Sonoma Coast does a great Pinot Noir.
- Littorai—that's Ted Lemon—over in Sonoma.
- Marcassin—that's Helen Turley's wine—is from delicious grapes.
- Shafer is one of my favorite wineries.
- Sloan, which is above Auberge, is a hillside vineyard I really like a lot.

Mustards
(NV) 7399 St. Helena Highway, Yountville, (707) 944-2424, www.mustardsgrill.com; $$; Open: L, D daily; Key: KIDS
SORRY, EVERYTHING HAS BEEN DELICIOUS SINCE 1983, reads a sign outside Cindy Pawlcyn's Napa restaurant, Mustards. While this statement is a bit peculiar and a lot cheeky, the truth is, Pawlcyn is probably Napa's most consistent, long-standing source of delicious food. Mustards is still a fan favorite,

From Caviar to Macaroni: Chef Thomas Keller's Reign Talks about Humble Gestures, Gracious Guests, and Mind-blowing Haute Cuisine

TT: What's your favorite thing about Napa?
TK: It's the only place in the country where people go specifically to eat and drink. From a consumer's or a chef's point of view, that's equally fabulous.

TT: It's commonly accepted that you've elevated Napa cuisine to a new level—but how has Napa elevated you?
TK: California overall is extraordinary. The quality of ingredients out here is just remarkable. Fast-forward ten years later after I got here: We have our own gardens and our own orchards. That has a big impact on food. But fresh food, wherever it comes from, is inspiring.

TT: Can you discuss whether the chef or sommelier drives the process of the food and wine pairing at French Laundry?
TK: I don't like to do a lot of pairings, because I think the guest is left out of that equation. When we make recommendations, we want to first get to know the guest and what he or she likes. That's a better approach than serving wine and saying, "Here's what goes best."

TT: What person or situation did you see in your dining room that gave you one of those, "Wow, how did I get here?" moments?
TK: Alain Ducasse and Jean-Louis Paladin . . . Julia Child and Robert Mondavi. When someone who's been a mentor, or an icon in our industry, comes into the restaurant, it's nerve-racking. You're extraordinarily nervous, making sure everyone's on their A game.

TT: What about when it's all over, and it's gone well, and they've shaken your hand and thanked you?
TK: It's almost like playing a sport and winning the world championship. You're pumped up; you can't go to sleep. There's a great sense of gratification when someone you have such respect for has a good experience.

(continued)

TT: Can we discuss the value of simple food in your life today?
TK: Simple foods are the foods that we have the most reference points to. Roast chicken, macaroni and cheese—[these] are things we remember from a very young age. As you get older, it becomes more layered, because you accumulate more memories surrounding those foods. They're memories of a moment, not memories of a chicken. I think it's a wonderful thing that people can have those memories—and typically, they're about simple things. If you have a mind-blowing haute cuisine experience at French Laundry, you have a different kind of memory. You have no reference points, because it was unique. Napa is the premier place in America that people come to in order to have those experiences and walk away with those memories.

TT: And finally, can we discuss the role humble gestures play in your life?
TK: My whole life is based around giving people great experiences, being hospitable, and nurturing them. I like to go out there and be with people. It's enjoyable.

although having celebrated its twenty-fifth birthday in 2008, it's looking a wee bit worn and torn. The parquet floors in the front bar are scuffed, and the low ceilings with sloped eaves don't seem fancy enough to match the proper white tablecloths. Then again, it doesn't seem like the management frets too much about those details. The Mustards bill of fare is dubbed "deluxe truck stop"—by implication, the decor is allowed a few imperfections. The menu changes regularly, and the food is sublime: Sweet corn tamales, Mongolian pork chops, and wood-grilled Sonoma rabbit are three of the standbys. In addition to thirty by-the-glass wine selections, the drink menu has microbrewed beers and specialty "highballs" (past-generation speak for cocktails).

Ubuntu
(NA) 1140 Main Street, Napa, (707) 251-5656, www.ubuntunapa.com; $$$; Open: L, weekends, D, daily; Yoga studio hours: Daily; Key: SCENE, VEG, RR weekends
The extreme zeitgeistiness of a vegetarian restaurant that also has its own biodynamic gardens and second-floor yoga studio (walk-ins welcome; just come by 10 minutes early to fill out a minimal waiver) is . . . well, it's enough to make LA and NYC restaurateurs very, *very* jealous. The big-city critics have certainly taken

notice: Though it only opened in the fall of 2007, Ubuntu was invited to cook for the 2008 James Beard Awards. It was one of the first few restaurants ever to earn the honor. For the ten days the awards ran, the exact same menu was served back in Napa—however, as soon as they ended, the menu went away, much to customers' dismay. It couldn't be helped, though: Because the ingredients come from the garden, Ubuntu's menu changes almost every day.

Michael Dellar says: "Chef Jeremy Fox just made the cover of *Food & Wine*. Sandy Lawrence, who's the owner, had a vision. She wanted to create a great vegetarian restaurant. She's not a vegetarian, and neither is the chef. I introduced them to their farmer."

LENA STAMP: *The photo collages on the walls are made from the owner's personal collection. She had them done in Paris. Customers have actually inquired after purchasing the pieces—in which case the owner furnishes them with the number of her Parisian contact so that they can get their own.*

Big Change in Small Town Napa: Michael Dellar, CEO, Lark Creek Restaurant Group

Though his Lark Creek Restaurant Group owns restaurants around the Bay Area and Las Vegas, Michael Dellar hasn't yet found the right venture in Napa County. In the meantime, he's a patron of many local spots—and an enthusiastic supporter of the downtown Napa revitalization.

"Napa's the place the people who work in the other areas live," he explains. "It's a fairly small town, but it services the needs of the general Napa Valley population: grocery store, beauty salon, car dealerships, the place you get your kids' school uniforms . . ."

Like many Napa citizens, Dellar anticipates the Riverfront's completion—not because it will bring luxury retail brands, but because it will give people a centralized downtown nucleus. "It creates more of a sense of community," he explains. "It's more vital, more lively, and centered around what Napa stands for: food, wine, and hospitality."

River Walk public areas are open every day during harvest, and retail outlets opened in March 2009. Chef's markets are Thursday nights in summer.

La Luna Market & Taqueria
(NV) 1153 Rutherford Road, Rutherford, (707) 963-3211; $; Open: L, D daily
As a rule of thumb, winemakers never agree on anything . . . but this no-frills lunch counter in a Mexican grocery store is the exception. Consensus is it's hands-down the best taqueria in the county. Every day at lunchtime, the place is packed with wine industry people, from CEOs and owners to admins and cellar employees. The brief menu has rice and beans, tacos, burritos, quesadillas . . . and the cheapest thing on it is under $2.

Violet Grgich says: "I like the quesadillas."

Mike Reynolds says: "Super steak burritos. Not only do they have great food but also great local character."

Taylor's Automatic Refresher
(SH) 933 Main Street, St Helena, (707) 963-3486, www.taylorsrefresher.com; $; Open: L, D daily; Key: KIDS
"No other burger stand in the country," locals quip, "offers $100 bottles of wine to go with your cheeseburger and fries." This is probably true, but what makes Taylor's so special isn't that it *has* the $100 bottles—it's that the clientele actually *wants* them, regularly. This ain't no Vegas gimmick; a regular night will find every table full of people happily chowing down on patty melts and chili cheese dogs while drinking Caymus Cabernet by the glass ($20) or bottle ($80). Organic Belgian wheat beer balances out the blue-collar Budweiser bottles. Even the shakes are Double Rainbow, in flavors like white pistachio and espresso bean. Outside seating only. There are heaters, and even when it's raining a few diehards huddle under whatever meager shelter they can find and make the best of it. Second location in Napa at 644 First Street—"but it isn't the same," according to those in the know.

Butter Cream Bakery
(NA) 2297 Jefferson Street, Napa, (707) 255-6700, www.buttercreambakery.com; $; Open: B, L daily; Key: KIDS
Grab yourself a doughnut or a Scandinavian-style pastry at this frumpy institution just outside of Napa's renovation district.

Michael Dellar says: "Where all the parents get their kids' birthday cake. We call it the Pink Palace because it's pink and white candy striped."

ENTERTAINMENT AND NIGHTLIFE

Arts Council Napa Valley
www.nvarts.org
Napa is not a hopping after-hours cultural destination—in fact, no wine-making region really is—but it does get a certain amount of performing arts and music. The Arts Council has created the Web site listed here as a reference point to learn what's going on in the Valley arts and culture scene.

SHOPPING

Oxbow Public Market
(NA) 610 & 644 First Street, (707) 226-6529, www.oxbowpublicmarket.com; Open: Daily; Key: KIDS
On the outside visitors see contemporary architecture with lots of gleaming metal and glass, but inside, this is a market hall similar to what's existed for hundreds of years in Europe. The market has everything from fresh-roasted coffee to organic ice cream to fresh fish. It's a great lunch spot.

Michael Dellar says: "The Fatted Calf charcuterie inside Oxbow makes awesome sandwiches. They get a beautiful long Italian loaf from the bakery next door and top it with very thinly sliced baby artichokes and luscious juicy pork loin on top. They put the sandwiches out on a platter, stack 'em in a pyramid, and sell them by the piece."

I. Wolk Gallery
(SH) 1354 Main Street, St Helena, (707) 963-8800, www.iwolkgallery.com; Open: Daily
Local artists and unknown talents get the spotlight at this longtime local favorite. It's a clean, well-lighted, and colorful place where art aficionados gather. There are three other locations: Auberge du Soleil, Cliff Lede, MacArthur Place in Sonoma.

Mike Reynolds says: "A St. Helena tradition. Wonderful exhibitions of mostly contemporary art."

Sunshine Foods
(SH) 1115 Main Street, St. Helena, (707) 963-7070, www.sunshinefoodsmarket.com; Open: Daily; Key: VEG
This is the un-supermarket, serving sophisticated St. Helena palates for years with nary a misstep. Sandwiches and pastries on the simple side, sushi and certified organic produce on the other.

Violet Grgich says: "If you can't figure out what to have for lunch, you can go there because they seem to have it all.

Mike Reynolds says: "Lunch destination for the whole staff, almost every day."

ACCOMMODATIONS

Napa River Inn
(NA) 500 Main Street, Napa, (707) 251-8500, www.napariverinn.com; $$-$$$
The "new" downtown Napa is literally springing forth all around this hotel, which was part of the first development wave that preceded the Riverfront, Westin Verasa, etc. It's housed in the historic Napa Mill building. It has an interesting layout: Guest rooms and common areas are in three separate buildings arranged around a central courtyard. They are so near the neighboring Riverfront development that it's hard to tell where one property ends and the next begins. Rooms in the historic Hatt Building have the most character; many of them date back to Victorian times in decor as well as architecture. The "Nautical" building features yacht-inspired room decor and a common front patio area for guests to gather within view of the Riverfront. The final "wine country" building doesn't have much of a theme, but it is comfortable enough. Businesses in the same complex include Sweetie Pies, Celadon restaurant, and a new tasting bar/jazz club.

Auberge du Soleil
(NV) 180 Rutherford Hill Road, Rutherford, (707) 963-1211, www.aubergedusoleil.com; $$$$; Key: SCENE, DS
This is the classic romantic splurge spot in all of Napa County. Even the outside tables in the bar see a lot of proposals, while the restaurant employees could write the authoritative guide. Ornaments in the lobby seem illuminated from within, the

landscape out the windows is flawless, and even the wax melting down the sides of decorative candle holders seems to have been choreographed just so. Add in a bit of French electronic down tempo and it's the perfect setting for wine country seduction.

Mike Reynolds says: "A marvelous place. Have a drink or dessert, hang out, and watch the sun set."

LENA STAMP: Bliss. Huge rooms. I love the art installations, especially the zebra sculpture on the patio.

Harvest Inn

(SH) One Main Street, St. Helena, (800) 950-8466, www.harvestinn.com; $$$$; Key: SCENE, SF

St. Helena is the epicenter of wine country in its most expensive, socially regimented form, and this property is at the epicenter of St. Helena. What this means is that the chances of a snob encounter are high, but so are the odds of having a truly luxe, memorable vacation experience. This hotel has been around since 1979 but doesn't show its age; thanks to a regular slate of expansions and additions, its rural/regal style is timeless.

Meadowood

(SH) 900 Meadowood Lane, St. Helena, (800) 458-8080, www.meadowood.com; $$$$; KEY: SF, AT, SCENE

Admittedly, it is the be-all and end-all of Napa wine country hangouts. The clientele are older, sports jackets are de rigueur in the dining room, and many of the staff have Euro aristocrat accents of indeterminable origin. However, there is no better place to get a crash course on wine, culture, and upper-crust manners. The expert and highly professional staff teach custom classes on everything from varietals to etiquette. Wine dinners and tastings are impeccably planned and executed. Originally a private residence club, Meadowood still keeps a lot of its country manor perks including an on-site tennis pro and croquet pro.

LENA STAMP: Director of Wine Education Gilles du Chambure is a connoisseur extraordinaire, an articulate speaker, and an enthusiastic teacher. Not to mention, a foxy beast who was basically born to wear custom-tailored Savile Row suits. Not that I was looking.

Cuddle and Canoodle

When Cupid's got you in his back pocket, and you can go punch-drunk just from looking in a certain someone's eyes, then quite frankly Napa's best vintages are wasted on you and you should leave them to someone else. Opt instead for these atmospheric, inviting, off-the-beaten-path places, where love's young dream is more cherished than a To Kalon Cabernet.

WINERIES

Castello di Amorosa

(NN) 4045 North Street, Helena Highway, Calistoga, (707) 967-6272, www.castellodiamorosa.com; Fee: Y; Open: Daily; KEY: TH, DS

Dario Sattui is one of Napa's great dreamers. But more than that, he's someone who knows how to bring dreams to life, no matter how big they are, how long it takes to achieve them, or how many of his neighbors tell him he's out of his mind. This property is the latest and greatest of Sattui's accomplishments: A 107-room Tuscan castle built true to twelfth-century standards, it spans 121,000 square feet in the Calistoga hills. It took Sattui fifteen years to build—and for the first ten, nothing could be seen above ground. This is because the bottom four levels of the Castello are underground: a labyrinth of wine caves, dimly lit by wall sconces and holding thousands of bottles of estate wine. Guided tours visit the caves, halls, and antechambers before winding up in one of many tasting rooms for the wine portion of the experience.

Twomey

(NA) 1183 Dunaweal Lane, Calistoga, (800) 505-4850, www.twomeycellars.com; Fee: Y; Open: Mon-Sat; Key: DS

A pretty little cluster of white storybook cottages tucked on a country lane in northern Napa, this winery is artisan but not dirt under the fingernails. Its flagship wine is Merlot, made in the *soutirage* traditional style of Bordeaux, France. *Soutirage* is the semiannual transfer by hand of barrel-aging wine from container to container to eliminate the lees. Technically, it softens the tannins. Psychologically, it adds to the charm of this small, intimate facility with a pergola and white flower. However, since *soutirage* is only performed roughly once a year, there's little chance you'll actually witness it.

Domaine Chandon

(NV) 1 California Drive, Yountville, (707) 944-2280, www.chandon.com; Fee: Y; Open: Daily; KEY: TH, DS

This classic winery's statement on romance is summed up in two words—and posted in highly visible spots up and down Highway 29: OYSTERS. BUBBLES. What more does a loving couple on

Castello—Behind the Scenes of an Epic Dream

For 15 years, most people in Napa thought Castello di Amorosa was Dario Sattui's folly—a project too massive, expensive, and completely random to ever come to fruition. But Sattui showed them otherwise. Now, not only does he have a castle to rival Hearst's, but also enough anecdotes to merit a full book. Here are a few little snippets that are just too good to stay in the "notes" file.

- Not only is all the stone and iron detail work done by hand, but it's done to look like it was built over many centuries, as is the case with authentic medieval castles.
- The bricks used to make the pedestrian thoroughfares are several hundred years old and imported from Italy. Newer stones were hand-carved from a rock quarry that Sattui rented for several months.
- The castle quarters include a Great Room, Knights' Room, barrel rooms, a chapel, and a dungeon with its own 300-year-old iron maiden, which Sattui found in the town of Arezzo.
- Bottles are stacked using the old horizontal interlock method rather than modern-day shelving. The bottles hold themselves up—pull the wrong one out, and 1,000 will fall.
- Dario Sattui started his Napa wine-making career as a young man with nothing but $8,000, a Volkswagen van, memories of his father, and the unshakable notion that growing grapes at the future site of original winery V. Sattui would be a *very smart thing* to do.

Castello di Amorosa—Napa's very own medieval castle.

- Disney filmed the Adam Sandler movie *Bedtime Stories* at Castello di Amorosa. The studio first came to Sattui asking for permission in February 2008, and he turned them down—mostly because he didn't want to inconvenience the neighors. The company kept coming back, and when he asked "Why?" they responded, "We looked all over the world for a castle that would be authentic but usable, and we could only find one other. In Scotland."
- Arnold Schwarzenegger paid a visit on Father's Day, with his children. He wanted them to see authentic Old World architecture without having to travel to Europe.
- Castello di Amorosa makes its own olive oil from the olive groves on the property.
- Twenty years ago, Sattui got a brochure from an Austrian master cellar builder. It took him five years to answer, but finally, on a cold February evening, he went to the man's house in Austria. At the sight of him, the cellar builder doubled up laughing. "Why are you laughing?" Sattui demanded. The man responded, "Five years ago I sent two thousand brochures to the U.S. Nobody responded. Now, five years later, you show up at my house in a snowstorm and tell me 'I want to build a castle!' I thought I was crazy, but . . . YOU are crazy." Then he accepted the job.
- Sattui brought master stonemasons over from Italy to supervise the Castello's construction. After three weeks of no progress, they admitted that the medieval architecture Sattui demanded was beyond their expertise. He sent them home, but the Austrian cellar master stayed at Sattui's home—along with his team—long enough to build the first two rooms of the Castello.

---

a weekend getaway need? Of French parentage but distinctly Californian in its fun-loving approach, this gorgeous winery has been a local and tourist favorite for decades. An elegant fine-dining restaurant is located on the property.

Cupid's Little Helpers

Hallmark, take note: The following wineries have created signature wines or experiences that tap into the very essence of romance—and they bottle it up for people to enjoy.

Terra Valentine
(NN) 3787 Spring Mountain Road, St. Helena, (707) 967-8340, www.terravalentine.com; Fee: Y, Open: By appt.; Key: DS
Within a beautiful stone and stained-glass building on Spring Mountain, young (and modest!) winemaker Sam Baxter crafts "blowaway" wines (to quote one insider). The venue feels like a historic Old Country monument, but is both approachable and youthful.

O'Brien Estate
(NA) 1200 Orchard Avenue, Napa, (707) 252-8463, www.obrienfamilyvineyard.com; Fee: Y; Open: Mon-Sat by appt.; Key: DS
The flagship blend at this estate is the Seduction, and the hospitality program includes "movie nights" and other romantic themed-events.

Connie Gore says: "They just had a Date Night; my husband and I went out there and watched a movie in the former barn."

Frazier
(NA) 70 Rapp Lane, Napa, (707) 255-1399, www.frazierwinery.com; Fee: Y; Open: By appt.; Key: DS
The staff make guests at this little Napa winery feel appreciated and adored. They're quick to follow up on questions, and will do whatever they can to make an occasion memorable.

Connie Gore says: "Beautiful caves, great presentation. Known for red wine. This boutique winery is able to customize a visit."

Love Is in the Air . . . But Where?

If anyone would know, it's Kate Stanley. The ebullient event designer has handled everything from exclusive banquets for a dozen executives to the star-studded, perennially sold out Napa Valley Wine Auction. Special occasions are her stock in trade, and Calistoga, one of her favorite places to plan one. Below, Kate's ultimate North Napa lovey-dovey picks:

- Tofanelli—This (cute!) winemaker used to sell grapes to the likes of Cakebread and Duckhorn. He's made his own wine since 2000. He works his own land, and takes a few visitors by appointment only. (www.tofanelliwine.com)
- Clos Pegase—Beautiful modern design, art and sculptures by Michael Graves (www.clospegase.com)
- Cuvaison—Beautiful picnic area! (www.cuvaison.com)
- August Briggs—The wine is incredible. (www.augustbriggswines.com)
- Golden Haven Hot Springs—Couples' massage (www.goldenhaven.com)

ATTRACTIONS

Indian Springs Resort & Spa
(NN) 1712 Lincoln Avenue, Calistoga, (707) 942-4913, www.indianspringscalistoga.com; $$$; Open: By appt.; KEY: DS
How's this for ironic? Calistoga's most remarkable natural feature isn't the *terroir;* it's the hot springs. Back when Calistoga was the last stop on the Calistoga railroad line, San Francisco residents used to catch the train out for a weekend of relaxation and healing waters. This spa resort was the original one in Calistoga; the row of palm trees lining the driveway dates back to the very first spa and is named after Sam Brannan, one of Calistoga's founding fathers. A relaxed property where most guests are in robes and swimsuits. Cozy cottage and lodge-style accommodations are available on the 16-acre property.

Kate Stanley says: "Little cottages just for two. Beautiful Buddhist meditation pool with lounge chairs and water features."

Lavender Hills Spa
(NN) 1015 Foothill Boulevard, Calistoga, (707) 942-4495, www.lavenderhillspa.com; $$; Open: By appt.; KEY: DS
Snuggled up against a hillside populated by tall shade trees, this adorable little day spa is a North County haven that glows with good feelings and pretty

Indian Spring's Buddha pond.

purple paint. Authentic Buddhist statuary gazes benevolently from their stations in the garden, the foyer, and the main spa room. The signature couples' treatment is the side-by-side immersion bath, which uses water mixed with a light white clay compound rather than mud. Choice of six different natural infusions including tangerine, jasmine, and coconut milk. Reserve two weeks in advance for a weekend, or before that if you want a specific treatment and time.

Old Faithful Geyser
(NN) 1299 Tubbs Lane, Calistoga, (707) 942-6463, www.oldfaithfulgeyser.com; Fee: Y; Open: Daily; KEY: TH
A peculiar phenomenon has happened with this attraction: The public knows the name, which has even become part of the modern vernacular, but few people know what—or where—the actual place is. The answer is, it's a geyser. Geysers are formed when water from a deep underground river flows over molten magma, boiling and evaporating inexorably upward, finding its way through cavities and fissures in the underground rock. Finally it reaches the surface, where it shoots up a tower of steam followed by an explosion of boiling water. There are actually only three geysers that erupt with the clockwork-like regularity that gives them the "Old Faithful" designation: one in New Zealand, a second in Yellowstone, and the third one here. Minimal fee—absolutely worth it.

RESTAURANTS

Bouchon
(NV) 6534 Washington Street, Yountville, (707) 944-8037, www.bouchonbistro.com; $$; Open: L, D daily; Key: DS, PU, GAY, SCENE OWL
It isn't exactly right to call this the French Laundry's little sister, even though it is Thomas Keller's younger, less expensive restaurant. The French Laundry has only one speed, whereas Bouchon is a smooth-shifting hybrid that can fulfill many moods for many people, simultaneously. A clatter of plates and chatter of voices greet you when you open the door, but at certain tables (Keller mentions number seven in the main dining room or the alcove table at the picture window in the bar) the noise of the outside world drops away as you're enfolded in a romantic cloud.

Since it closes past midnight every night, Bouchon is most locals' fallback dining venue, especially late at night when everything else is closed. Local restaurant employees head there after work, winery owners go low profile at the bar, and business-people from neighboring cities drop by for their roast chicken fix. It's good to book ahead of time so the staff can do their part to prepare for your big date night. While there are many options on the menu, this is the best oyster bar in the Valley, and with shellfish and a great Muscadet or Sancerre, you really can't go wrong. If you're there around sunset, try to snag one of the outside tables with a view across the valley.

Bistro Don Giovanni

(NV) 4110 Howard Lane, Napa, (707) 224-3300, www.bistrodon giovanni.com; $$$; Open: L, D daily; Key: DS, SF

While it doesn't pretend to be a bow-low-before-ye-enter-here culinary temple, this Italian standby has lots of foodie followers who appreciate its Old Country cookery and fresh-from-the-garden produce. The compact menu includes several pastas, pizzas, and wood oven-grilled meats like dry-aged prime steak and Sonoma duck. Though the location is within sight of Highway 29, the decor inside is rustic Italian.

Violet Grgich says: "I always get their pasta and carpaccio. I'm sort of picky about pastas, but I love their sauces. Being Croatian, we're very into Mediterranean cuisine."

Bistro Jeanty

(NV) 6510 Washington Street, Yountville, (707) 944-0103, www.bistrojeanty.com; $$; Open: L, D Mon-Sat; Key: DS

The former executive chef at Chandon Restaurant owns this chi-chi French bistro in downtown Yountville. With flower boxes outside the windows and an old bicycle in front, it offers classic French bistro fare: steak frites, mussels, cassoulet, and coq au vin. Recipes are decadent and rich, never skimping on the buttercream. During a pouring winter Nor Cal night, there's no better place to escape the chill, dry your feet, and warm your stomach . . .

Angele Restaurant & Bar

(NA) 540 Main Street, Napa, (707) 252-8115, www.angele restaurant.com; $$$; Open: L, D daily

French country dining by Bettina Ruas, whose father Maurice started Auberge du Soleil. The indoor/outdoor dining room with its exposed beam ceiling and vivid wall art is the warmest, most upscale barn in the West. And it's riverfront! Classic recipes like tomato bread salad, roast chicken, and roast lamb loin are prepared with fresh garden ingredients and presented beautifully.

Michael Dellar says: "Wonderful old building and outdoor patio right on the river."

La Toque

(NA) 1314 McKinstry Street, Napa, (707) 257-5157, www.latoque.com; $$$$; Open: D, daily; Key: RR, SCENE, XP, SF, LN

One of the most telling acknowledgments of the Napa renaissance is this restaurant's move down valley into the new Westin Verasa. Behind the French Laundry, it's the most expensive and high-concept venue in the Valley. Northern California seasonal cuisine features Niman ranch beef, Liberty Farms duck, and other name-recognizable ingredients. It keeps the same chef and remains as high-end as it was before—if not higher. Insiders say this one will be the hot ticket of Napa destination dining for quite a while, so reserve your table a month in advance for weekends—three weeks for a weekday.

Violet Grgich says: "The all-truffle dinner they do right after New Year's is really absolutely necessary if you love truffles."

ENTERTAINMENT AND NIGHTLIFE

Brannan's
(NN) 1374 Lincoln Avenue, Calistoga, (707) 942-2233, www.brannansgrill.com; $$; Open: L, D daily; Key: DS, SCENE

The centerpiece of the handsome front lounge area is an antique wooden bar that was shipped from San Francisco about a hundred years ago. The dining room is big, open, and old-school elegant: you'd think it had been around for seventy years, not barely a decade. This is a Calistoga standby for good drinks, great ambiance, and live music. Food is less reliable, though many people have good experiences.

Kate Stanley says: "Very old San Francisco, with a gorgeous bar."

Calistoga Inn Restaurant & Brewery
(NN) 1250 Lincoln Avenue, Calistoga, (707) 942-4101, www.calistogainn.com; $$$; Key: DS

This is an iconic property, with the best weekend brunches in town. It's a hotel, but locals think of it as more of a restaurant and hangout spot. You have a whole slate of picturesque places to plant yourself: the jazz-serenaded outdoor patio, cozy pub, adjacent historic Napa Valley Brewing Company, or old-fashioned hotel dining room.

Kate Stanley says: "Amazing weekend brunches. Mimosas and champagne by the creek."

SHOPPING

V Marketplace
(NV) 6525 Washington Street, Yountville, (707) 944-2451, www.vmarketplace.com; Open: Daily; Key: TH, DS

Lots of cool shops in a converted old winery near Villagio and Bouchon. You may never see a local shopping here, but for trinkets, souvenirs, and pricey gifts, it hits visitors' sweet spot.

Historic Napa Mill
(NA) 500 Main Street, Napa, (877) 251-8500, www.napariverinn.com/napamill.php; Open: Daily; Key: TH, DS

This converted landmark on the riverfront is a great place to stroll, shop, dine, and relax. It has a bakery, an old-fashioned candy shop, a wine bar, and two popular indoor-outdoor restaurants: Celadon, which serves contemporary California small plates, and Angele, which looks like a French country barn.

ACCOMMODATIONS

Milliken Creek Inn and Spa
(NA) 1815 Silverado Trail, Napa, (800) 835-6112, (707) 255-1197, www.millikencreekinn.com; $$$; Key: DS

This inn is truly an authority on romantic getaways—it's built a Web site just to give helpful hints to people planning a vacation. Tucked alongside its namesake creek a few minutes off Napa's Silverado Trail, Milliken is a beautiful, inviting place. The staff specializes in creating customized romantic experiences (see sidebar below). However, if your needs are simple in that regard, you'll be satisfied with their regularly scheduled programming: sunset "Magic Hour" wine and cheese, creekside breakfast, evening port, and a newly renovated spa.

Villagio Inn and Spa
(NV) 6481 Washington Street, Yountville, (800) 351-1133, (707) 944-8877, www.villagio.com; $$$$; Key: DS

Kitty-corner to Bouchon, this picturesque property is in the middle of expansion. It gets the local thumbs-up for the most romantic place in Yountville.

Cottage Grove Inn

(NN) 1711 Lincoln Avenue, Calistoga, (800) 799-2284, (707) 942-8400, www.cottagegrove.com; $$; Key: DS

Little cottages line a storybook lane so exquisitely charming, it seems one of the classic Disney cartoon couples might stroll by at any minute, complete with bluebirds whistling a happy tune. Each cottage has a name: Audobon, Botanical, and so on. Wicker rocking chairs sit on each front porch, while inside is a lovebird's haven. Flower petals bestrew the bed, original artwork adorns the walls, and chilled champagne on ice awaits the next happy couple. Of course the bathrooms boast deep soaking tubs built for two. Anyone who actually gets motivated enough to leave the property can borrow bicycles at the front lobby.

LENA STAMP: As a person who never makes it to breakfast, I appreciate the fresh-baked cookies and iced tea served mid-afternoon in the breakfast room.

Solage

(NN) 755 Silverado Trail, Calistoga, (866) 942-7442, www.solagecalistoga.com; $$$$; Key: DS, SCENE

The first property in a new brand owned by the Auberge group. It is similarly evocative of the wine country luxe life, but it's slightly hipper and more youthful. It's also a bit simpler, with modern "studio" accommodations.

Romantic Inspirations

Connie Gore, General Manager, Milliken Creek

- A sunset picnic by the river, with chilled rosé or Chardonnay, gourmet cheeses, and olives.
- Chocolate fondue for two, in-room, by the fireplace: strawberries, shortbread, blackberries, finger food, and chilled champagne to drink.
- Candlelit couples massage. Flower petals strewn around and mood music on the stereo. Take it back to your suite for in-room bath a deux.
- Commemorate your magic moments: Napa photographers reproduce your romantic memories with black-and-white portraits shot in the vineyard.
- Take a motorized rickshaw tour of downtown Napa tasting rooms and/or wineries. Lunch at the winery of your choice with a bottle you just bought.

Cab Hunters

There are people who come to Napa with one purpose only: To track down and buy the best, most pedigreed, and most under-the-radar Cabernets that they can find. The smaller the producer, the more obscure the facility, the more hidden the path . . . the happier they are. For the Cab Hunter, it's all part of the fun. The following section is big fun for big red hunters—and best of luck finding your prize.

WINERIES

Caymus Vineyards
(NV) 8700 Conn Creek Road, Rutherford, (707) 963-4204, www.caymus.com; Fee: Y; Open: By appt.; Key: SCENE, AT

Cab, all Cab, and nothing but the Cab—such is the credo of Caymus, an iconic winery founded in 1972. A specialist since the early days, Caymus has won some of the most prestigious awards in the wine business over the past twenty-five years. It continues to position itself as a single-varietal winery. Oddly, though, the Conundrum, a white blend produced by the same group, earns nearly as much recognition for the brand, even though it's marketed under its own label.

Eclectic Cabs: Three to Go On
David Rasmussen

Family-owned luxury tour company Eclectic Tours is a quality outfit that's built relationships with quality wineries all around the county. Their reputation and Rolodex are the foundations of their business. Many thanks to founder David Rasmussen for recommending the three following wineries, with venue notes in his own words.

Kelham Vineyards
(SH) 360 Zinfandel Lane, St. Helena, (707) 963-2000, www.kelhamvineyards.com; Fee: Y; Open: By appt.; Key: RR

"Susanna Kelham is the matriarch of the winery. Her two sons, Ham and Ron, make the wine. Between the three of them, they entertain all winery guests. Every time you go there, you'll meet one of the Kelhams. You get your choice of tasting, or lunch paired with wine. You get to taste seven or eight different wines, but we recommend that you don't drink them all unless you've got someone else to drive you. They used to sell their grapes to the likes of Opus and Duckhorn."

Keenan
(NN) 3660 Spring Mountain Road, St. Helena, (707) 963-9177, www.keenanwinery.com; Fee: Y; Open: By appt.; Key: FO, LN

"This is the quintessential mountain vineyard. They do a very small production—about 7,000 cases annually. About 1,800 feet up, off Spring Mountain Road, a long winding track leads you deep down into the forest, with beautiful views to the right and vineyards on both sides. You go over a cattle grade, down a one-lane track. Then it opens up and you see this old ghost winery that was abandoned during Prohibition and put back together again. Picnic there and decompress. Laura is the fourth generation Napa gal who runs the tasting room. Her husband, Randy, is the assistant winemaker, and they live on the property. Even when it's foggy in the valley, it's clear sunshine up there."

LENA STAMP: Grapes are sustainably farmed . . . doubly impressive when you consider how difficult mountain terrain is to begin with.

Constant Wine
(NN) 2121 Diamond Mountain Road, Calistoga, (707) 942-0707, www.constantwine.com; Fee: N; Open: By appt.; Key: FO, XP
"Owned and operated by Fred and Mary Constant, this winery is located at the very top of Diamond Mountain Road, three miles up from the valley floor. Tastings are done in the "pool house" overlooking Mount St. Helena, a dormant volcano, and a further three counties. The Diamond Mountain Appellation is well-known for its intense Cabernet fruit. The weather is generally hot and dry with very rocky soil, which stresses the vines and causes the berries to be much smaller and more flavorful. Fred and Mary are very gracious hosts. The views are stunning, and the wine is spectacular! Visits are strictly by appointment, and it is recommended that a guide accompany you, as the road is one lane and quite steep at times."

LENA STAMP: Fred is fantastic, and his wines are outstanding—expensive, but come on, you're drinking diamond juice.

Stag's Leap Wine Cellars
(NA) 5766 Silverado Trail, Napa, (800) 422-7523, (707) 261-6441, www.cask23.com; Fee: Y; Open: By appt.; Key: SCENE, RR
The iconic Napa winery ever since it beat out all the big ol' French burgundies in the famous Paris tasting event in 1976. The recently released film *Bottle Shock* purported to tell the Paris story, but instead focused on Chateau Montelena, the Calistoga winery that won the same tasting for Chardonnay. However, Stag's Leap's triumph in the big red category was the one that truly established Napa on the world wine stage, and connoisseurs in the know have always been aware of that. Founder Warren Winiarski is known for being a pillar, of the lo-

cal wine scene, and even though he recently sold Stag's Leap to an Italian wine conglomerate, he continues to remain involved. Amidst too many Napa Valley wineries that give nothing but attitude, Stag's Leap Wine Cellars provides a wonderful experience from the minute you walk in the door—regardless of whether you're wealthy enough to walk out with a case of their reserve Cabernet.

LENA STAMP: Wonderful staff, warm atmosphere, beautiful wines. I love this place.

Shafer Vineyards
(NA) 6154 Silverado Trail, Napa, (707) 944-2877, www.shafervineyards.com; Fee: Y; Open: By appt.
Almost every respected wine critic in the world raves about this boutique winery, as do culinary figures like Thomas Keller. It is a low-key, family-owned winery that consistently releases knockout wines.

Cliff Lede
(NA) 1473 Yountville Cross Road, Yountville, (800) 428-2259, (707) 944-8642, www.cliffledevineyards.com; Fee: Y; Open: Daily; Key: AT, XP
This new winery specializes in elegant, expensive Cabernet. Vineyard blocks are named after rock songs ("Ziggy Stardust," "Cinnamon Girl"), and the new red blend series is named accordingly: "Cinnamon Stardust '05." There is a small but elegant tasting room, which is transitioning over to appointment only. The winery is in the process of rolling out new, high-end hospitality programs including cave tastings, food and wine pairings, and so on.

Mark Pope says: "Their Poetry and other Cabernet-based wines are really delicious."

Mark Pope Recommends

Mark Pope is the original wine country Bounty Hunter, and an encyclopedic authority on Napa Cabernet. Everyone needs a wine merchant like him in their corner—particularly when seeking out heavy-hitter wines on a budget. The following producers are included in Mark's latest "Legends of the Fall" boutique collection—see his notes on the following pages. By all means, try to get in for a tasting . . . but if you fail, Mark has got a place on his mailing list for you.

Palmaz Vineyards
(NA) 4029 Hagen Road, Napa, (800) 592-2306, (707) 226-5587, www.palmazvineyards.com; Fee: Y; Open: By appt.; Key: RR
"The 'wow' factor is amazing—the experience will blow you away. Largest underground caves in California. The wines are well crafted and well balanced and have a long finish, great fruit source, and a lot of heart."

Seven Stones Winery
(SH) P.O. Box 2013, St. Helena, (707) 963-0993, www.sevenstoneswinery.com; Open: By appt.; Key: LN
"Some of the most powerful fruit. Wine is very well balanced, with a long, lingering finish."

LENA STAMP: This is a tough one to get into. There's even a wait list to get on the mailing list. The best way to make requests is by e-mail.

Gemstone Vineyard
(NV) P.O. Box 2014, St. Helena, (707) 944-0944, www.gemstonewine.com; Fee: N; Open: N.; Key: LN
"The insider's insider. In the Stag's Leap district."

LENA STAMP: There is a wait list to get on the mailing list—at time of print, the wait time is approximately one year.

Hartwell Vineyards
(NA) 5795 Silverado Trail, Napa, (707) 255-4269, www.hartwellvineyards.com; Fee: Y; Open: By appt.; Key: XP
"On my short list. Appointments available. In the Stag's Leap district."

Justice Vineyards
(NA) 975 First Street, Napa, (800) 943-9463, www.justicevineyards.com; Fee: Y; Open: Daily at Bounty Hunter.
"This just happens to be my series. I sourced grapes at Beckstoffer's To Kalon Vineyard."

LENA STAMP: Of course you want to taste this! Mark is the man, and Napa grapes are his specialty. Available by the taste or glass at Bounty Hunter.

Parallel Wines
(NA) 2920 Spring Mountain Road, Suite A, St. Helena, (707) 486-1100, www.parallelwines.com; Fee: Y; Open: By appt.
"[The Oakville Cabernet embodies] well-endowed lavish fruit, completely in balance. Sells for $45, but holds court with wines that sell for three times that."

LENA STAMP: There's a treacherous road up to this little boutique winery, so the owners make this wine available to taste at Vintners Collective. They are really nice people.

Hourglass
(SH) 1104 Adams Street, Suite 103, St. Helena, (707) 968-9332, www.hourglasswines.com; Fee: N; Open: By appt.

"Just delicious. Made by Bob Foley, the winemaker at Pride."

LENA STAMP: There is no tasting room, but customers can taste in the office. Sign up for the waiting list/ mailing list online.

Martin Estate
(NV) P.O. Box 390, Rutherford, (707) 967-0300, www.martin estate.com; Fee: No; Open: By appt. only; Key: LN

"In an old stone winery building that's more of a medieval fortress, with incredible Spanish conquistador arms and armaments. Totally a museum. They make a reserve and an estate."

LENA STAMP: Not another boring winery—not by a long shot. Wine geeks won't just want to visit this place, they'll want to move in. Shoutout to Petra the proprietress for answering her phone at random hours of the day and/or night.

PlumpJack Winery
(NV) 620 Oakville Cross Road, Oakville, (707) 945-1220, www .plumpjack.com; Fee: Y; Open: Daily; Key: SCENE

It's a little bit ironic and a little bit cool to think that, although PlumpJack started out as a wine merchant, these days most people only think of the name in association with its own proprietary-labeled wines. The estate is down a dirt road in Oakville, with direction markers done in PlumpJack's little coat-of-arms logo. The winery is small and not imposing, as fits the company profile. The wines are major award winners, and have acquired a stellar reputation and pretty serious prices. They're estate-grown in the Valley and consistently yum.

Rockledge Vineyards
(SH) 360 Taplin Road, St. Helena, (707) 963-5488, www.rockledge vineyards.com; Fee: N; Open: By appt.; Key: LN

Winegrower Peter Snowden's project is located just east of the Silverado Trail southeast of St. Helena, within the St. Helena AVA. On the eastern slopes, about 600 feet above the Napa Valley floor is a saddle covered with loose, rocky soil that extends down the benchland. The twelve-acre Rockledge Estate Vineyard is perched on this precipitous ledge. Winemaker Mike Hirby (Realm, Relic, Sherwin Family, St. Helena Road) has been the winemaker since 2004. Mike likes to inter-

To Cab Hunters, Love Gillian and PlumpJack

Founded on the basic tenets that wine connoisseurship should be fun, accessible, and affordable, San Francisco–based PlumpJack Group has a huge following among Bay Area epicureans. At its inception it mostly had a twenty- and thirty-something fan base, but as the years pass, it continues to reach a wider cross-section: Original customers are maturing but staying loyal, while new ones continue to latch onto the brand. First as wine merchants, then restaurateurs, then vintner/winemakers, and now hoteliers (Carneros Inn, PlumpJack Squaw Valley Inn), PlumpJack champions quality, value, discovery, and great style. Wine director Gillian Balance spends her whole life in search of tomorrow's great discoveries—it is not just her job but her passion. Below, check out Balance's thesis-length pick list of the "Next Cult Cabs"—and note, all these up-and-comers are ready to meet serious collectors.

vene as little as possible to preserve fruit flavors. Wine lots typically have extended maceration, less contact, and little racking and are bottled unfined and unfiltered. The wine is aged about twenty months in new French barrels.

There were less than 500 cases of 2004 "the Rocks." It has a deep ruby red, almost black color. Enticing aromas of anise, blackberry, raspberry, chocolate, and clove emanate from the glass, and the texture is rich and unctuous, with very soft, velvety tannins and a really lengthy finish.

LENASTAMP: Extremely hard to wiggle your way in to this tiny, but well regarded, garage winery. Sign up online now for the mailing list or wait list, and when you're coming to Napa, call Peter Snowden ahead of time to make your case for a visit.

Realm Cellars

(SH) 3468 Silverado Trail, St. Helena, (707) 967-0226, www.realmcellars.com; Fee: Y; Open: By appt.; Key: LN

Since the debut vintage in 2002, Realm Cellars has consistently pursued a simple mission: to produce hand-crafted Bordeaux-style wines of superior quality in small amounts, with grapes sourced from the most distinctive Napa Valley vineyards. Their wines are some of the top artisanal Cabernet blends being produced in the Valley. Partners Wendell Laidley and Juan Mercado have provided the notes for the current releases. The 2005s are the best efforts to date, and I truly believe that these wines are some of the best being produced in Napa Valley. The wines currently being made at Chateau Boswell and featured in that St. Helena tasting room include the following:

- 2005 The Tempest Napa Valley Red Wine. This year's blend consists of 52 percent Cabernet Sauvignon, 30 percent Merlot, and 18 percent Petit Verdot. Historically their homage to Bordeaux's Right Bank, the addition of some very dark and rich Cabernet Sauvignon from Coombsville, along with some very ripe Petit Verdot from St. Helena, gives the 2005 Tempest more black-fruit flavors and aromas than ever before. Bottled unfined and unfiltered.
- 2005 Beckstoffer Dr. Crane Vineyard Cabernet Sauvignon. This site on the west side of St. Helena (in the vicinity of the famous Hayne Vineyard) is extremely gravelly, yielding a rich wine with elegant tannins and great aromatics. Bottled unfined and unfiltered.

Orin Swift

(SH) 1352 Main Street, Napa, (707) 967-9179, www.orinswift.com; Fee: Y; Open: By appt.

Former political science student Dave Phinney worked many harvests at Robert Mondavi before founding his own label, Orin Swift. Today his flagship wine "the Prisoner" is rapidly becoming a cult find for people who love great Zinfandel. The Cabernet Sauvignon "Mercury Head" is also exquisite. With the purchase of forty-eight acres in the hills above Oakville, expect more great wines in the future. Now is the time to get on this list! They have a tasting room right in downtown St. Helena at the Odd Fellows Lodge.

- 2006 Red Wine The Prisoner
  The 2006 blends the lush berry flavors of Zinfandel (51 percent), the power and concentration of Cabernet Sauvignon (23 percent), the dark black fruit of Syrah (12 percent), the intensity and structure of Petit Sirah (6 percent), the flesh of Charbono (6 percent), and a hint of Grenache (2 percent) to create a decadent wine with great complexity.
- 2005 Cabernet Sauvignon Mercury Head
  Cabernet Sauvignon is one of the easier varieties to grow as well as make. The old saying, "Great Cabernet Sauvignon makes itself," rings true. These grapes are sourced mostly from the famed Morisoli

Vineyard—the wine is very lush and extracted, with layers of cassis and mocha.

Anomaly Vineyards
(SH) P.O. Box 741, St. Helena, (707) 967-8448, www.anomaly vineyards.com; Fee: Y; Open: By appt. only to people on the mailing list; Key: RR
Anomaly Vineyards specializes in the production of the highest-quality Cabernet Sauvignon. Their first release consisted of 300 cases and sold out immediately. Each subsequent release is of a larger quantity, as more fruit from the vines became available. Winemaker Mark Porembski's notes on the 2005 Anomaly Vineyards Cabernet Sauvignon:

"Loaded with dark fruit flavors of blackberry and plum. It begins with smooth and approachable scents of Darjeeling tea, confectionary notes, and island spice. The wine is smooth and dense with dessert-like flavors of *panna cotta* (cooked cream) and caramel. The tannins are relaxed, round, and amiable, leading to Anomaly's signature velvety finish."

LENA STAMP: Small private winery. Only allows mailing list members and special groups (rare). Sign up on the mailing list and make arrangements well ahead of time.

ATTRACTIONS

Vintners Collective
(NA) 1245 Main Street, Napa, (707) 255-7150, www.vintners collective.com; Fee: Y; Open: Daily; Key: LN
Come in, pay $20, and taste four or five boutique wines from local producers so new or small you can't find them anywhere else. This kind of place is beloved by the wine geek, and there aren't too many of them in Napa. It's a casual setup housed in a historic stone building. Customers stand up at the bar, often chatting with one of the winemakers who's just popped by for a second to show off his latest no-label bottling. (Note: gets the Logistical Nightmare mark because of the downtown locale—very tough to find parking.)

Connie Gore says: "Cellar for very boutique winemakers who don't actually have a winery. Milliken does customized private experiences with seating."

di Rosa Preserve: Art & Nature
(NA) 5200 Sonoma Highway 121, Napa, (707) 226-5991, www.dirosapreserve.org; Fee: Y; Open: Tue–Fri; Key: LN

Open sporadically, this quirky art compound in Carneros is owned by a former vintner and major patron of the arts. Not too many people know much about this place, but it's always recommended, and the founder is highly regarded. A nice little reservoir acts as a reflecting pond in the midst of the 217-acre venue, while approximately 2,200 art pieces are displayed around it, some in the Gatehouse Gallery onsite and some outdoors. Parking is limited, so carpooling is encouraged.

RESTAURANTS

Cindy's Backstreet Kitchen
(SH) 1327 Railroad Avenue, St. Helena, (707) 963-1200, www.cindysbackstreetkitchen.com; $$; Open: L, D daily; Key: SCENE, SF, PU, LN

Just like big sister Mustards, this restaurant features garden-fresh California comfort cuisine—lighter and more contemporary than traditional American comfort food but based on a lot of the same recipes. Oven-grilled meats—the duck is a signature—fresh fish, and gourmet sandwiches hold down the menu, while weekly whimsies run the gamut from fried green tomatoes to stuffed peppers. Cindy specializes in once-upon-a-time Southwest recipes that have been Northern California–ized beyond all Mexican borders. Housed in a renovated two-story Craftsman, the restaurant appears tiny at first—just a bar area and a few tables. However, that opens onto a much larger dining room . . . and another . . . and then upstairs, another. All the rooms are usually busy, with tons of St. Helena locals on any given night. However, Wednesday's traditional "Cindy's Supper Club" ($40 for four courses, though every course is available a la carte) draws a particularly festive and chatty (for St. Helena) crowd.

LENA STAMP: Sat at the bar: Service was fantastic, cocktails were too good (could have drunk five Lemon Drop martinis in fifteen minutes), the oysters were outstanding, the duck burger was mmmm . . . and there was even a nice crowd!

Rutherford Grill

(NV) 1180 Rutherford Road, Rutherford, (707) 963-1792, www.hillstone.com; $$; Open: L, D daily; Key: SCENE

No matter what time of year, this restaurant sees the who's who of Napa Valley wine making every day at lunch. Evenings are also slammed, but with more of a mixed crowd. Either way, service is brisk (though nice) and the atmosphere buzzing with the kind of energy that comes when 50 percent of the guests want to make the scene, be seated, get fed, and hit the road again within thirty minutes flat.

Mike Reynolds says: "I call this 'the yoo-hoo place,' because you walk in at lunch and see everybody you know."

Boon Fly Café

(NA) 4048 Sonoma Highway, Napa, (707) 299-4870, www.thecarnerosinn.com; $; Open: B, L, D daily; Key: KIDS

One local describes this casual eatery in the Carneros Inn as "some of the best eavesdropping in the Valley." Typically there are more wine industry folks than tourists eating lunch here, and the tables are *thisclose.* Plus the atmosphere is so friendly, you might not even have to eavesdrop—a stranger comes up, says how-de-do, and the next thing you know, you're deep in conversation about the winery he runs. The food is American: down-home with a gourmet twist that mostly comes from extra-special care with the ingredients. Eggs Benedict is made with thick-cut ham; doughnuts are made fresh (and are famous!).

LENA STAMP: I'm crazy about the hash browns here. The potatoes are par-baked, grated, and fried in clarified butter (pure butterfat, with milk solids removed)—as perfect as hash browns can be. And I would know. I had to make 'em every Sunday for ten years.

Tra Vigne

(SH) 1050 Charter Oak Avenue, St. Helena, (707) 963-4444, www.travignerestaurant.com; $$; Open: L, D daily, B Sun, Key: SCENE

One of the old faithfuls of Napa Valley, this restaurant has its ups and downs, food-wise, but the handsome, high-ceilinged, open dining room remains a fave. In fact front-of-house staffers say it's one of the hardest rooms in Napa to work simply because it's so huge and busy. Guests can pick up a little bit of this frenetic energy, but it's fun, not stressful. After a brief lull, cuisine here may be on an upswing, thanks to a new (as of 2008) chef who spent two months in Italy studying before donning his Tra Vigne apron. The current California/Mediterranean menu is big on housemade pastas and wood-oven pizzas. Approximately 350 wines are available, but only twenty by the glass. Twelve seats at the bar are on a first-come, first-served basis and see a lot of local traffic. Adjacent wine bar Cantinetta and neighboring Pizzeria Tra Vigne are part of same restaurant family.

Martini House
(SH) 1245 Spring Street, St. Helena, (707) 963-2233, www.martinihouse.com; $$$ Open: L Fri-Sun, D nightly; Key: DS, PU, SCENE
It's named after the Martinis that owned the place, not the drink—but still, it's a bold move to adopt a cocktail moniker in a wine industry town. This place can back it up, though: Its California cuisine is excellent, and its wine list is amazing. Then there's an entire menu's worth of sophisticated but fun top-shelf cocktails. Like the Bounty Hunter, this place takes a witty but intellectual approach toward its wine and spirits—reading the menu is like taking a journey. The downstairs bar is a collection point, especially in fall and winter. It's warm and fairly dark, with fireplaces and colorful wall hangings. Open till midnight with lots of boisterous late-night conversation, it's a fun place to go with groups, but equally fun if you're on a date or on your own. "It's always an occasion," says one local.

W F Giugni & Son Grocery Co.
(SH) 1227 Main Street, St. Helena, (707) 963-3421; $; Open: B, L daily; Key: LN
Pronounced "Juney's," this is a standby sandwich spot—and some faithful customers will tell you that it's much more than that. This kitschy Italian-inspired storefront is known for the sandwich dressing called "Juney Juice," and fans aver that there is no substitute. Even though there's no seating and you can't call in an order, they'll stand in line and go through the whole traditional lunch counter process just to get their juice fix.

Mike Reynolds says: "I don't know what's in the 'Juney Juice,' but some people swear by it."

ENTERTAINMENT AND NIGHTLIFE

Bounty Hunter Rare Wine & Provisions
(NA) 975 First Street, Napa, (800) 943-9463, (707) 255-0622, www.bountyhunterwine.com; $$; Open: Daily; Key: SCENE, PU
Although this wine merchant/bar/barbecue spot could fit into many categories, we're putting it in "Nightlife" because it's one of the only places in town that's hopping after 9 p.m. Every seat in the place is occupied. People from every corner of the world are talking (shouting?), laughing, and drinking. Wonderful wine is literally everywhere you look. The staff is on point, but if you don't want to consult with them, the wine list is brilliantly laid out and will point you where you need to go. Mouthwatering barbecue, an unpretentious vibe . . . this is a haven for the wine geek. Large groups and solo travelers will be equally well taken care of. Save some time to shop the retail store. Owner Mark Pope runs one of the best boutique Cabernet wine clubs in the world.

Michael Dellar says: "Awesome barbecue, pulled pork, plus these great kosher dill pickles. Very noisy though. Fabulous wine program. You're guaranteed that every wine's going to be a winner."

SHOPPING

Wine Garage

(NN) 1020 Foothill Boulevard, #C, Calistoga, (888) 690-WINE, (707) 942-5332; www.winegarage.net; $; Open: Daily

It's not strictly Cabernet, but cool enough to sneak in anyway on the hunch that you won't mind. The scoop is this: 250 wines, all under $25. The selection changes all the time, and owner Todd Miller employs various time-honored methods to procure what he feels are great picks: He canvasses the countryside, seeks out small winemakers, woos up-and-comers, and haggles shamelessly for the best price. His stock runs the gamut from Russian River Pinot to Sangiovese to old vine Gamay Noir, but all are from California. A good percentage of the wines are Cabernets, though the exact number of producers and labels changes from week to week.

ACCOMMODATIONS

Carneros Inn

(NA) 4048 Sonoma Highway, Napa, (888) 400-9000, (707) 299-4900, www.thecarnerosinn.com; $$$; Key: DS, GAY

Just off the Sonoma Highway, but officially within Napa County lines, this resort is within fifteen minutes of hundreds of wineries. It's really neither in Napa nor Sonoma, but Carneros—an officially designated sub-AVA and world unto itself. Carneros overlaps both counties, and its nickname is "the Switzerland of wine country." These days it's a prestigious AVA for Chardonnay and Pinot, but just a few decades ago no one thought the soil could grow vines. The landscape was stark and quiet, with tall grass, wandering cows, and corrugated metal barns here and there. People actually used it as a dumping ground.

At some point vintners began to realize the district's grape-growing potential, but even so, when the Carneros Inn developers conceived of this project, the land was mostly unoccupied and its residents did not want a resort in the neighborhood. The developers went door-to-door explaining their vision and getting feedback as to what sort of place would be appropriate. The result is a rambling, whimsical, luxe-casual resort that remains true to the region's farm-country roots. It's a cheerful village fashioned of many corrugated metal buildings. There's a "town square" with shops, a meeting hall, and two great restaurants—Farm and Boon Fly—that locals frequent as much as tourists. Rooms are simple and sophisticated, with many touches from the Northern California-country home: heated tile bathroom floors, indoor/outdoor showers, private back porches, sun decks in the residential units. The pool deck is a sunny, convivial spot for guests to mingle, but eight lounge chairs overlook the Carneros landscape: gorgeous vineyard vistas surrounded by sweeping dry-grass meadows and vast silence.

LENA STAMP: When the spa was coming up with its signature scent, the spa director asked locals to bring in what they thought Carneros smelled like. Among other things they brought in grapes, goat's milk, lavender, fresh honey, and various types of dirt.

Westin Verasa

(NA) 1141 First Street, Napa, (800) 509-8090, www.verasanapa.com; $$$; Key: SCENE, LN

Opened in fall 2008, this is the newest flagship Westin and the pride of downtown Napa. Its coming marks the dawn of a new day in downtown Napa. No longer just the place where locals come to get their brakes tuned up, it's now officially the site of most of the distinctive new luxury developments in the Valley. This hotel's signature restaurant is La Toque, an expensive and exquisite place second only to French Laundry in local rankings.

El Bonita

(SH) 195 Main Street, St. Helena, (800) 541-3284, (707) 963-3216, www.elbonita.com; $; Key: CHEESE

It doesn't look like much—and online it's even less impressive—but this motor lodge is surprisingly cute inside. And more important, it's *clean.* It even has a pool. It's just inside the St. Helena town borders, surrounded by vineyards on both sides. Look for the neon sign and old-fashioned metal gates. It's the best bargain in Napa.

Silverado Resort

(NV) 1600 Atlas Peak Road, Napa, (707) 257-0200, www.silveradoresort.com; $$; Key: KIDS, SF

Good location, not directly on any beaten path, but only a minute away from several. This property is as much about its two Robert Trent Jones, Jr.–designed golf courses as its wine country proximity. The courses and the main public space (aka "The Mansion") have both completed recent multi-million dollar updates. Caters to multi-generational groups.

Poetry Inn—Cliff Lede
(NV) 6380 Silverado Trail, Napa, (707) 944-0646, www.poetryinn.com, $$$$; Key: XP, DS, AT
Ultimate luxury in a stunning villa inn perched on a hilltop. No room is smaller than 1,000 square feet, and there are three butlers to serve the four total guest rooms. Outfitted with wood-burning stoves, indoor/outdoor showers, and Italian linens, these accommodations emulate a winemaker guest house, but at a level only the wealthiest winemakers could aspire to.

TOUR PROVIDERS

Eclectic Tour
(ALL) 1330 Diamond Mountain Road, Calistoga, (888) 411-TOUR or (707) 224-2265, www.eclectictour.com; Fee: Y; Open: Daily; Key: RR
This family-owned and operated private tour provider is friendly, knowledgeable, and expert in providing a relaxed luxury experience. Tours are always customized, and as a rule, at least one stop will be to a boutique producer that offers one-on-one winemaker interaction and "discovery" wines. Known and liked by people in the local industry. For "Cab hunters," this company will get you into exclusive places (often the winemakers' home), but you must have a serious commitment to seeking out and procuring the wines.

Napa Valley Tours & Transportation
(NV) 1325 W. Imola Avenue, Napa, (888) 946-3859 or (707) 251-9463, www.nvtt.net; Fee: Y; Open: Daily
The preferred limo and tour company of several Napa hotel concierges, this outfit is reliable, reasonably priced, and able to customize experiences.

SUGGESTED TWO-DAY ITINERARIES

{LEGENDARY NAPA}

DAY ONE

From Napa

Morning: Grab breakfast and a picnic at Oxbow. On the way out of town, stop for a morning photo opportunity at Westwood Hills, where you will get a bird's-eye view of Napa.

Mid-morning: Taste at Rubicon *or* have a glass of wine in their wine bar, Mammarella, if you don't want the stand-up tasting-room experience. Taste Joseph Phelps.

Afternoon: Picnic at Hall, then taste.

Late afternoon: Tour, taste, and food pairings at Quintessa *or* taste at Grgich Hills.

Evening: Have dinner at Mustards.

DAY TWO

From Napa, Yountville, St. Helena

Early morning: Go to Butter Cream for doughnuts.

Mid-morning/afternoon: Take a guided tour to mountain wineries: Schramsberg, Smith-Madrone, Paloma, Pride.

Afternoon: Have lunch arranged by the tour company.

Evening: Dinner at French Laundry *or* at Taylor's *or* at one of the Napa Riverfront restaurants (Celadon, Angele).

{CUDDLE AND CANOODLE}

DAY ONE

From Napa or Yountville

Early morning: Have breakfast in bed.

Mid-morning: Taste at O'Brien.

Afternoon: Oysters and champagne at Domaine Chandon.

Late afternoon: Taste at Terra Valentine *or* cocktails at Auberge du Soleil.

Evening: Go to Bouchon.

Late evening: In-room chocolate fondue.

DAY TWO

From Calistoga

Early morning: Have breakfast at hotel.

Mid-morning: Tour and taste at Castello di Amorosa.

Afternoon: Picnic on the grounds.

Late afternoon: Enjoy a couples' spa treatment at Lavender Hills Spa.

Evening: Creekside picnic (prearrange with the concierge) for dinner.

{CAB HUNTERS}

DAY ONE

From Napa

Early morning: Breakfast at Boon Fly.

Mid-morning: Visit Stag's Leap Wine Cellars, Shafer, and Caymus.

Afternoon: Have lunch at Rutherford Grill.

Mid-afternoon: Visit Hartwell and Cliff Lede.

Evening: Have dinner at Bounty Hunter.

DAY TWO

From St. Helena

Morning: Arrange guided tour (Eclectic, preferred company) of appointment-only wineries like Keenan, Constant, Anomaly, and Palmaz.

Afternoon: Have lunch arranged by tour company *or* pick up sandwiches Guigni's.

Evening: Have drinks and dinner at Martini House.

CALENDAR OF EVENTS

FEBRUARY-MARCH

- Napa Valley Mustard Festival
  www.mustardfestival.com

MAY

- Tour de Cure
  tour.diabetes.org

JUNE

- Auction Napa Valley
  www.napavintners.com

JULY

- Napa County Fair
  www.napacountyfairgrounds.com/fair.htm
- Napa Valley Shakespeare Festival
  www.napashakespeare.org
- Wine Country Film Festival
  www.winecountryfilmfest.com
- Domaine Chandon Bastille Day Celebrations
  www.chandon.com

AUGUST

- Music in the Vineyards
  www.napavalleymusic.org
- Napa Town and Country Fair
  www.napavalleyexpo.com

OCTOBER

- Yountville Days Festival & Parade
  www.yountville.com

NOVEMBER

- Yountville Festival of Lights
  www.yountville.com

DECEMBER

- Annual Holiday Candlelight Tour
  www.napacountylandmarks.org
- Carols in the Caves
  www.carolsinthecaves.com

RESOURCES

www.napavintners.com
www.napagrowers.org
www.napavalley.org
www.yountville.com
www.calistogafun.com
www.carneros.com
www.rutherforddust.org
www.howellmountain.org
www.atlaspeakappellation.com
www.mtveederwines.com
www.oakvillewinegrowers.org
www.appellationsthelena.org
www.stagsleapdistrict.com
www.springmountaindistrict.com
www.localwineevents.com

SONOMA

Sonoma occupies a cushy position, geographically and socially . . .

within not only California but the entire universe. It's a land of mild temperatures, liberal policies, vast acreage (approximately the size of Rhode Island, according to the literature), and modern box-like construction. "The City" (San Francisco) is close enough for comfort, but not so near that it harshes the overall mellow. The land is fertile. The social structure is flexible—or at least it wants to be. People come to Sonoma County to "do their thing," whether that be apple farming, grape growing, or underwater basket weaving. Personal passions and quirks are encouraged . . . although steely, tooth-gritting ambitions don't usually go over too well. They interfere with the overall happy-go-lucky, roundabout way of things.

The wine industry in Sonoma is influenced by its farm-country roots, hippie tendencies, and unacknowledged capitalist influences. People historically come here looking for a better quality of life. They want to start family wineries, grow crops organically, or live out the dreams that harsher lands or tougher cities wouldn't allow. They want to enjoy every sunset with a glass of Chardonnay in hand. They want to hand harvest the vines and host an annual grape stomp at Crush. However, they also want to earn an annual income several times higher than the national average and ensure their children get a university education, private violin lessons, and the best teeth money can buy. Thus, the debate about "going corporate" has always been emotionally fraught for Sonoma's winemakers.

A lot of people who are probably perfectly intelligent in other areas have proven their ignorance of all things Northern California by calling Sonoma County "Napa's little sister" or "the next Napa." This is about as sensible as calling Snow White "the next Pocahontas." They're two different entities that just happen to inhabit the same sphere in public consciousness. There's crossover, but no clear

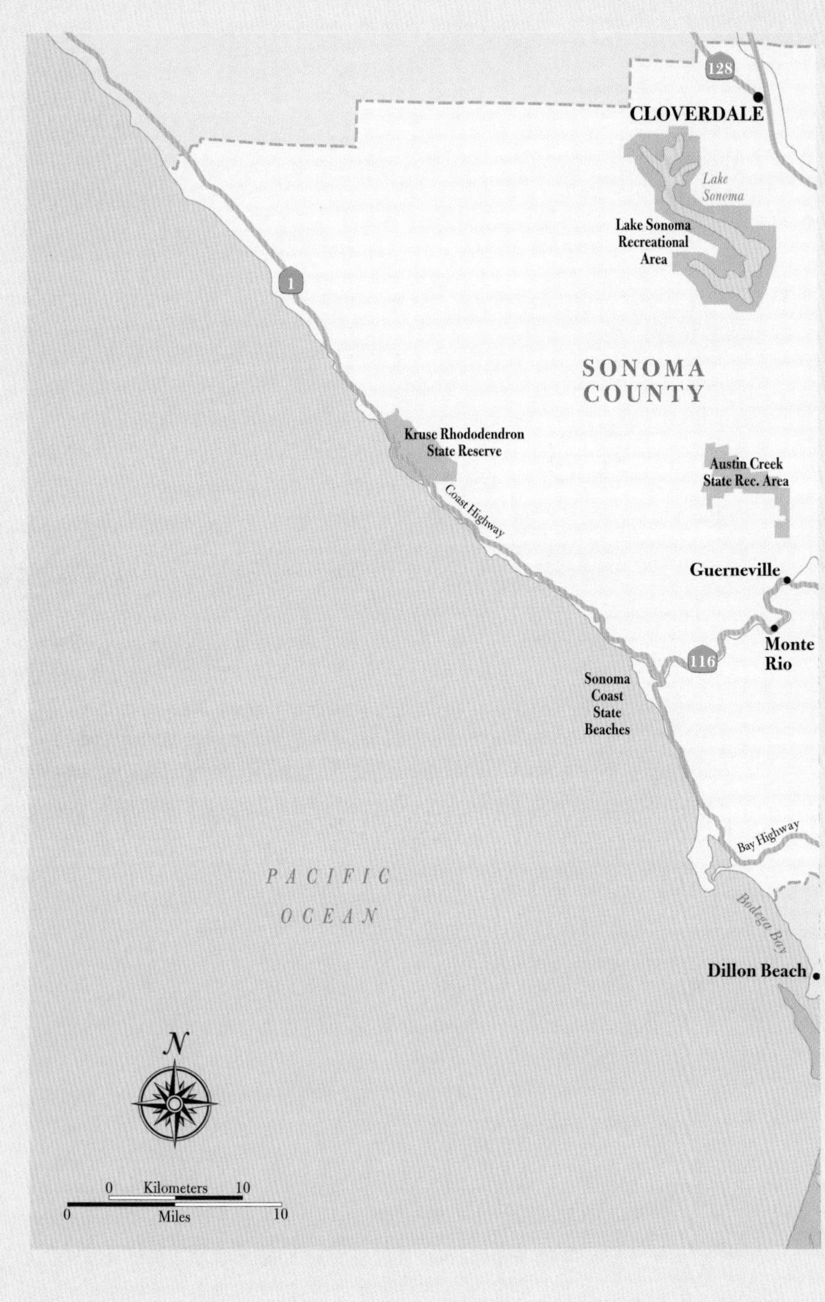
128
CLOVERDALE
Lake Sonoma
Lake Sonoma Recreational Area
1
SONOMA COUNTY
Kruse Rhododendron State Reserve
Austin Creek State Rec. Area
Coast Highway
Guerneville
Monte Rio
116
Sonoma Coast State Beaches
Bay Highway
PACIFIC OCEAN
Bodega Bay
Dillon Beach
N
0 Kilometers 10
0 Miles 10

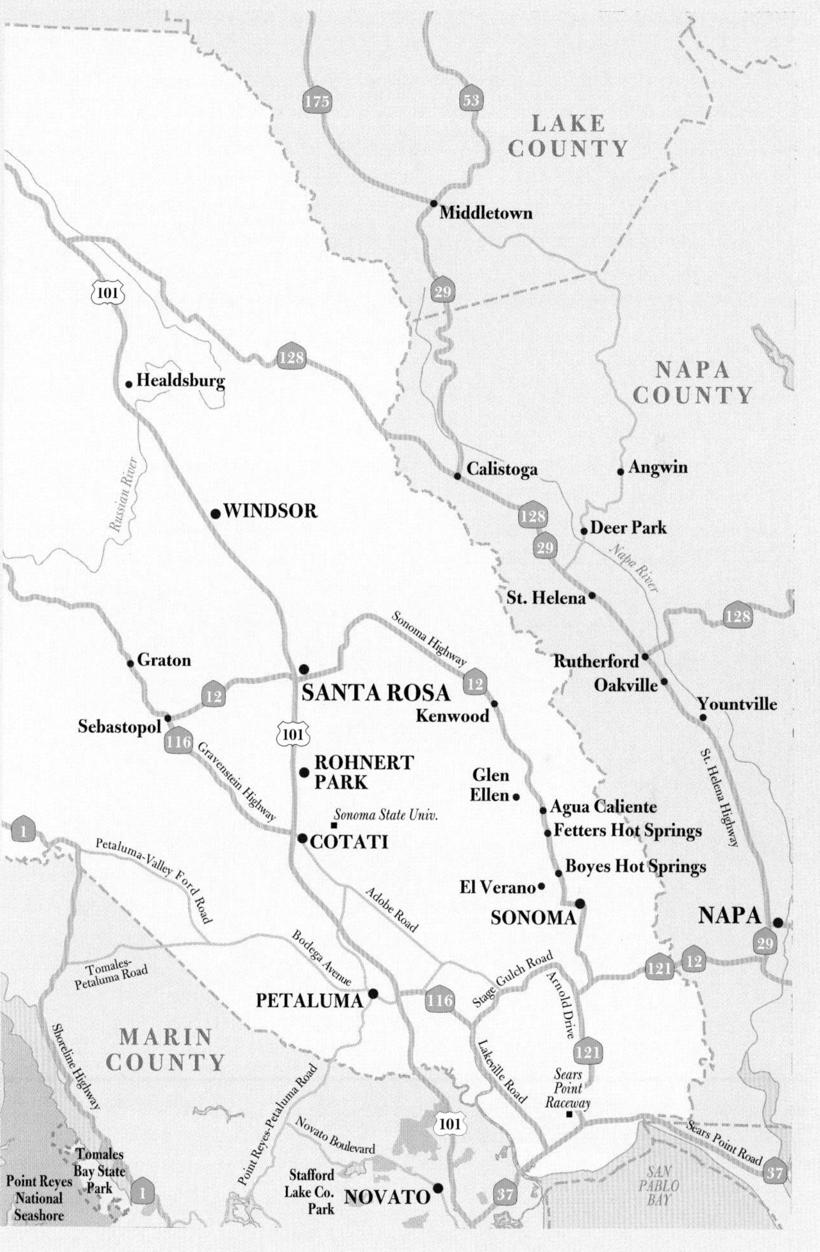

LAKE COUNTY
NAPA COUNTY
MARIN COUNTY
Middletown
Healdsburg
Calistoga
Angwin
Deer Park
WINDSOR
Russian River
Napa River
St. Helena
Sonoma Highway
Graton
SANTA ROSA
Rutherford
Oakville
Yountville
Kenwood
Sebastopol
Gravenstein Highway
ROHNERT PARK
Glen Ellen
St. Helena Highway
Sonoma State Univ.
Agua Caliente
Fetters Hot Springs
COTATI
Petaluma-Valley Ford Road
Boyes Hot Springs
El Verano
Adobe Road
SONOMA
NAPA
Bodega Avenue
Tomales-Petaluma Road
Stage Gulch Road
Arnold Drive
PETALUMA
Shoreline Highway
Lakeville Road
Sears Point Raceway
Point Reyes-Petaluma Road
Novato Boulevard
Sears Point Road
SAN PABLO BAY
Tomales Bay State Park
Point Reyes National Seashore
Stafford Lake Co. Park
NOVATO
175
53
29
101
128
12
116
1
121
37

hierarchy in terms of which one's older or better looking or has more to offer. One thing to remember is that Sonoma's a lot bigger. Only a portion of it is "Wine Country." The rest is backcountry, farm country, or in surprisingly large areas, ugly sprawling suburbs that might as well be in Michigan or Arizona.

Getting Here

Charles M. Schultz Airport shows potential to become a short-haul commercial airport, but presently San Francisco International is the main point of connection. Oakland and Sacramento are preferable, because the airports are less congested and the freeway routes are a bit more direct.

Weather

As a rule it is always twenty degrees cooler in the morning than in the afternoon. Summer starts late and hits its apex in August, with warm temperatures lingering through mid-October. Rainy season is November to February.

Recommended Transportation

The villages are walkable; the cities (Santa Rosa, Petaluma)

The days of wine and roses are plentiful at places like Foppiano, pictured above.

aren't. Tour companies upsell their product by offering "customized tours," but they're probably not taking you anywhere off the regular wine routes. Either hire a driver for the day or get your own car and a designated ~~sucker~~ driver.

Style

There is an odd misconception lately that Sonoma's a snobby sport jacket sort of place. *Not true.* Dress is casual, shorts are fine, hippie skirts are better, and khakis mark you as a yuppie—who hopefully will spend tons of money and is, therefore, to be courted but not trusted.

Fees

Generally there is a $10–$20 tasting fee, give or take.

Bird's-eye View

This is a huge county with a coast and a river, varied topography, mysterious microclimates, and a lot more cookie-cutter suburbs than the publicity would have you believe.

Right at the southern border is Petaluma, a funky-clunky retro town and former chicken-raising hub which gets a decent amount of wine tourism traffic because it's the closest to San Francisco. From there, Highway 101 leads to Cotati, Rohnert Park, Santa Rosa—all suburban towns with traffic, strip malls, and motels packed together in an ugly concrete grid crisscrossed by freeway overpasses. Cotati can be cute, as it's more of a college town. Rohnert Park and Santa Rosa can be skipped altogether.

Jaunt east on Highway 116 and you'll get to Carneros, which is a peculiar AVA because it spans the Sonoma/Napa County border. Heading north on Highway 12 are the villages of Sonoma, Boyes Hot Springs, Glen Ellen, and Kenwood, all of which are cute and picturesque and cluttered with wineries—many of them quite famous.

Highway 12 East takes you through Sebastopol, and from there, either farther east to the hippie towns of Occidental and Freestone, or north to the recently famous "West County," where dozens of picturesque and/or famous wineries flourish nearby the Russian River, surrounded by woods and nudists, Haight-Ashbury holdouts and the last few remaining orchards.

Windsor marks the beginning of North County. It used to be a fairly ugly town, but recent overhauls leave it looking far more like somewhere you'd want to actually visit on vacation. It has to be: It's the gateway to Healdsburg, which is the shining star in the Sonoma County wine tourism spectrum. Once known only for its Raven Theater and walkable square, this town's become a bona fide media darling. We won't rehash everything you've already read about it.

Keep heading north and you'll hit Geyserville, with Dry Creek toward the west and Alexander Valley in the east. This area still has uncontrived bucolic charm and affordable prices. The focus remains on wine making, not new luxury inns and celebrity restaurants. Because of this, lodgings are more limited, but those that exist are unique and charming.

Area Key:
12E = Carneros, Sonoma, Boyes Hot Springs, Glen Ellen, Kenwood
CS = Central Sonoma County: Petaluma, Santa Rosa, Rohnert Park, Cotati
WC = West County including Sebastopol, Graton, Forestville, Monte Rio, Occidental, Guerneville, Rio Nido, Fulton
RR = Russian River area including Windsor, Healdsburg, Green Valley
NC = North County including Geyserville, Dry Creek, Alexander Valley

The Panel

Chris Benziger, Benziger Family Winery

Jeff Bundschu, Gundlach Bundschu Winery

Mark Caldwell, executive chef, Bubble Lounge at J Vineyards & Winery

Peter Fodor, concierge, Gaige House

Nick Frey, Sonoma County Winegrape Commission

Gina Gallo, Gallo Family Wine

Liza Graves, owner, Beautiful Places

Chris Sawyer, consulting "film sommelier" and sommelier at the Lodge at Sonoma

Welcome to the Good Life

Sonoma County residents have always known how to have a good time. They appreciate quality food and booze, performing arts and culture, friends and family. They know how to slow down and appreciate life—and, especially in the following venues and places, visitors are encouraged and even shown how to do the same.

Wine Grapes 101

Nick Frey, Sonoma County Winegrapes Commission

Take away the alcohol and what in wine are you actually tasting for? Perhaps the best way to learn is by getting to know the grapes—by taste, look, smell, and feel. Wine grapes are 24½ percent to 26½ percent sugar. They're very sweet compared to table grapes. Tannins and seeds have a nutty flavor when ripe.

Chardonnay: Usually a larger berry than red varietals. Chard tends to be exposed to the sun. That sun exposure turns the grape from green to golden yellow on the skin and also has a bit of an impact on the flavor profile.

Gewurtzraminer: Tough-skinned berries with distinct, sugar-concentrated flavors.

Cabernet: These grapes have the most tannins, which is why Cab ages the best. The dominating taste is a veggie, almost bell pepper flavor that will dissipate over time. Even when it's ripe, it is squeaky on the teeth and dries your mouth out. Winemakers check to see if tannins are at the stage they want them: not too stringent, but with some structure. The grapes can be puckery if tannins haven't started to mature.

Pinot Noir: Softer skin, low tannins, a little lighter. Small berries. More toward red fruit and cherry.

Zinfandel: Of the red grapes, the best flavor is in the Zinfandel. It's black fruit and not as peppery as the grapes are. Zin grapes are larger as well. In the old days Zinfandel could possibly be dual-purpose grapes (for wine and the table).

Sauvignon Blanc: If it's not exposed to sun, you get a little grassiness and herbal flavor, the same as you'd get from the wine. The more you expose it to sun, the more you get tropical fruit or pear, though it's harder to tell in the grape.

Syrah: More toward the black fruit; not as much tannin as Cab. Often as they get ripe, the skin dimples and shrivels a bit.

Where to taste: Sonoma County Harvest Fair, Grape Camp, www.sonomawinegrape.org

WINERIES

Cline Cellars
(12E) 24737 Arnold Drive/Highway 121, Sonoma, (707) 940-4030, www.clinecellars.com; Fee: Y; Open: Daily; Key: DS
One of the closest wineries to the south county border, Cline nonetheless never seems like it's been overtaken by a tourist stampede. There's a pleasant tasting room and a couple picnic tables that are better suited for sharing a bottle than laying out a whole picnic spread.

Chris Sawyer says: "Great for Rhône varietals and Zinfandel."

LENA STAMP: Every now and again, though not with predictable regularity, they produce swoon-inspiring dessert wines, both red and white.

Jacuzzi
(12E) 24724 Arnold Drive/Highway 121, Sonoma, (707) 931-7575, www.jacuzziwines.com; Fee: Y; Open: Daily
This new Cline offshoot right across the road from the original property offers California-style Italian wines. Everything is farmed organically, without pesticides and sustainably.

Chris Sawyer says: "Fred Cline's family legacy came from inventing the Jacuzzi hot tub, and this winery is named in homage. Zingy, spicy Zinfandels and really lush, lovely Rhône varietals."

Hanzell
(12E) 18596 Lomita Avenue, Sonoma, (707) 996-3860, www.hanzell.com; Fee: Y; Open: By appt.; Key: XP, RR
A historically significant, critically acclaimed winery that rests quietly at the end of a lane, one mile north of the Sonoma town square. Library wines reach back to the 1950s.

Liza Graves says: "Stunning Chardonnay and Pinot Noir."

Iron Horse Vineyards
(WC) 9786 Ross Station Road, Sebastopol, (707) 887-1507, www.ironhorsevineyards.com; Fee: Y; Open: By appt.; Key: DS
This spot is peaceful, beautiful, and petite, with rose gardens and hillside vineyards. It's an under-the-radar classic in a lush countryside setting.

Liza Graves says: "Beautiful winery tucked away on top of a hill."

LENA STAMP: Its sparkling wines are my favorite and everybody else's, though it also does Chardonnay and Pinot Noir.

J Vineyards & Winery
(RR) 11447 Old Redwood Highway, Healdsburg, (707) 431-3646, www.jwine.com; Fee: Y; Open: Bubble Lounge Thu-Tue; Key: XP, DS
The younger sister to iconic Jordan Winery on Alexander Valley Road, J has become just as beloved in the decade since its inception. It specializes in sparkling wine and has created a sophisticated tasting experience to showcase the wine. Sit-down flights are accompanied by gourmet food pairings, served with pomp—and expense—that even the Napa wineries respect. The winery runs tours daily by appointment.

J's food and wine pourings are a splurge in a scenic setting.

Trentadue
(NC) 19170 Geyserville Avenue, Geyserville, (707) 433-3104, www.trentadue.com; Fee: N; Open: Daily
Out of dozens of wineries in the Geyserville area, this is one of the most recommended because it still does hospitality the old-fashioned way. It's primarily grown reds since its inception in the 1960s. The winery shares ties, property, and grapes with neighboring Ridge Vineyards. (Note: Ridge Vineyards is located in Dry Creek Valley and is owned by Ridge/Lytton Springs out of the South Bay. It grows a cult Zinfandel.)

Pedroncelli
(NC) 1220 Canyon Road, Geyserville, (800) 836-3894, (707) 857-3531, www.pedroncelli.com; Fee: N; Open: Daily; Key: DS
Strong local ties and a love for the land define this family-owned holdout in Dry Creek Valley. After chasing the boom like everyone else in the 1970s, the family scaled back and refocused on single-vineyard wines. It is the oldest tasting room in Dry Creek Valley, with a local artist exhibit room, bocce courts, and a picnic area.

Nick Frey says: "Well priced, well made. Not overpowering. Nicely balanced food wines."

Sbragia Family Vineyards
(NC) 9990 Dry Creek Road, Geyserville, (707) 473-2992, www.sbragia.com; Fee: Y; Open: Daily; Key: FO
Secreted away in the northern reaches of Dry Creek Valley, this winery has a patio with a beautiful hillside overlook.

Nick Frey says: "A family winery owned by the longtime winemaker at Beringer."

Eco Defined

Chris Benziger, Benziger Family Winery

With *green* and *eco* as the buzzwords of the day, it helps to understand what they mean if you want to know what you're buying—and, by proxy, buying into.

Green wraps up a whole philosophy. If you're green, you're thinking about what kind of water your employees are drinking, your corporate philosophy, whether your consumption of a product is cutting down trees, and so on. Unfortunately, since there's no government or third-party standard for "green," just about anyone can slap a GREEN sticker on their product.

Organic wine is a label that came from the government. It means the winemaker hasn't added sulfites.

Organically grown means there's been no chemical input. The real benefit to growing organically is that the crops evoke the flavor of the place. When you use synthetic fertilizers, the roots are fed at the surface of the soil. If you don't, they have to reach farther, prompting deep root growth. Grapes grown organically reflect the *terroir,* or "sense of place," much more distinctly, and that carries over into the wine.

Biodynamic encompasses organic farming's chemical-free principles and also dictates that the entire ecosystem of a farm (or vineyard) be self-sustaining and a "closed circle." In a biodynamic vineyard, every shrub, plant, and animal is there for a reason.

Sustainability (in any business) hinges on three principles. It's actually a pyramid. The bottom of the pyramid is that you try to do the most environmentally sensitive things possible. Everyone's vineyard is different, so what applies for one doesn't apply for another. Products that are sustainably grown won't necessarily be organic, and vice versa. The middle rung revolves around social responsibility: the way you treat your employees and resources and, farther up the supply chain, the way your contracted suppliers treat their people and resources. The top of the pyramid is economic viability. You do no good if you go out of business.

Benziger Family Winery
(12E) 1883 London Ranch Road, Glen Ellen, (888) 490-2739, (707) 935-3000, www.benziger.com; Fee: Y; Open: Daily; Key: DS, TH
Ride a tram powered by french-fry oil all around the hilly vineyards, herb gardens, and insectories. The grounds are gorgeous, but for those über-private moments, Chris Benziger recommends a late-afternoon walk up to the "Acropolis," a Greek-style gazebo built on the Benziger ranch by the hippies who owned the property before them.

Adds Benziger: "Pull in at 4:30. The tours shut down, but the winery doesn't shut down for another hour. Nobody's up there, and we don't bother anybody. Just you, your girlfriend, and a bottle of wine. . . . It's the most romantic spot in wine country. During that one hour, people propose, have impromptu weddings, do the dirty. . . . It's awesome."

Recommended wines include the 2004 "Sunny Slope" Cabernet, made from grapes grown on the slopes of the Mayacamas mountain range; the 2006 Sauvignon Blanc "Estate Paraiso de Maria," which emulates the style of a Sancerre ("I'd drink it on my Coco Puffs," Benziger claims); and the 2004 "Tribute," which honors past-generation Benzigers.

ATTRACTIONS

Family Wineries of Dry Creek Valley
(RR) 4791 Dry Creek Road, Healdsburg, (888) 433-6555, www.familywines.com; Fee: Y; Open: Daily
Six small independent wineries are part of this co-op tasting room. More than twenty wines are on pour from Collier Falls, Mietz, Dashe Cellars, and others. It has a cute, farm-cottage tasting room with specialty foods and gift items. There are bocce courts and a picnic area outside. The affiliated East County co-op is Family Wineries of Kenwood (see same Web site).

Sonoma Segway
(12E) 524 Broadway, Sonoma, (707) 938-2080, www.sonomasegway.com; Fee: Y; Open: Daily; Key: CHEESE, RR
If a golf cart and pogo stick had a steamy love affair, this weird little transporter would be the result. They only go about ten

miles an hour, and you don't have to pedal, which makes them an ideal way to get around the vineyard roads. The only problem is, there's no drinking on the organized tours. Hourly rentals are another option.

Peter Fodor says, "A young couple put together the business. You spend the first half-hour learning to ride the Segway. Then they take you on a tour through the back part of Sonoma and through the vineyards."

Cornerstone Place
(12E) 23570 Highway 121, Sonoma, (707) 933-3020, www.cornerstonegardens.com; Fee: N; Open: Daily; Key: FO
An upside-down picket fence, a large tree festooned with blue Ping-Pong balls, and other ever-changing oddball installations are the main attraction at this unique garden/retail/wine-tasting facility.

Peter Fodor says: "Multiple landscape architects have designed relatively avant garde gardens. They have a tasting room, an excellent little deli/café, and shops where you can purchase upscale garden accents—not necessarily the same things you'd find in a chain store."

RESTAURANTS

Garden Court
(12E) 13647 Arnold Drive, Glen Ellen, (707) 935-1565, www.gardencourtcafe.com; $; Open: B, L Wed-Mon; Key: PETS
A mom-and-pop-and-dog shop serving American standards made from local ingredients. Pet menu available for pups.

Chris Benziger says: "Best Eggs Benny in the world."

Café LaHaye
(12E) 140 E. Napa Street, Sonoma, (707) 935-5994, www.cafelahaye.com; $$; Open: D Tue-Sat; Key: SCENE
From the art on the walls to the

fresh and flavorful food, this Sonoma Square kitchen offers the kind of colorful experience visitors crave. There's a slight Italian influence to the food, though often it's overwhelmed by California cuisine stylings.

Peter Fodor says: "My favorite place, and a wonderful wine country experience. The food is always excellent. Every time I send guests, I get raves. Chef Norman Owens works out of a kitchen the size of a closet."

La Hacienda

(NC) 134 N. Cloverdale Boulevard, Cloverdale, (707) 894-9365; $; Open: L, D daily; Key: FO

A Michoacan native does authentic Mexican in this little restaurant, which has something like legendary status in spite of its out-of-the-way locale.

Chris Benziger says: "A fair combination of gringos and Mexicans, but great food. It's where the locals hang. You'll have a great time."

Syrah Bistro

(CS) 205 Fifth Street, Santa Rosa, (707) 568-4002, www.syrahbistro.com; $$$; Open: L Tue-Sat, D daily; Key: AT, DS, RR on weekends

At this Railroad Square restaurant, the servers have tattooed San Fran style and a hint of Parisian attitude that probably comes from reading about themselves in the papers too much. The food is outstanding enough to make up for their shortcomings (and the fact that the dining room is packed claustrophobically tight). The chef's a Slow Food follower who uses organic or free-range meats raised close to home (Liberty Farms duck, Fulton Valley chicken, Sonoma lamb), along with produce and herbs at the peak of their season. Four- or seven-course tasting menus are available.

Restaurant Mirepoix

(RR) 275 Windsor River Road, Windsor, (707) 838-0162, www.restaurantmirepoix.com; $$; Open: L, D Tue-Sat; Key: DS

Long before Sonoma County became a media darling, this was Mariposa—one of the few fine dining outposts within fifty miles. Now, to compete with its newly arrived Food Network-honored neighbors, it's turned into a tres sophisticated bistro gem in a residential neighborhood.

Gina Gallo says: "Windsor's done a good job in terms of how they developed the town. This is in an older home but very top-notch. I like the paté."

Food and Wine Pairing: An Interview with Mark Caldwell, Executive Chef, Bubble Lounge at J Vineyards

TT: Please resolve the eternal debate over red for meat, white for chicken/fish. Is it really set in stone?
MC: It's a good general guideline to follow when you're first learning. But it really comes down to the sauces and the marinades.

TT: Is there a science or do you follow your nose?
MC: The biggest thing is to work the acidity in the food against the acidity in the wine or with the acidity of the wine. When you first start drinking wine and pairing, pay attention to the first few bites and sips—what works and interacts well. After a while, it is a matter of instinct.

TT: So what about rosé?
MC: It falls right in the middle. It's pretty versatile. Dryer ones go with smoked or grilled meats; sweeter go with seafood dishes or even chicken.

TT: How do you pair sparkling wines with food?
MC: With sparkling wine, in general, it's safe to go with seafood. Lighter dishes, creamy sauces, and fried dishes usually work very well with a sparkling menu. I pair soft-shell crab in season with a vintage Brut. People don't realize that sparkling wine can carry you all the way through a meal.

TT: How do you pair wine with cheese?
MC: This could go on forever, because there are so many variables. Sparkling wine is the fallback with salty cheeses, creamy or blue. A Pinot Noir works well with lighter cheese, because it's a lighter red. With a strong cheese (i.e., a Stilton), a dessert wine, such as our Ratafia, would go well. One rule of thumb with a cheese from Europe is to pair it with a wine from the same region.

TT: How do you pair with soup or stew as a main course?
MC: A bisque goes well with sparkling rosé or sparkling vintage Brut. The creaminess of bisque and citrus notes in Brut complement each other, and the effervescence cleanses the palate. My mom makes an Italian wedding soup, and she pours in some Pinot, so naturally that has the affinity to go with Pinot. A big thick stew (beef Bourguignon) goes well with a big, thick red wine. Cioppino could go with a Pinot Gris or a sparkling wine. Depending on spices, it might also go with a Pinot.

Taverna Santi
(NC) 21047 Geyserville Avenue, Geyserville, (707) 857-1790, www.tavernasanti.com; $$$; Open: L Wed–Sat, D daily; Key: DS, SF
The wave of good feeling in this place hits you like a warm tide when you open the door. The bar has an exposed brick back wall with a little stone arch over mirrors. The dining room is elegant, with Tuscan stylings, slanted ceilings, and a fireplace. The wooden back deck is strung with fairy lights. This is the social hub of downtown Geyserville—or it used to be before the owners opened Diavola Pizza a few doors down. Santi's hearty yet sophisticated Northern Italian cuisine (grilled rib eye, brick-oven chicken, house-cured Salumi) is more expensive and more special occasion than Diavola's brick-oven pizzas. Both places are wonderful and serve a need in the neighborhood, however.

ENTERTAINMENT AND NIGHTLIFE

Saloon at the Jack London Lodge
(12E) 13740 Arnold Drive, Glen Ellen, (707) 938-8510, www.jacklondonlodge.com; $; Open: PM, OWL; Key: PU
A jukebox, a cue ball, local color, and good company. Jack London would have approved of this tavern located in "his" hotel.

Chris Benziger says: "Drunks are at the bar doing shooters, kids are playing pool. A good piece of wood, as my father used to say."

El Dorado Kitchen
(12E) 405 First Street West, Sonoma, (707) 996-3030, www.eldoradosonoma.com; $$$; Open: AM, PM; Key: PU, SCENE
A full bar and a fabulous patio draw people to this buzzy restaurant/lounge. Live music, wine tastings, and other events are geared toward enhancing the social scene as much as showcasing local wines and food. This venue is inside a little downtown hotel, so if you get too drunk to find your way to your own bed, you may be able to score one upstairs.

Peter Fodor says: "One of the few places that has a bar scene. Going for hip and trendy."

SHOPPING

Cheese Shop
(RR) 423 Center Street, Healdsburg, (707) 433-4998, www.doraliceimports.com; Open: Mon-Sat

A picnic becomes a gourmet experience when you set foot in this chef's pick, which has a weekly changing selection of fromagerie from places near and far—as well as some made just for the house. Art exhibits by different local artists rotate monthly.

Mark Caldwell says: "This is the one I use. An amazing selection of cheeses from all over the world."

Windsor Wine Shop
(RR) 9058 Windsor Road, Windsor, (707) 838-9378, www.windsorwineshop.net; Open: Daily, PM/OWL Fri-Sat; Key: SCENE

An affable local retailer that switch-hits as a neighborhood bar, small-plates cafe, and music venue. Locals say owners Stephanie and Tony Marti are the unofficial mayors of the town—which makes sense, being that they control the vino.

LENA STAMP: Live music till 11 p.m. on Friday and Saturday nights. This is what I call doing your duty for the community.

ACCOMMODATIONS

Gaige House Inn
(12E) 13540 Arnold Drive, Glen Ellen, (800) 935-0237, (707) 935-0237, www.gaige.com; $$$$; Key: AT, XP

Sleek and serene—a classic local inn renovated in the chic manner of Thompson Hotels. This international brand mostly does luxury boutique hotels in big cities. Though the staff contends this is still a "wine country inn," it's not even a little bit country. It does have the fireplaces and oversize bathtubs, but they're contemporary and sophisticated, just like everything else. It's as if a San Francisco boutique hotel went to the countryside for the weekend and tried to blend in with the locals. However, San Francisco (and Los Angeles, and New York, and London . . .) dwellers who are doing that very thing will feel quite at home here.

Geyserville Inn
(NC) 21714 Geyserville Avenue, Geyserville, (877) 857-4343, www.geyservilleinn.com; $$; Key: FO
Just off Highway 101 (the 101), moments from Sonoma County's northern border, this unpretentious property provides comfortable, reasonably priced lodgings in the unsung heartland of wine country. Geyser Peak, Pedroncelli, Trentadue, and scores of other famous wineries are within a few miles. Looks-wise, the exterior is somewhere between a Victorian mansion and a motor inn. Inside it leans more toward deluxe motel—except for in the upstairs king rooms, which are gradually being made over in glossy "wine resort" style (flat screen TVs, soaking tubs, gas fireplace, and so on). Adjacent restaurant Hoffman House serves breakfast and lunch daily, dinner on weekends only.

Scenes from a Wine Country Idyll

Liza Graves, Owner, Beautiful Places

The Wine Country lifestyle is about enjoying natural beauty and garnering an appreciation for the process that leads from grape to glass. It's about reconnecting with spouses, friends, and family. It's about relishing tastes, flavors, and sensations. And it isn't relegated to a particular property. As Liza Graves can tell you better than anyone, this lifestyle suits a myriad of beautiful places. Here's her list of six picture-perfect wine country scenarios:

- An alfresco luncheon—everyone pitches in doing what they're best at, whether that's making salad, whipping up a *beurre blanc,* or keeping their friends' wine glasses full.
- A late-night vineyard dinner under a huge harvest moon, after you've helped a small winery destem their grapes or punch down the fermenting juice.
- Early morning at the local farmers' market: the jovial hunt for the pick of local produce and fish from the Pacific, sausages from Sonoma, handcrafted cheeses, and artisan breads.
- Bringing in the dawn with a private yoga class, where the instructor comes to your villa and the incredible views imbue your body and spirit with grace.
- Sunset in a private hot tub, with a bottle of wine, good friends, and free-flowing conversation.
- Cuddling by a fire at 10 p.m., having conversations you couldn't have in a hotel.

Beautiful Places
(MULTIPLE) 539 First Street West, Sonoma, (800) 495-9961, www.beautiful-places.com; $$$$; Key: XP, DS
Villa and home rentals all around Sonoma and Napa counties are the easiest way to pretend like you're a wealthy local with a multimillion-dollar home. This is well suited to small groups who want to stay together, cook together, hot tub together, and avoid people they don't know.

Bella Villa Messina
(RR) 316 Burgundy Road, Healdsburg, (707) 433-6655, www.villamessina.com; $$$; Key: DS
Only a few rooms are available at this funky, unpretentious B&B, which treats guests like friends and has plenty of sunny spaces to picnic and relax.

Mark Caldwell says: "A fun one. Decorated antique style, the dogs are ambassadors, and the owners are fun. It's like you're visiting someone you know."

As Seen on TV

If you've only seen Sonoma County in newspapers or the pages of *US Weekly* or on television, here are some familiar places to start off your exploration of this great big photogenic county.

WINERIES

Keller Estate
(CS) 5875 Lakeville Highway, Petaluma, (707) 765-2117, www.kellerestate.com; Fee: Y; Open: Thur-Sat or by appt.

At this impressive new winery, exceptional wines and gorgeous classic cars reflect the personal tastes of the owner.

Chris Sawyer says: "The owner made his fortune designing the interiors of Alfa Romeo and Ferrari. He put down a vineyard and originally wanted to make a racetrack, but realized he was growing great grapes and decided to get a winemaker and go all the way. Walk in the front door and you might see a cherried-out Woody or a 1956 Mercedes."

Adobe Road Winery
(CS) 1995 S. McDowell Boulevard, Petaluma, (707) 939-7967, www.adoberoadwines.com; Fee: Y; Open: By appt.; Key: CHEESE

This winery's in a nondescript warehousey area, but inside, a collection of super-hot Porsches greets the unsuspecting visitor.

Chris Sawyer says: "This one's a little bit more *Talladega Nights*—you know, the whole thrill of victory. Kevin owns a stock car company and a Porsche company. He also owns racing teams. I like their Cabernet Franc a lot."

SoCo on the Screen

Chris Sawyer, Sommelier,
the Lodge at Sonoma, and Consulting "Film Sommelier"

From as far back as the 1950s, Sonoma County has had its place on the silver screen. A film buff as well as a sommelier, Chris Sawyer knows all film locations, famous and obscure. A few he suggests you look out for:

Peggy Sue Got Married was filmed in Petaluma and based in the 1950s. There's a walking tour you can take that brings you to all historic houses built in the same time period.

Downtown Petaluma is the cruising lane in *American Graffiti,* where the guys were driving the cars, trying to pick up girls. All the buildings are still there.

Bodega Head is great to go up and eat oysters. Driving back is the same route the ravens flew in Hitchcock's *The Birds.*

Gloria Ferrer

(12E) 23555 Carneros Highway, Sonoma, (707) 996-7256, www.gloriaferrer.com; Fee: Y; Open: Daily; Key: TH, DS

One of the foremost sparkling wineries in the area, this property has a postcard feel about it, with caves and a scenic outlook. Locals suggest you end the day there with a flute of fabulous bubbly. The tour is a good way to learn about *methode champenoise* (traditional French method for making sparkling wine).

Chris Sawyer says: "I did a very cool thing with *Batman* and their Carneros Cuvee, which comes in this gorgeous black curvaceous bottle. When Michael Keaton came here for the film festival, I unveiled a whole row of wine and revealed that I was going to pair his films with wines and have them drink it up on stage."

Great sparklers come from the Gloria Ferrer Estate.

Sonoma-Cutrer

(RR) 4401 Slusser Road, Windsor (888) 766-2770; www.sonomacutrer.com; Fee: Y; Open: By appt.; Key: DS

One of the classic Sonoma County wineries, this estate has been closed to the public for years. It's opening in phases—first to Wine Club members only, but hopefully it will become a go-to destination. In the meantime, it may be worth it to become a member just to play a few games of croquet on the perfectly maintained lawn court.

Chalk Hill Estate

(RR) 10300 Chalk Hill Road, Healdsburg, (800) 838-4306, (707) 838-4306, www.chalkhill.com; Fee: Y; Open: By appt.; Key: DS

A health retreat . . . an artist's inspiration . . . a farm . . . an award-winning sustainable wine estate. This property has been many things over the years, all of which focus around the singular qualities of its beautiful, nurturing lands. Of its wine portfolio, the estate Chardonnay—particularly from the Founder's Block—is a connoisseur's pick.

Liza Graves says: "This appointment-only 1,477-acre winery is one of the most beautiful estates that we have ever seen. For a special treat, book the 1½-hour culinary tour of the vineyards and estate culinary garden followed by a wine and small plates pairing prepared by the estate's chef."

Kunde
(12E) 9825 Sonoma Highway 12, Kenwood, (707) 833-5501, www.kunde.com; Fee: Y; Open: Daily; Key: TH

This fifth-generation family winery is a huge proponent of sustainable farming. Learn more about it on an ecotour, which is not for the faint of foot—it's actually a hike through the mountainside property. Much of the movie *Bottle Shock* was filmed here, though the movie was actually about Napa.

LENA STAMP: Kunde's wines are excellent, but my favorite grape, the Malvasia Blanca, which is only grown on this property of all the places in the county, doesn't show up as its own varietal on the release list.

ATTRACTIONS

Jack London State Park
(12E) London Ranch Road, Glen Ellen, (707) 938-5216, www.jacklondonpark.com; Fee: Y; Open: Daily; Key: TH

One of Sonoma's most famous citizens, the author Jack London, loved his 1,000-acre Beauty Ranch with a fervor that any vintner can appreciate. Now part of the park system, Beauty Ranch is protected land, as is London's gravesite and the ruins of Wolf House, the "dream home" in which he never actually got to live. Docent-led tours visit all kinds of significant sites, including the piggery that was one of London's most talked about projects. A museum is also located on the grounds.

Green String Farm
(CS) 3571 Old Adobe Road, Petaluma, (707) 778-7500, www.greenstringfarm.com; $; Open: Daily; Key: VEG

This certified organic and sustainable farm is on the road that leads from Petaluma to Sonoma—a convenient pit stop that's also in the center of a classic film shot. The owner is a green gardener of long standing. He sells all sorts of certified organic vegetables for $2 a pound.

Chris Sawyer says: "Right in the middle of the long strip of road where they did the drag racing in *American Graffiti*."

RESTAURANTS

Dry Creek Kitchen
(RR) 317 Healdsburg Avenue (in Hotel Healdsburg), Healdsburg, (707) 431-0330, www.charlie palmer.com; $$$; Open: L Fri–Sun, D daily; Key: SCENE, DS
Sonoma County pulled off a culinary coup when this Charlie Palmer restaurant arrived on the scene—particularly since, unlike many big city restaurants with a marquee-name chef, this one actually has its famous owner on-site and overseeing the day-to-day operations much of the time. According to locals, Palmer fell in love with the county and its focus on artisan cuisine, and thus decided to make Healdsburg his home base. Sonoma duck, Painted Hill beef, Love Farms produce, and mountain-picked mushrooms make regular appearances on the table. The Sonoma Neighbor Menu is a three-course prix fixe served Monday through Thursday—definitely it's the best bargain from a culinary superstar.

Gina Gallo says: "He's part of the community, very present."

Cyrus
(RR) 29 North Street, Healdsburg, (707) 433-3311, www.cyrus restaurant.com; $$$$; Open: D daily; Key: XP, DS, SCENE, AT
When even the winemakers describe a place as "only for people with money," you know it's formidable. Nonetheless, ask about fine dining in the area and this California-French stunner is the first name off everyone's lips. Possibly it's due to the superformal service by tuxedo-clad servers, possibly because of the prices, and possibly because there's a separate menu for champagne and caviar, but Cyrus has an undeniable "wow" factor. Foie gras and lamb loin, lobster salad and sea bass . . . the menu is a laundry list of special-occasion treats. The wine service includes custom pairing flights as well as standard bottle suggestions, which is a very nice touch—particularly since the 600-label cellar merits some in-depth exploration.

Zazu
(CS) 3535 Guerneville Road, Santa Rosa, (707) 523-4814, www.zazurestaurant.com; $$; Open: D Wed–Sun; Key: TH, VEG
With its quaint looks and personable chef/owner Duskie Estes, this restaurant is a low-key charmer. Its homegrown, back-to-the-roots Slow Food philosophies just happened to dovetail perfectly with the collective national urge to "go green," inspiring a tremendous amount of great press, including a *Wine Spectator* cover. The menu changes just about every day and features whatever Duskie harvested from her garden or found at the market, but the Pinot & Pizza pairing proved so popular that it now happens three times a week.

Gina Gallo says: "Adorable—looks like a little red barn."

ENTERTAINMENT AND NIGHTLIFE

Volpi's
(CS) 124 Washington Street, Petaluma, (707) 762-2371; $; Open: Wed–Sun AM/PM/OWL; Key: SKETCH
A colorful neighborhood bar attached to an Italian restaurant. Deer heads, ram heads, and various other dubious ornaments occupy the walls, and dollar bills are tacked to the ceiling. The clientele is a potpourri, and the evening's "entertainment" may consist of the Volpi family playing the accordion.

Chris Sawyer says: "You really feel that you're in *American Graffiti.* Old Swiss-Italian style speakeasy. Kids with Mohawks, winemakers, old farmers. A very nostalgic place."

SHOPPING

Jack London Village
(12E) 14301 Arnold Drive, Glen Ellen, (707) 933-3055, www.jacklondonshops.com; Open: Varied; Key: TH
This former sawmill has transformed halfway into a bustling commercial collective, and it seems to be holding steady, just a few notches short of actual bustle. The various merchants—a wine country chocolatier, a Nepalese restaurant, Raymond & Co. cheese monger, an olive press,

a tasting room—are a casual collection of neighbors. There's no strip-mall feel to this place—hallelujah!

LENA STAMP: Sonoma Creek runs along one side of the building, with lots of walking trails nearby.

Sonoma Cheese Factory
(12E) 2 Spain Street (Sonoma Plaza), Sonoma, (800) 535-2855, www.sonomacheesefactory.com; $; Open: Daily; Key: TH, KIDS
It's touristy as can be, and in the direct path of pedestrian flow, but this place has been around forever, and if there were a special designation for food landmarks, it would get one. Long before Sonoma was a culinary destination of any kind, the Cheese Factory served locals and visitors who were out for the weekend, cruising the wine country trails. Yes, these days it has a bit of a superdeli feel, but for foodie gift shopping and casual luncheons, it's still a standby.

LENA STAMP: Picnics in my family consisted of pepper jack cheese, summer sausage, and crackers . . . and this is where we got supplies.

ACCOMMODATIONS

The Lodge at Sonoma
(12E) 1325 Broadway, Sonoma, (707) 935-6600, www.thelodgeat sonoma.com; $$$$; Key: SCENE
Sophisticated and contemporary, this place shows the aesthetic effects of a recent $2 million revamp. With a subtle but tangible emphasis on the social aspects of wine country vacationing, this hotel livens up the serene east Sonoma landscape. Guest rooms or cottages are available. Chris Sawyer is the sommelier at the hotel's Carneros Bistro and runs an extensive Sonoma County–centric wine program: thirty-five wines by the glass and 425 by the bottle—the vast majority from the county, with a few European labels just to mix things up. There's live jazz and a groovy cocktail scene in the lounge Friday and Saturday nights.

Fairmont Sonoma Mission Inn & Spa
(12E) 100 Boyes Boulevard, Sonoma, (866) 540-4499, (707) 938-9000, www.fairmont.com /sonoma; $$$$; Key: XP, DS, SF
Even before it came into the illustrious Fairmont fold, this hotel was a Sonoma County classic. It was built in the 1920s, and people

Alfresco dining at Carneros Bistro.

who have been coming here since the early days say it's changed . . . almost entirely. The decor looks nothing like it did in the grand old days. Some things remain consistent though: the graceful exterior, the name, the top-rate service, and the thermal mineral springs. There are lots of destination spas in the country, but only a handful still have that legendarily healing water on tap. This is a special-occasion spot for visitors on getaway and local families celebrating birthdays, engagements, and holiday dinners.

Hotel Healdsburg

(RR) 25 Matheson Street, Healdsburg, (707) 431-2800, www.hotelhealdsburg.com; $$$; Key: SCENE

When it first opened, this property redefined ritzy for the region. Since then, one newcomer after another keeps upping the ante—however, Hotel Healdsburg holds a place at the top of the "it" list. Both the bar and Charlie Palmer's Dry Creek Kitchen have a sizeable local following to balance out the tourism ebb and flow. The hotel is right on the square and maximizes the see-and-be-seen potential with French doors in the restaurant that open out onto the square, and oversize windows looking out on it. The bar has outdoor tables as well, but only on the side, so not quite the same prime people watching. Excellent cocktails and great bartenders.

Grass Roots Legacies

The term *family winery* tends to evoke mom-and-pop operations, small farms, a daily dirt-under-the-fingernails struggle to stay alive as an "indie" in a big-money corporate game. That's why it's so satisfying to see so many of the oldest Sonoma County wine families not only surviving, but dominating the scene. The names you see on the label are the same ones working in the fields, the crush pads, the tasting rooms, and the boardroom roundtables. They bring passion, character, and commitment that corporations just can't match.

WINERIES

Foppiano
(NC) 12707 Old Redwood Highway, Healdsburg, (707) 433-7272, www.foppiano.com; Fee: Y; Open: Daily

This is a classic winery run by a classic family. Everyone in town knows Louis Foppiano, and depending whom you ask, he's either "a grumpy codger" or "the greatest guy in the world." The winemaking facility has been here since 1937, when the label first started bottling and labeling its wine (before that wines were sold in bulk). The Foppiano name has always been known for red wines—first blends and then single varietals in the mid-1960s.

Petite Sirah was the first and still is one of the main varietals produced. Other grapes come and go—in fact, all the whites are gone now—although Cabernet is fairly consistent. Pinot Noir is one of the current focuses. And in the way things have of coming full circle, red blends are back: "Lot 96" (named in honor of the Foppiano's first year here—1896) is a spring 2008 release that Louis recommends for its inexpensive price tag, excellent packaging, and drinkable, food-friendly characteristics.

Gundlach Bundschu
(12E) 2000 Denmark Street, Sonoma, (707) 938-5277, www.gunbun.com; Fee: Y; Open: Daily; Key: TH

This sixth-generation, 100 percent family-owned winery has a unique vineyard. It's about 300 acres, and though it's technically in Sonoma Valley, it borders Sonoma and Napa. It was founded in 1858. It does a number of different varietals: Chardonnays and Pinots that are typical of the region, but Cabs and Merlots as well. The visitor areas offer expansive views of the whole surrounding area. By prearrangement, the winery will

Empty wine barrels awaiting their next journey.

Louis Remembers: The Oral History of the Russian River

Louis Foppiano, Fourth-Generation California Winemaker and One of Healdsburg's Living Legends

In the 1850s, my great-grandfather emigrated from Italy to California for the Gold Rush, via the Isthmus of Panama. By the late 1860s he ended up in Healdsburg, farming fruit. In 1896 a ranch came up for sale two miles south of Healdsburg—the eighty-acre Riverside Farm. It had a winery on it already. We're still there, on that ranch.

My grandfather [Louis A.] ran the ranch. In those days wine was delivered by barrel to grocery stores; customers would bring a jug and fill it up. In 1905 a grocery store owner invited Louis A. for dinner, but neglected to mention that his sister was visiting from Italy. My grandfather met her, proposed, and married her within two weeks. Some stories say he married her the first week and proposed the first night. His decisiveness was deemed "very un-Italian."

In 1910 my great-grandfather and grandfather were fighting, and my great-grandfather sold the ranch. My grandfather borrowed money from his father-in-law and bought it back. During their final meeting, he took my great-grandfather's portrait off the wall, threw it on the ground, and stomped on it. They never spoke again.

Around the year 1920, the Howard Street Gang from San Francisco came to hide out from the law on the west side of Santa Rosa. When the sheriff went to arrest them, they lynched him. Thirty vigilantes—including my grandfather—formed a posse and took the outlaws down. The last person who participated in that died this winter [2007].

Foppiano kept making wine through Prohibition. Northern California was pretty loose as far as that went. There was no Golden Gate Bridge. San Francisco, where all the revenuers were, was a long way away. We got busted once or twice and dumped 50,000 or maybe 100,000 barrels. People could make wine up in the hills, and there were also brandy stills up there. The sheriff would put you in jail if he had to, but it was a fairly light deal. I understand the second floor of the jail was for bootleggers—they'd play cards all day and the jailer's wife would cook for them.

When it looked like Roosevelt was going to be elected, everyone started making wine so they'd have it ready to go after the repeal. My father, Louis, got the winery going in 1933. In 1937 he took a gamble, tore down the original winery—

which was basically just a barn—and built the winery that exists today. Also in 1937 we started bottling our own label. In 1945 we bought Sotoyome Vineyards and doubled the size of the ranch.

Rio Nido was a summer resort area, and in the 1930s and 1940s big bands like Glenn Miller and Benny Goodman would play around there and Guerneville. In the 1960s all these summer homes in that river area were not being used, and when all the hippies left Haight-Ashbury, they moved there and into the unoccupied cabins. At the time there wasn't even a thought of a wine region.

Louis Foppiano and granddaughter.

bring people out to the vineyard in a Pinzgauer (fifteen-person Swiss Army vehicle . . . very popular among winemakers) for tastings and an educational tour. "Get out, get in the dirt, touch the vines, drink some wine in the context of the vines, and then come back to the winery," suggests Jeff Bundschu.

St. Francis
(CS) 100 Pythian Road, Santa Rosa, (888) 675-9463, (707) 833-0242, www.stfranciswinery.com; Fee: Y; Open: Daily; Key: DS, TH
Classic winery with deep Sonoma roots and mission architecture.

Peter Fodor says: "My favorite. Also a beautiful winery to visit. Specializes in big reds."

Buena Vista
(12E) 18000 Old Winery Road, Sonoma, (800) 926-1266, www.buenavistawinery.com; Fee: Y; Open: Daily; Key: XP, DS
If you ever got caught up in the whole Napa vs Sonoma showdown hype, a sociological study of this winery will put it to rest forever. Both counties feel affectionate and proprietary toward Buena Vista, which ignores all of it and proudly proclaims its association with the Carneros subappellation first, foremost, and forever. Established in 1857, the winery's known for Chardonnay and Pinot.

Peter Fodor says: "One of the oldest wineries; beautiful to visit."

Gallo Family Vineyards
(RR) 320 Center Street, Healdsburg, (707) 433-2458, www.gallosonoma.com; Fee: Y; Open: Daily; Key: TH
When the Gallos celebrated their winery's seventy-fifth birthday in 2008, they held a party on the winery grounds for all the employees and their families. About 15,000 people showed up. This is an indication of just how big—and yet how tightly knit—Sonoma's most famous wine family is. Everyone knows the brand, even if he or she mostly associates it with the "value" bottles sold at the supermarket. However, the latest generation of Gallos are moving more and more into the premium market—third-generation winemaker Gina Gallo wins rave reviews from customers for her reserve, estate, and single vineyard releases.

Carneros: What's in the Name?

Jeff Bundschu, Gundlach Bundschu Winery

Over the last few years, Carneros has become a cache name, with implications of great quality and mystique (and subsequently, expense). If pressed, though, few people would know whether it's a vineyard, a county, or an offshore island run by a puppet government. In fact it's a sub-appellation that, for empirical scientific reasons, really deserves its own designation. Jeff Bundschu, a fifth-generation winemaker whose father helped establish the Carneros AVA and then decided *not* to be a part of it, explains:

> Carneros is one of the first established noncounty AVAs in California. It was developed in the early 1970s, during what we call the initial boom of the premium wine industry in California. New wineries were popping up all over, and people were paying attention to the factors that made wine special.
>
> You would judge the climate of Carneros on an east-west running line. As soon as you get far enough north, stick a line in the sand, and everything north would be Sonoma or Napa.
>
> Because of Carneros's proximity to the top of the San Francisco Bay and its position in the direct firing line of Pacific Ocean fog, it was easy to distinguish. In June and July you wake up to the fog—you can almost set your watch to it. And it comes back in the evening. It provides rich ripening conditions wherein during the middle of the day, plants soak up sunlight and create sugar, and then are shut down dramatically by fog, which acts as natural air-conditioning and causes acid levels to peak.

Barrel storage at Gundlach Bundschu.

The Ties That Vine'd - Q&A with Gina Gallo

In the Gallo Family Winery, siblings play nice, kids respect their elders, blood ties don't excuse bad manners, and current generations look out for the ones yet to come. According to third-generation owner/winemaker Gina Gallo, these simple rules are what have made her family one of the largest and most influential wine concerns in the country.

TT: What is your definition of family *from a business perspective?*
GG: The employees are the extended family, the greater family, so to speak—which is pretty obvious, because we're spending so much time together, with similar challenges and similar goals. It's about all of us working together and being together. We just celebrated our seventy-fifth birthday, which was a milestone. We had one big celebration on the winery grounds, with 15,000 people retrospecting. We looked at all the wines that ever were created, the advertising history from the 1930s through the 1950s. We showed movies of Ernest and my grandfather Julio; it was very powerful to see and hear them speaking. There's a famous and wonderful saying: "To understand where you're going, you have to understand where you've come from." I think that gives you great strength.

TT: Does the personal/professional overlap make things easier or harder?
GG: It's hard for me to judge, because it's the only life I've lived. I work with my brother, and people ask, "How do you do that?" But my relationship with him has become so much richer because of having commonality. The wine business is probably one of the perfect family-owned businesses, because it's such a long-term, long-thinking vision. It's five years from when you plant grapes to when you see the wine. We're not under the pressure of reporting to stockholders. Plus, it's fun. The hottest thing right now is food and wine. It's not like we're making widgets.

TT: It's common for close relatives to be less considerate and/or less rational with each other than they are with anyone else—the logic being, blood ties are always going to hold. Have you never had that kind of family drama?
GG: I'm sure Grandpa and Uncle Ernest had some drop-dead knockout fights, but one thing they learned is not to make a decision until both of them agreed. They'd stay up all night, and if they couldn't agree, they'd go home, process everything, and return to the issue the next day. Also, we respect each other's areas of expertise. My brother, Matt, is the vineyard manager; I'm very focused on wine making. Depending on the situation, he'll defer to me or I'll defer to him. But there's still a

challenge. One thing about family: They'll always tell you the truth. I think that's what keeps you grounded.

TT: America's such a transitory culture—even in other local wine-making families, the second or third generation doesn't necessarily join the business. How do you keep the multigenerational mentality?

GG: Grandpa and Uncle Ernest built a very strong foundation, which we keep alive. Not everyone in my family is in the business, but those who are learned from them. Our parents were building something for the next generation. When you feel that, you want to be a part of it and take care of the *next* generation. The question is, how do you do it and have fun? What's worked for us is that everyone's managed to find an area they really enjoy. People have to have enough space to spread their wings.

TT: How do family values lend themselves toward sociological sustainability?

GG: We look at that as social equity: acting in a way that strengthens the local communities. We encourage mutual respect and shared goals based on individual responsibility. We aim to provide meaningful work in a financially viable business model. Decisions made within our company affect communities, both from an ecological and sociological perspective. So we weigh most decisions from a green or sustainable bent.

TT: Other winemakers struggle to go from an artisan brand to a supermarket brand. Over the last ten years, you've done the opposite. Why?

GG: In 1973 the biggest challenge was to introduce wine to a population that didn't drink it or know much about it. It was literally ground zero. Our first goal was to share wine with the consumer. If we'd come out with top-end wine, no one would have drunk it. My friends never grew up with wine at the table. When I was in school, wine coolers were so hot. There was no demand for top-end wine until recently. There still isn't much, but it's the fastest-growing sector—mostly, I think, due to cooking shows. People are open to it.

TT: Where do you plan to take your company in the next ten years?

GG: The California wine industry has so much potential—we want to play a responsible role in its evolution. For our family, we know there's so much more to do. We're looking at the clock saying, "How many more years do we have?" The beautiful thing about America is the entrepreneurial, pioneering spirit. We're keeping that spirit alive—and keeping our eyes open.

ATTRACTIONS

Kozlowski Farms
(WC) 5566 Gravenstein Highway 116, Forestville, (800) 473-2767, www.kozlowskifarms.com; Fee: N; Open: Daily; Key: TH, KIDS
This is one of the original Sonoma County farms—and also the one most likely to appear in your Christmas and birthday gift baskets. Awesome blackberry jam, boysenberry jam, fudge sauce, pumpkin butter . . . mmm. Certified organic since the early 1980s. If you're visiting, go for the fresh-baked pies, cookies, and such, since those are the products you can't get anywhere else. There's a fairly huge retail store stocking more Kozlowski products than you ever dreamed existed. Outside, you can picnic at tables on the lawn.

Tuesdays in the Plaza
(RR) Healdsburg Avenue, between Plaza Street and Matheson Street, Healdsburg, (707) 431-3300, www.ci.healdsburg.ca.us; Fee: N; Open: Tue 6–8 p.m., Key: KIDS, SF
This free weekly summer concert series is put on by the city of Healdsburg and sponsored by a different local business every week. After the Tuesday afternoon farmers' market in the square, people head to the park for an evening of live entertainment in a friendly outdoor setting. The lineup includes every genre from jazz to blues to Irish barn dances.

Louis Foppiano says: "Everyone comes, brings dinner and wine, blankets, and everything else."

Summer Jazz at Rodney Strong Vineyards
(RR) 11455 Old Redwood Highway, Healdsburg, (707) 431-1533, www.rodneystrong.com; Fee: Y; Open: Varied; Key: LN, DS, SF
Though it's on an irregular schedule, the summertime afternoon jazz series at this landmark winery is a local favorite. Concerts take place about every two weeks to a month, from June through the end of September. Shows start anywhere between 3 p.m. and 5 p.m. Past performers include Chris Isaak and Boz Scaggs. Lawn seating and VIP seats (i.e., chairs) available. "We never even sit down; we're just dancing in our chairs," says one regular attendee. Most people bring their own picnic supplies but buy wine on-site. Also, it's smart to take a taxi—parking can be a hassle.

RESTAURANTS

Kenwood Restaurant
(12E) 9900 Highway 12, Kenwood, (707) 833-6326, www.kenwoodrestaurant.com; $$$; Open: L, D Wed–Sun; Key: SF, SCENE, AT

Back in the day this was a down-home family restaurant serving Southern fried chicken. Ain't it funny how things change? To accommodate the plethora of nearby winemakers and the Boomer residents of Oakmont (a fifty-five-plus community) across the street, the space has turned into a pricey "power" dining spot serving contemporary American cuisine. There are three formal dining rooms, but you can also eat at the bar or on the patio.

Chris Benziger says: "Where all the winemakers hold court."

The Fig Café & Wine Bar
(12E) 13690 Arnold Drive, Glen Ellen, (707) 938-2130, www.thegirlandthefig.com; $$; Open: Brunch Sat–Sun, D daily; Key: DS, VEG

An offshoot of the Girl & the Fig, this airy, cheerful California bistro is *the* Glen Ellen brunch spot of choice. A casual yet innovative menu features thin-crust pizzas, homemade soups, pastas, and entrée salads.

Chris Benziger says: "Bryan is the chef. Killer fries, breakfast pizza, French toast. They have Bellinis, mimosas . . . and for two months at harvest, they blend champagne with fresh grape juice, and it's amazing."

LENA STAMP: This is a wine bar . . . that does not charge corkage if you BYOB. Illogical, Captain, but I love it.

Madrona Manor
(RR) 1001 Westside Road, Healdsburg, (800) 258-4003, www.madronamanor.com; $$$–$$$$; Open: D Wed–Sun; Key: DS, SF

Always a popular special-occasion place for locals, whether for a wedding, a corporate event, or a lengthy dinner—and all the more since a 1999 change of ownership and renovation. Not just a restaurant or lounge, but a classic wine country inn housed in a historic Victorian mansion. According to local gossip, current proprietors Bill and Trudi Konrad enlisted their son, who's a renowned landscape designer, to add a few design touches to the revamped property. However, Master Gardener Geno Ceccato continues to oversee the eight-acre estate garden and organic kitchen garden, as he has for approximately a quarter of a century.

Gina Gallo says: "A wonderful setting for a glass of bubbles. It's nice to eat on that veranda. It's bizarre because you don't feel like you're in Sonoma County."

ENTERTAINMENT AND NIGHTLIFE

Barn Diva
(RR) 231 Center Street, Healdsburg, (707) 431-0100, www.barndiva.com; $$; Open: Wed-Sun; Key: PU, SCENE
Popular hangout for thirty- and forty-somethings, helmed by an energetic and dynamic management team. Owner Jil Hales, head bartender/winemaker Dan Fitzgerald, and general manager/local foodie personality Lukka Feldman create a buzzing social scene powered by top-shelf drinks, 250 wine selections, and contemporary California comfort nibbles. The aesthetic is hipster art barn: a front deck, decomposed granite on the ground, decorative light strands in the trees. It's hip and festive, especially after everyone's had a few specialty cocktails.

Gina Gallo says: "I think Lukka is doing an amazing job. He's got a great personality and is always out front, talking to people. There's a fabulous curry dish on the menu. French fries with homemade ketchup are over the top. They make a really nice strawberry margarita with fresh local strawberries."

SHOPPING

Dry Creek General Store
(NC) 3495 Dry Creek Road, Healdsburg, (707) 433-4171, www.dcgstore.com; $; Open: Daily; Key: SCENE
Sandwiches, wine, *panini,* and charcuterie on the northern wine trail. The store stocks about 85 percent local products, 15 percent the very best of international imports (i.e., Italian Parma ham, reggiano cheese). It's been

around since 1881, but Gina Gallo bought it a few years back when the previous owners were looking to offload.

Gina Gallo says: "It's my little hobby. There's such a cast of characters there. It's a meeting place for locals, but then you see the tourists pulling up in limos. I go there and stock shelves when I need to relax."

Artists and Farmers
(RR) 237 Center Street, Healdsburg, (707) 431-7404, www.artistsandfarmers.com; Open: Daily
Before diving into your top-shelf cups at Barn Diva, check out this adjacent gallery/retail store, which is under the same ownership and evinces a similar sort of enthusiasm for aesthetics, quality, and story. In order for a piece to make it in the gallery, it has to evoke a sense of the place it came from, and it has to tap into the owners' personal connection. The same rules apply to everything from handblown glass ornaments to French farm antiques.

Glen Ellen Village Market
(12E) 13751 Arnold Drive, Glen Ellen, (707) 996-6728, www.sonoma-glenellenmkt.com; $; Open: Daily
This is an "extraordinary" deli for wine-trail travelers in search of gourmet picnic supplies.

ACCOMMODATIONS

Vintners Inn
(CS) 4350 Barnes Road, Santa Rosa, (800) 421-2584, (707) 575-7350, www.vintnersinn.com; $$$; Key: SCENE
One of the original Sonoma County wine country properties, and still perennially popular in spite of all the competition from glamorous newcomers. It helps that it's owned by Ferrari-Carano, one of the county's first winemaking families, instead of some faraway corporation. Also, the signature restaurant, John Ash & Co, has been a gourmet mainstay for about a quarter of a century. Every accommodation in the county promises a taste of "the wine country lifestyle," but this one really knows how to deliver.

Sonoma Hotel
(12E) 110 W. Spain Street, Sonoma, (800) 468-6016, www.sonomahotel.com; $; Key: LN
Locals refer to this landmark inn as "Sonoma Hotel on the Plaza"

because it has anchored one corner of the town square for as long as anyone remembers. Adjacent restaurant the Girl and the Fig is a standby for farm-fresh California fare. The sixteen-room property is recently refurbished and under new ownership.

TOUR PROVIDERS

Extranomical Adventures
(ALL) 690 Fifth Street, Suite #205, San Francisco, (866) 231-3752, www.extranomical.com; Fee: Y; Open: By appt.
For group tours or partially customized one-day tours departing/returning to San Francisco, this company is highly recommended. Very friendly staff and good tour packages that offer an authentic wine country experience even in a group setting. Some itineraries combine wine tasting with redwood hikes, or other popular tourist activities.

Jake's Valley Wine Tours
(ALL) 1208 Los Robles Drive, Sonoma, (707) 975-6462, www.valleywinetours.com; Fee: Y; Open: By appt.
Group tours or customized full-day private tours of Sonoma County. Nice outfit. Will pick up/drop off in San Francisco for a (steep) additional fee.

Beau Wine Tours
(ALL) 21707 Eighth Street East, Sonoma, (800) 387-2328, www.beauwinetours.com; Fee: Y; Open: By appt.
This Sonoma-based tour company offers all varieties of tour experiences and is flexible in terms of group size. Fleet includes every vehicle option from town cars to limo buses.

SUGGESTED TWO-DAY ITINERARIES

{WELCOME TO THE GOOD LIFE}

DAY ONE

From Geyersville

Early morning: Pick up breakfast burritos and picnic supplies (optional) at Dry Creek General Store.

Mid-morning: Taste at Trentadue, Sbragia.

Afternoon: Taste and picnic at Pedroncelli *or* taste, then eat La Hacienda.

Late afternoon: Taste at Family Wineries co-op.

Evening: Drinks and dinner at Taverna Santi.

DAY TWO

From Geyersville or Windsor

Morning: Taste at Iron Horse, Rodney Strong.

Mid-morning/afternoon: Taste at J Vineyards, food pairings at Bubble Lounge *or* shop at Windsor Wine Shop and eat lunch in store.

Late afternoon: Explore downtown Healdsburg, Cheese Shop, and so on, and then drive to Santa Rosa.

Evening: Have dinner at Syrah in Railroad Square, Santa Rosa.

BONUS: DAY THREE

From Sonoma or Glen Ellen

Early morning: Have breakfast at Garden Court.

Morning: Taste at Benziger.

Late Morning: Private taste at Hanzell (book ahead).

Afternoon: Have lunch at Cornerstone.

Mid-afternoon: Explore Cornerstone.

Late afternoon: Taste at Cline and Jacuzzi.

Evening: Have dinner at Café LaHaye *or* El Dorado.

Late evening: Have drinks at El Dorado.

{AS SEEN ON TV}

DAY ONE

From San Francisco, Napa, or Carneros

Morning: Taste at Keller Estate, Adobe Road Winery.

Afternoon: Have lunch at Carneros Bistro (upscale) and then tour Gloria Ferrer, followed by a bottle of Ferrer champagne on the property.

Late afternoon: Shopping and tasting at Jack London Village.

Evening: Have dinner at Zazu.

DAY TWO

From San Francisco, Napa, or Carneros

Morning: Taste at Kunde, Sonoma-Cutrer.

Afternoon: Have a picnic lunch at Sonoma Cutrer *or* wine and food pairings at St. Francis.

Afternoon: Taste at St. Francis, if you haven't already.

Late afternoon: Taste at Chalk Hill Estate and explore downtown Healdsburg.

Evening: Have dinner at Dry Creek Kitchen or Cyrus (advance reservations recommended).

{GRASS ROOTS LEGACIES}

DAY ONE

From Sonoma

Morning: Have brunch at Fig Café (weekends only) *or* pick up snacks Glen Ellen Village Market.

Afternoon: Taste and tour Buena Vista, Gundlach Bundschu.

Mid-afternoon (optional): Have a picnic *or* lunch at Kenwood Restaurant.

Late afternoon: Explore Sonoma town square *or* visit St. Francis (from Itinerary 2) if you haven't already.

Evening: Have cocktails at The Girl & the Fig at Sonoma Hotel on the square and dinner at Kenwood Restaurant if you haven't eaten there, or at Vintners Inn, John Ash.

DAY TWO

From Sonoma

Morning: Buy snacks at Dry Creek General Store for breakfast.

Mid-morning: Taste and tour at Gallo.

Afternoon: Taste at Foppiano and a picnic lunch *or* go to Kozlowski Farms, followed by taste, tour, shopping.

Late afternoon: Shop at Artists & Farmers.

Evening: Have cocktails at Barn Diva and dinner at Barn Diva *or* Madrona Manor.

CALENDAR OF EVENTS

FEBRUARY

- Sonoma County Olive Festival www.sonomavalley.com OliveFestival
- PS I Love You (Petite Sirah celebration) www.psiloveyou.org

MARCH

- Savor Sonoma Valley Annual Barrel Tasting www.heartofsonomavalley.com

APRIL

- Apple Blossom Festival & Parade www.sebastopolappleblossom.org
- Passport to Dry Creek Valley

MAY

- Annual Architectural Tour & Tasting www.simsc.org

JUNE

- Sonoma County Fair www.sonoma-marinfair.org

JULY

- Art & Garden Festival, Petaluma
- Wine Country Film Festival

AUGUST

- Gravenstein Apple Fair www.farmtrails.org

- Bodega Seafood, Art & Wine Festival
  www.winecountryfestivals.com
- Grapes to Glass, Russian River Valley
- Sonoma Wine Country Weekend
  www.sonomawinecountry weekend.com

SEPTEMBER

- Kendall Jackson Heirloom Tomato Festival
  www.kj.com
- Russian River Food & Winefest
  www.russianriverfoodandwine fest.com
- Harvest Fair
  www.harvestfair.org
- Russian River Jazz Festival
  www.rrfestivals.com
- Valley of the Moon Vintage Festival
  www.sonomavinfest.org
- Spotlight on Zinfandel
- Sonoma Grape Camp
  www.sonomagrapecamp.com

OCTOBER

- Pinot on the River
  www.pinotfestival.com

RESOURCES

www.alexandervalley.org
www.carneros.com
www.ci.healdsburg.ca.us
www.farmtrails.org
www.geyservillecc.com
www.healdsburg.org
www.heartofsonomavalley.com
www.petalumadowntown.com
www.rrvw.org
www.sonomacounty.com
www.sonomawine.com
www.sonomavalleywine.com
www.sonoma.com
www.sonomauncorked.com
www.sonomavalley.com
www.townofwindsor.com
www.wdcv.com

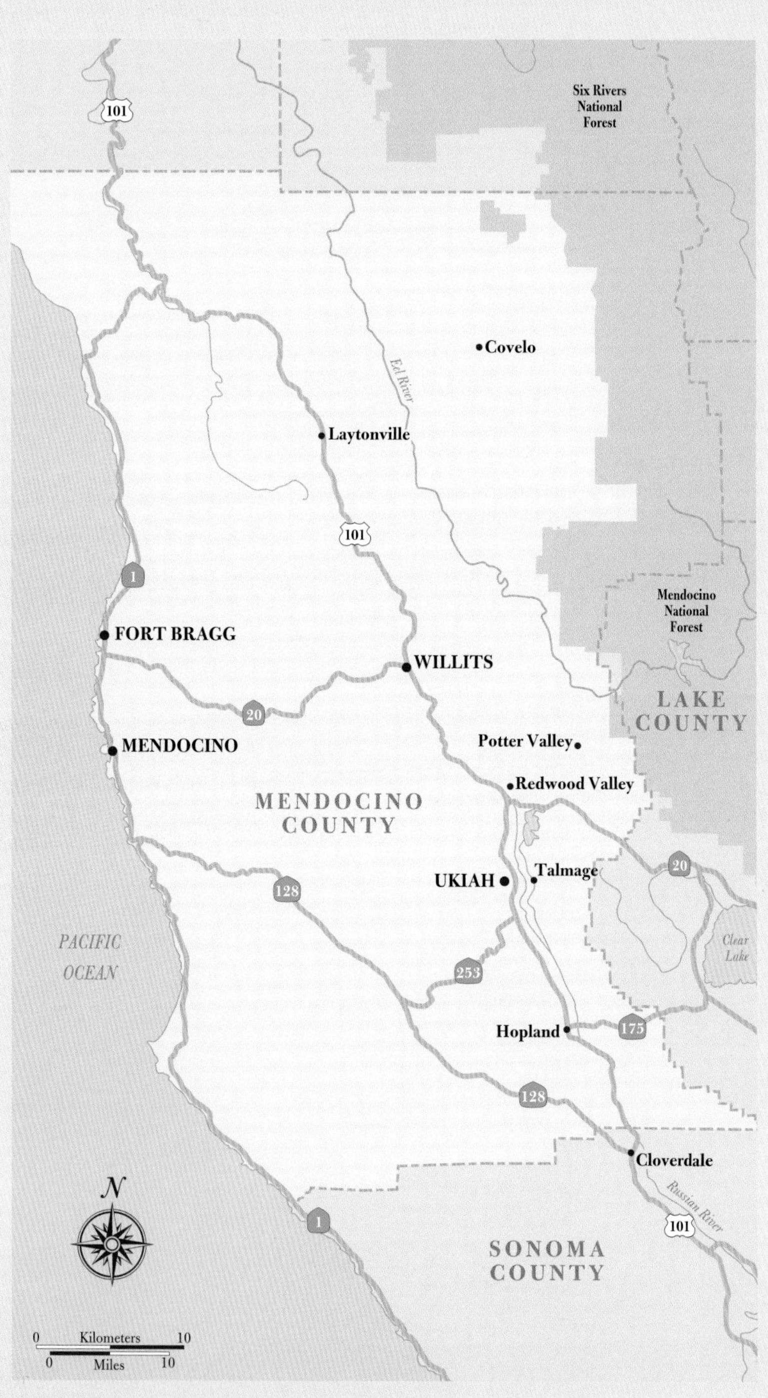

101
Six Rivers
National
Forest
Covelo
Ed River
Laytonville
101
1
FORT BRAGG
WILLITS
Mendocino
National
Forest
20
LAKE
COUNTY
MENDOCINO
Potter Valley
Redwood Valley
MENDOCINO
COUNTY
20
UKIAH
Talmage
128
PACIFIC
OCEAN
Clear
Lake
253
Hopland
175
128
Cloverdale
N
1
Russian River
101
SONOMA
COUNTY
0
Kilometers
10
0
Miles
10

MENDOCINO

It's a trip you'll want to take over and over.

You think I've been brainwashed by a pack of marauding destination marketers? Ah, no. Even jaded skeptics can be won over by Mendocino's heart-stoppingly beautiful landscape, interesting wine-scape, and quirky, nonconformist citizens. The land isn't just unspoiled; in the far reaches, it's downright uncivilized. The people are passionate in their beliefs and close-knit in their communities. However, they're not closed to outsiders. In the Anderson Valley, which is the main wine region, shops still sell a dictionary of *Boontling,* the Swedish chef–sounding made-up language that locals a few generations back spoke so outsiders couldn't understand them.

Mendocino proudly identifies itself as "America's Greenest Wine Region." Two of the biggest wineries in the county, Fetzer and Frey, have been on the forefront of the organic-grown movement for twenty-plus years. Parducci is the first carbon-neutral winery in the country. Almost all wineries follow some sustainable, biodynamic, or organic tenets. It's also artsy: There are artist colonies in Mendocino and Gualala that were established decades ago and have somehow managed to become famous without ever going commercial.

Mendocino's tourism industry isn't a slick machine. Residents are chatty without being particularly eager to sell you anything. Main topics of interest include sustainable gardening practices, solar power, gossip about the neighbors, where you came from, and whether you're planning to move here. In any of the Anderson Valley wineries, the owner/winemaker will pull up a stool (or a hay bale) and tell you as much as you want to know about his or her product. No one's ever snooty or in a rush; at worst, they will be . . . dreadlocked.

Getting Here

It's about a two-hour drive on Highway 101 (the 101) from San Francisco, which is where the closest major airport is. There's another airport in Santa Rosa (Sonoma County), but few routes service it, and it won't make much difference to your drive time.

Weather

The coast is not hot even in summer, when temperatures hover in the mid-60s. September is the warmest month and sees spikes into the 70s. Winters are chilly and damp; nighttime temperatures dip below freezing. Inland weather is ten to fifteen degrees warmer, but coastal breezes keep Anderson Valley temperatures from being too extreme. It's rare for summer highs to hit 100°F—though it usually happens a few times a year.

Recommended Transportation

You have no choice but to drive in wine country. And concerned local citizens politely remind you that "slower drivers need to pull over for faster ones." Mendocino village is easily walkable.

Style

Wear anything you want . . . seriously . . . no one's paying attention.

Fees

Complimentary tastings at some places, but they are usually about $5.

Bird's-eye View

There is a great deal to explore in this county, and a myriad of adventures to have. However, for wine tourism purposes, we're focusing on only a few areas. First is the southern region around Hopland, where there are several wineries just off the 101. Second, and most important, is Anderson Valley. The main route here is Highway 128. It cuts through the heart of the valley, passing through several dinky one-horse towns and connecting most of the county's wineries. The last part of it winds into the redwoods and eventually connects with the coastal route, Highway 1. Third are the coastal towns of Mendocino Village and Fort Bragg, both of which have a significant wine and food scene, plus active cultural scenes. Note: Mendocino County is a natural treasure, and half its land is protected. The Highway 1 route is famously nicknamed "the Lost Coast." Its parklands and old-growth redwood forests are a world unto themselves—well-nigh impossible to incorporate into a wine weekend. However, this side of Mendo is so worth exploring, we've devoted an entire section to it in the SUN Guide.

Area Key:
101 = South County, Hopland
128 = Anderson Valley, Yorkville Highlands
HW1 = Mendocino, Fort Bragg, Little River

The Panel

- Bernadette Byrne, SIP Mendocino
- Deborah Cahn, owner, Navarro Winery
- Anna Kvinsland, executive director, Arts Council of Mendocino County
- Kevin Milligan, local artist and owner, Coastside Gallery
- Jeff Stanford, owner, Stanford Inn
- Arnaud Weyrich, winemaker, Roederer Estate

The Artistic Palate

Art and wine historically have a complementary relationship, and in Mendocino you can't really get one without having a little of the other. You must drive through the heart of Anderson Valley to get to the coastal villages and art colonies. Gorgeous vineyards and friendly tasting rooms tempt visitors off the main road to sample the Pinot Noir, Zinfandel, and sparkling wine for which Anderson Valley is known.

Though this is the polar opposite of a metropolitan art scene, art aficionados and oenophiles can experience a different sort of thrill: that of exploration and possibility. For the most part artists and winemakers alike are unconcerned with marketing or self-promotion, so it's the fan's job to find them. Further throwing a wrench into the system: Nothing's very expensive. You often identify the "best" wines not by the price tag, but by the fact that they're already sold out by the release date. Those are only the well-known ones, though. There are plenty of discoveries still to be made.

WINERIES

Roederer Estate
(128) 4501 Highway 128, Philo, (707) 894-2288, www.roedererestate.com; Fee: Y; Open: Daily; Key: DS

This is the California counterpart to a historic French champagne house. It produces four sparkling wines, two of which are rosé. Winemaker Arnaud Weyrich blends aged wine in with the newly fermented lots—in fact, that's how the rosé gets its lovely hue. He also ages the wine "on the yeast," (e.g., in the bottle) for two years before releasing it, because he believes it creates a distinctive and heightened flavor profile.

The Roederer Web site says its winery is rustic, but, um, it isn't—at least not for this century/continent. Crowning a massive hill of vineyards, it's impressive from the first glimpse. It looks like the kind of country farmhouse that movie stars rent out when they want to play at escaping Hollywood.

CORO, CORO: Mendocino's Heritage Red

Recently a group of vintners who had been in the county for thirty to forty years decided to collaborate and create a "heritage wine"—a blend to be their signature and the ultimate expression of what the region could produce. They settled upon a red blend based on Zinfandel, one with a lot of history. (Zin was first planted in Mendocino one hundred years ago.) They called the blend CORO, which means "chorus" in either Spanish or Italian. The name is in honor of the collective spirit of area winemakers.

Winemakers who participate in the CORO annually submit vintages they feel are worthy of the CORO Mendocino label. Wine production must adhere to specific protocols, many of which are based on Old World traditions. The wines are then judged in a series of blind tastings. Those that are deemed worthy get a special certification from the Mendocino Winegrowers Alliance and are packaged under the CORO umbrella. Participating wineries include Fetzer, Parducci, and Pacific Star. For more information visit the Web site www.coromendocino.com.

LENA STAMP: When I drink the Brut Rosé NV, the wine aficionado in me says, "Crisp, light on the palate, not too tart." The girly girl says, "Pinkbubbly pinkbubbly pink! Mmm." Tops on my birthday wish list (in case you were keeping notes): a case of vintage, limited-production L'Ermitage Rosé.

Scharffenberger Cellars

(128) 8501 Highway 128, Philo, (707) 895-2957, www.scharffenbergercellars.com; Fee: Y; Open: Daily; Key: DS

First of all, the wine brand has nothing to do with the chocolate. It has name recognition of its own, particularly among people who appreciate excellent sparkling wines priced under $30. Although it's had a turbulent history—ownership changes, name changes, and even a brief halt to sparkling wine production—its reputation saves it. The latest owners even decided to go back to the original name.

The winery doesn't look like it's been through turmoil and tear. It's a serene, pretty property surrounded by gardens and shaded by plum trees. Rocking chairs sit on the wraparound porch; a bench in the back garden encourages quiet meditation. The tasting room also serves as an art gallery and usually contains exhibits by two local artists. Sculptures or accent pieces sometimes are displayed outdoors, which can be confusing, as they tend to blend right into the topiary.

Bernadette Byrne says: "A very established, high-quality sparkling wine facility."

Handley Cellars

(128) 3151 Highway 128, Philo, (800) 733-3151, www.handleycellars.com; Fee: N; Open: Daily

This place has the coolest chairs ever! Carved from solid old-growth teak, they're in the likeness of magnificent miniature elephants—polished to a gleam, eye-catching, and exotic—and not for sale. There are less than twenty such pieces in the world, and three of them are in the Handley tasting room. Along with a fifteen-foot ceremonial wood-carved crocodile canoe, they're the best pieces in the founder's folk art collection, which he spent decades amassing. Most of the other good pieces are in a gallery in San Francisco, leaving the tasting room free to display smaller, much more affordable pieces by (mostly) local artists. Try the estate Pinot, Gewürztraminer, or Chardonnay—made from grapes grown organically just outside the tasting room. The winery went solar in May 2008, and visitors are welcome to check out

The Road from Champagne

Arnaud Weyrich, Winemaker, Roederer Estate

Some people like to dis and dismiss California sparkling wine, but the fact is big French champagne houses own most of the best California sparkling labels. Their philosophies and centuries-old techniques are being applied to newly grown vines all over Anderson Valley. Educated in France but with eight years of experience in Anderson Valley, Roederer winemaker Arnaud Weyrich compares and contrasts the two.

Old World vs New World

Regions: In Europe, regions are very specialized. In the Champagne region, everybody does champagne. In Anderson Valley in the 1970s, everybody kind of planted a little bit of everything: Chardonnay, Gewurtz, Reisling. Nobody knew exactly what would be good, and there was a learning curve.

Identity: Everybody in France knows about champagne; it's the local wine and part of the way of life. Everybody drinks it. In California as a whole, there is not a single area that can say, "What we do here is one thing." People tend to focus on what's currently fashionable.

Rules and regulations: In Europe, because of those extremely old traditions, things are regulated. If you're supposed to plant Pinot, don't even think about putting Cabernet there! In California, there's no regulation to tell you what to do or not do. People have options, so they'll weigh the economics of the choice.

Land: Champagne has limestone-rich, high-calcium soils. Most of the North Coast soil is based on sandstone or shale, and there have been a lot of previous redwood forests. Most of these have evolved toward acidic soil.

Growing season: In Champagne, ninety to one hundred days is the "magic number": the number of days between bloom and harvest. Anderson Valley has almost the same "magic number."

Grapes: France relies mainly on Pinot Noir and Pinot Meunier for champagne. California relies mainly on Pinot Noir and Chardonnay.

Method: The technical method, the philosophy, the equipment are all the same, but we had to adapt to local environments and what the local fruit is giving us. So the blending is different.

The verdict: No clear winner. Ever. Whether everything is regulated and traditional, or whether you have a blank page to write your history, a winemaker's job is to adapt. Every year is slightly different, so every vintage is different. Nothing is set in stone.

the recently installed panels. This is the last winery you hit before you go into the redwoods. Also worth noting, Handley has two female winemakers: co-founder Milla Handley and assistant winemaker Kristen Barnhisel.

Bernadette Byrne says: "It's been around since the late 1970s. They have a cool tasting room, and they make excellent wines."

Goldeneye
(128) 9200 Highway 128, Philo, (800) 208-0438, www.goldeneyewinery.com; Fee: Y; Open: Daily; KEY: TH, AT, SCENE
Owned by Napa-based Duckhorn, this winery is all about Pinot Noir and has been for more than ten years. It's comprised of four vineyards, all planted to Pinot. The tasting room is located on Confluence Vineyard and is one of the most visible and popular stops on the wine trail. In addition to regular and reserve tastings, it does formal wine and cheese "Estate Tastings" a couple times a week and vineyard tours Friday and Sunday. Partners Gallery in Fort Bragg pours Goldeneye wines.

Bernadette Byrne says: "One of the most spectacular settings in Anderson Valley. Gorgeous vistas, rolling vineyards, redwoods,

Goldeneye patio—the perfect setting for a Goldeneye estate tasting.

and pines in the distance. It's a spectacular sight. This is a first-class operation."

Maple Creek Winery
(128) 20799 Highway 128, (707) 895-3001, www.maplecreekwine.com; Fee: Y; Open: Daily
Just as advertised, maple trees lend a New England note to the landscape at this rustic Yorkville Highlands winery. The proprietary wine brand here is Artevino, so named because the gorgeous labels designed by owner/vintner Tom Rodrigues are as distinctive as the wine itself. Tom and his partner/co-owner Linda Stutz are city escapees, and it's pretty easy to understand why they left when you look around their property, with its organic gardens, horse pasture, and picturesque creek.

Bernadette Byrne says: "Tom Rodrigues is an extremely well-known artist. They bought this winery probably about ten years ago. He's done portraits—has all these wonderful works in the tasting room. He does the labels. They have a wine called 'Buckin' Bronc,' and he did the pictures. It's a beautiful, charming destination. Friendly fun people, with good, quality wines."

Pacific Star Winery
(HW1) 33000 N. Highway 1, Fort Bragg, (707) 964-1155, www.pacificstarwinery.com; Fee: Y; Open: Daily; Key: FO
This winery is a half an hour from the village of Mendocino, and worth the drive according to everyone. It is the only ocean-side winery in California, and it utilizes its setting to the utmost, with picnic tables set up right on the bluff. The taste of the wine pairs with the pounding of the waves and the smell of salt air. It's located north of Fort Bragg about twelve miles.

Bernadette Byrne says: "A really spectacular setting. She makes a lot of Italian varietals, sourcing her grapes from inland Mendocino County. There's lore about how the pounding of the surf helps the wine age and breathe, so they'll move the barrels out to the bluff. Wine is such a living, breathing thing . . . maybe there could be some merit to it."

ATTRACTIONS

Triangle Tattoo and Museum
(HW1) 356-B North Main Street, Fort Bragg, (707) 964-8814, www.triangletattoo.com; Fee: N; Open: Daily; Key: SKETCH
A unique modern art museum housed within a tattoo parlor, this is a jaw-dropping compendium of tattoo history, all displayed neatly on the walls of an upstairs space in downtown Fort Bragg. "Art with a pulse" is the overarching theme, and all of tattooing's significant historic periods, movements, and cultural niches are explored. The walls flanking both sides of the steep front stairs are covered every square inch with tattoo art. Asian tattoos and sacred tattoos of the Solomon Islands, Russian prison tattoos, and a "Captain Jack" collection from 1920s San Francisco. Newspaper clippings, historic articles, and other text accompaniments provide background information and context. Proprietors Mr. G and Madame Chinchilla are surprisingly erudite and intellectual folks, who have written and published multiple books and contribute regularly to magazines. If you manage to catch one of them on-site (not a given), your gawkfest may turn into an impromptu sociology lesson.

LENA STAMP: Though it's not the most colorful display, the most disturbing one in my opinion is "Tattoos without Consent," which includes everything from ancient Japanese penal and punishment tattoos to Holocaust concentration camp numbers.

North Coast Artists Collective
(HW1) 362 North Main Street, Fort Bragg, (707) 964-8266, www.northcoastartists.org; Fee: N; Open: Daily; Key: SF, AT
Overheard while browsing/eavesdropping at this big, bright gallery space in historic Fort Bragg: "I've been coming here for twenty years, and every time, I find something new to like. It's been so fascinating to see artists evolve over the years." From silk screens to jewelry to ceramics to found object art, this gallery displays all sorts of media, most of which are unique but not so edgy they'd throw your living room decor out of wack.

Mendocino Art Center
(HW1) 45200 Little Lake Street, Mendocino, (800) 653-3328, (707) 937-5818, www.mendocinoartcenter.org; Fee: N; Open: Hours vary; Key: LN

More than a gallery or event space, this is really a hub of artistic activity in Mendocino. It nurtures artists, gives them a place to show their work, and supports the art community as a whole. The main gallery houses four exhibition spaces, which are usually used to showcase local artists. Classes, events, and art shows held regularly.

LENA STAMP: I love the staff, the community spirit, the reputation among locals . . . everything! However, I have to give it the "Logistical Nightmare" stamp because I did so many circles trying to find it, I started to feel like a human Slinky.

RESTAURANTS

Mendo Bistro
(HW1) 301 N. Main Street, Fort Bragg, (707) 964-4974, www.mendobistro.com; $$; Open: Nightly; Key: VEG, KIDS
A square second-story space that wraps around the balcony of the Company Store retail center, this restaurant features all Mendocino County wines and food made in-house from scratch. Everybody raves about the food, from fresh-baked bread to classic Italian pastas and lots of seasonal seafood. Most proteins are done in mix-and-match manner: Pick your steak/chicken/Portobello, the way you want it cooked, and the sauce of choice. Wall-to-wall windows save the place from being too rough-hewn.

Gray Whale at MacCallum
(HW1) 45020 Albion Street, Mendocino, (800) 609-0492, (707) 937-0289, www.maccallumhouse.com; $$$; Open: B, D daily; Key: DS, VEG
Even on a weeknight this place is packed, and rightly so: The food is absolutely outstanding. Seasonal, organic, and mostly local ingredients are used at their peak ripeness, even though it makes things harder from a sourcing and menu-planning perspective. Executive Chef Alan Kantor has a long-standing agreement with his vendors that if they wait to pick his produce until the moment it's ripe, he will not send back anything that's gone rotten. Thus, you get vine-ripened tomatoes, tree-ripened peaches, and sun-ripened blackberries. The food is fairly rich: Niman ranch steak

with melted bleu cheese is a favorite. A less-expensive but equally quality menu is served in the bar and draws a lot of local regulars.

LENA STAMP: This is not simple everyman cuisine, and you can't get it that way by special request either—thankfully. During my visit an overly protective mom's advance request to get "plain pasta" for her twelve-year-old child was politely stonewalled by the front desk hostess. She canceled her dinner reservation, and the hostess helped her find a more suitable restaurant.

North Coast Brewing Co.
(HW1) 455 North Main Street, Fort Bragg, (707) 964-2739, www.northcoastbrewing.com; $$; Open: L, D Wed-Sun; Key: KIDS
Modern and surprisingly pretty, this brewpub has no more than its fair share of moose heads on the walls. Belgian biere posters balance out the redneck accents, just like the families in the booths balance the woodsmen and cowboys at the bar. The restaurant is the starting-out point for the brewery's daily tours.

SHOPPING

Rookie-Too Gallery
(128) 14300 Highway 128, Boonville, (707) 895-2204
Mainly fine crafts, from a lot of local artists. Housed in a small, charming converted cottage, it gets lots of local recommendations—possibly because there isn't much competition.

Deborah Cahn says: "Beautiful handmade artisan things. The name means 'the quail' in Boontling."

Coastside Gallery
(HW1) 45055 Albion Street, Mendocino, (707) 937-4960, www.coastsidegallery.com
Owner Kevin Milligan will allow that he's "mainly a Plein Air painter," but you should never leave it at that. He paints from life, whether it be portrait, still life, or landscape. He shows other artists in addition to himself at his space behind the historic Mendocino Hotel, and he also houses a tasting room for LeVin Winery. When he's not in the gallery, he's usually out in some nearby field, waist-high in grass with his easel.

Mendocino and the Arts, an Interview with Artist Kevin Milligan

TT: How did Mendocino go from being a logging town to an artist colony?
KM: The founder of the artist community here was Bill Zacha. He was the trigger, the spark for the Mendocino switch from a Gold Rush logging town. It was founded in 1852 as a town that shipped wood all over the world—old-growth redwoods, in fact. He invited veteran artists from the Bay Area here in the 1950s and 1960s to newly identify it as an arts hub. And it still lives on.

TT: Do artists still find their way here, without such a dynamic front person?
KM: Yes. I've been [here] eleven years, and I've got a friend a few doors down who's been here about four years. You really see the arts community is supportive, not competitive. People really do try to help each other.

TT: What here nurtures artists and makes them stay?
KM: You have a lot of open space; the town is bounded by open space from the town to the headlands. It got historic status in the 1970s. There's an anti–chain store ordinance, buildings are preserved, and the place has character. It's the juxtaposition of a historic town with forests, the ocean, and nine-story cliffs. That's a pretty amazing backdrop.

TT: What's your favorite Mendocino scene to paint?
KM: You could go sit in your backyard, and it wouldn't be a bad subject. The view is cool everywhere you look. I'll be painting a scene in town, look in the other direction, and there's another great scene—whether it's a neighborhood in town, an open field, or a vineyard.

TT: Is there any kind of relationship or parallel between wineries and galleries?
KM: Wines and galleries have a symbiotic relationship. In the beginning people were headed to the Mendocino coast, not Anderson Valley. They'd come through and discover this great hidden wine region, and it would add to the experience, which is generally very peaceful and personal.

ACCOMMODATIONS

Boonville Hotel

(128) 14050 Highway 128, Boonville, (707) 895-2210, www.boonvillehotel.com; $; Key: PETS, VEG

The bar is also the restaurant's hostess stand and the hotel's check-in desk at this artsy-funky ten-room hotel. The vibe is shabby-chic/redwoods hick: The building facade looks vaguely saloonlike, but the lobby/living room has a larger-than-average lending library and a gift shop bordering on gallery-esque. Oh, and the garden is quite picturesque. (Yes, that was intended to rhyme.) Even the bar menu is California cuisine, with offerings like pork tenderloin and charcuterie. This is a good base for wine tasting in Anderson Valley, as the owner is very into local wine and local history. Note: there is a two-night mimimum stay on the weekends.

MacCallum House

(HW1) 45020 Albion Street, Mendocino, (800) 609-0492, (707) 937-0289, www.maccallumhouse.com; $$; Key: DS

The term "bed and breakfast" doesn't begin to do justice to this collection of village properties. From the elegant yet comfortable main house to the less-expensive Village Inn to the mansion suites, McCallum is the first and last word in luxe Mendocino lodgings by general consensus.

LENA STAMP: True story: My sister brought her husband here on his fortieth birthday. He brought her back when he proposed. Completely unaware of any of that, I booked the place for her final bachelorette getaway. That's not coincidence—it's the ineffable magnetism of clawfoot bathtubs, gourmet food, limo wine tours, and in-room massage.

North Cliff Hotel

(HW1) 1005 South Main Street, Fort Bragg, (707) 962-2500, www.fortbragg.org; $

Close to restaurants and shops, this hotel looks from afar like a row of gables perched on a hill. Rooms overlook the ocean.

Green Tasting

Toss away all notions of "green" as you know it, because you're about to enter a whole different realm. People in Mendocino are serious when it comes to matters of the earth and responsible living—they've been practicing it for years. Though their beliefs run the gamut from raw food to vegan to "you can only eat chicken you've killed in your backyard," they stand firmly behind the collective right to live off the land, be independent, and make good wines at reasonable prices.

WINERIES

Navarro
(128) 5601 Highway 128, Philo, (800) 537-9463, (707) 895-3686, www.navarrowine.com; Fee: N; Open: Daily; Key: KIDS

Deborah Cahn and Ted Bennett have been in Anderson Valley since 1974, and their winery is both a local landmark and a typical small farm, where everything from the chickens in the stew to the wine on the table came from the land right outside. Pinot Noir is what Navarro has always been known for—it's moderately priced by design and sells out before it even hits the shelves. Currently three different Pinots are produced, the best one being the "Méthode á l'Ancien," where the grapes are punched down by hand in a modification of the ancient French style (which was by stomping . . . the Health Department does not approve).

"Our customers enjoy wine and enjoy talking about it. A lot of academics are our customers; they appreciate wine and learning about it but don't have a lot of money to spend," says Cahn. The winery makes excellent Gewürztraminer and good

Babydoll sheep are part of the family at Navarro.

Pinot Noir: The Grape and Its Grower:

Deborah Cahn, Owner, Navarro Winery

In the beginning: When I first went into business, Pinot was referred to as a winemaker's wine. That was in 1973, and I was a grad student at Berkeley. When we first planted, it used to be easier to sell Gewurtzraminer than Pinot. Now my Pinot sells out before release. But all those things come in cycles.

Anderson Valley: It's hard for people to come here and do large planting to produce the cheapest Pinot in the world. That's not what Anderson Valley is about. It is a small valley with rugged terrain—that's what allows people to have boutique wineries.

The community: We're still a community in an old-fashioned way. People come out here to be farmers—but overall, they have an independent spirit.

The sensitive fruit: It is a relatively thin-skinned grape, with very small clusters. There are an enormous number of different clones. It's a very old grape.

The painstaking process: Pinot is a grape that requires a lot of intensive care in the vineyards and the winery. It lends itself to craftsman-style wine making rather than bulk wine making. You have to spend a lot of time balancing your crop level, which in our case involves going through the vineyard two or three times and thinning the crop by hand.

From the soil to the barrel: One of our favorite restaurants is Chez Panisse. What's wonderful about it is you can taste the ingredients and the authentic flavors. We want the flavor of the vineyards and grapes to show through in the wine.

The perfect Pinot: Ask one hundred winemakers what that is, and you'll get one hundred different opinions. We're aiming for a wine that reflects food like a mirror. We're more interested in complexity and finesse rather than tannins and power.

The point of it all: Wine is meant to be drunk every night—with dinner, with your family, and with friends. In my house we have a sense of place in everything we eat, and wine is just another one of those foods.

Chardonnay as well. Its nonalcoholic fresh grape juices are a refreshing treat. Picnic supplies such as smoked salmon and gourmet cheese are sold in the tasting room for you to enjoy at a picnic table under the trellis.

LENA STAMP: Beautiful ranch—full of colorful foliage and happy people.

Frey Vineyards
(FAR OUT) 14000 Tomki Road, Redwood Valley, (800) 760-3739, (707) 485-5177, www.freywine.com; Fee: N; Open: By appt.; Key: LN

Organic since it opened in the the 1980s, this quintessential Mendocino winery is heading in a biodynamic direction. It's the oldest organic winery in the country, winning awards for Zinfandel, Syrah, and biodynamic Petite Sirah, among other things. It produces no conventional wines. Founders Paul and Beba Frey have twelve children, many of whom live on the ranch (some with their spouses) and are involved in wine making. This is a must-visit experience for the serious student of organics—however, it is by appointment only.

Bernadette Byrne says: "Iconoclastic Berkeley throwback founders. Brilliant, charming, and on the forefront of organic farming. People from all over seek them out for that."

Toulouse Vineyards
(128) 8001 Highway 128, Philo, (707) 895-2828, www.toulousevineyards.com; Fee: N; Open: Daily

Who knew a retired firefighter could prove so versatile? Toulouse owner Vern Boltz has been a rising Anderson Valley star since the winery's first-ever Estate Pinot was the panel favorite at a *San Francisco Chronicle* wine competition. Also produced: Gewürztraminer, Riesling, and Rosé of Pinot Noir. Sustainable farming is a key focus, and wines are handcrafted in small lots. Although it has no official public tasting facility as yet, the winery itself is lovely, and the pooches are bigger crowd-pleasers than the winemakers are.

Bernadette Byrne says: "Stellar wines. Beautiful location, hasn't built a tasting room yet, but he's usually there with his dogs."

Jeriko
(101) 12141 Hewlitt and Sturtevant Road, Hopland, (707) 744-1140, www.jeriko.us; Fee: Y; Open: Daily; Key: DS

All grapes are estate grown—and organically grown to boot. This winery is owned by Danny Fetzer of the Fetzer wine-making family. The tasting room is just a mile north of Hopland, in a Tuscan-inspired villa.

Bernadette Byrne says: "Gorgeous estate—very high-end."

Parducci
(101) 501 Parducci Road, Ukiah, (888) 362-9463, (707) 463-5350, www.mendocinowineco.com; Fee: N; Open: Daily; KEY: TH
Its billing as a "carbon neutral" winery deserves a mention, particularly since guests can go behind the scenes and observe sustainable practices in action. This is one of few wineries in Mendocino that offers regular tours of production facilities. It also has a picnic area. It is owned by Mendocino Wine Company.

Bernadette Byrne says: "Great tasting room; extremely historic facility. Founded by the Parducci family in 1910."

ATTRACTIONS

Real Goods Solar Living Institute
(101) 13771 S. Highway 101, Hopland, (707) 774-2017, www.solarliving.org; Fee: N; Open: Daily; Key: VEG
A twenty-foot wicker woman guards the front gate, and a solar-powered carousel operates in the summer. A beautiful fountain marks the center of a sprawling property; brass poles are set at the sun's rising and setting points, and poplar trees are planted due north and south. Arbors, vines, and flowers flourish in the central courtyard, while the back garden, with its three aerated ponds, is positively idyllic. But this unique property is more than just a pretty park; it is a hub of ecoeducation and environmental awareness. With small signs and diagrams explaining all of the environmental and alt-energy installations that comprise the landscape, the center marries style and substance quite nicely. Everything's beautifully maintained—thanks mostly to the interns who live on-site and are responsible for the center's upkeep. Tours take place a couple times daily on weekends for a minimal fee; ditto for carousel rides. Numerous classes, workshops, and other events are held here; the schedule is available online or inside the gift shop.

Philo Apple Farm
(128) 18501 Greenwood Road, Philo, (707) 895-2333, www.philoapplefarm.com; $$-$$$; Open: Year-round (but according to season); Key: RR (for cottages and cooking classes)
Don and Sally Schmitt aren't fooling anybody: They may be selling

produce from a farm stand now, but back in the day they founded the French Laundry—the best restaurant in the country—and any foodie who comes within one hundred miles of Mendocino finds that out right away. The Schmitts' bucolic farm retreat has a few cottages that rent for modest prices; their cooking school, however, is priced at a premium and nonetheless sells out six months in advance.

Hendy Woods State Park
(128) Greenwood Road just off Highway 128, Boonville, (707) 895-3141, www.parks.ca.gov; Fee: N; Open: Call for hours
Hike through the redwoods, picnic by the Navarro River, or try to identify various local species on a self-guided nature walk. Just a half a mile away from the main highway, this is a local favorite that's easily accessible to out-of-towners if you know to turn off Highway 128 onto Philo-Greenwood Road and drive for a half a mile.

Deborah Cahn says: "Our own little redwood grove."

RESTAURANTS

Boont Berry Farm
(128) 13981 Highway 128, Boonville, (707) 895-3576; $; Open: L daily; Key: VEG
Sandwiches, salads, strawberries, and seaweed (various kinds—dried, of course) are among the munchies on offer at this natural food store and deli on the main Boonville drag. There are more dry goods than deli items, but a few tables are set up for diners. Staff is very nice, and a couple of them are—surprise!—all kinds of crunchy cute/hot.

Mendocino Café
(HW1) 10451 Lansing Street, Mendocino, (707) 937-6141, www.mendocinocafe.com; $$; Open: L and D daily; Key: KIDS, SCENE, VEG
This is the funky-fun-cool neighborhood standby where everybody goes when they don't feel like cooking. The menu's a mishmash of Americanized dishes from various parts of the globe. Anywhere else in the country, this would be a Cheesecake Factory branch. Since it's in Mendocino, it's an independent restaurant featuring local organic produce, free-range meats, house-baked desserts like apple blueberry crisp, and wild-harvested seafood. You can enter through the side door or via a pretty garden path that leads up to a little swinging gate—much cuter, but only convenient if you're on foot.

Raven's Restaurant at Stanford Inn
(HW1) Coast Highway and Comptche Ukiah Road, Mendocino, (800) 331-8884, (707) 937-5615, www.ravensrestaurant.com; $$; Open: B and D daily, brunch Sun; Key: VEG
A vegan restaurant (during dinner only) featuring organic produce from Big River Nurseries. Depending on the season, diners get kale, chard, greenhouse-grown heirloom tomatoes, and apples from a 150-year-old orchard. Breakfast service is vegetarian but not always vegan. This is a longtime favorite of Mendocino's eco-warrior contingent.

SHOPPING

SIP Mendocino
(101) 13420 S. 101 Highway, Hopland, (707) 744-8375, www.sipmendocino.com; Fee: Y; Open: Tasting daily; Key: VEG, SCENE
Mendocino's a big county with a lot of small-production wines, but Bernadette Byrne, proprietress of this Hopland wine shop, manages to wrap her arms around all of it. She moved here in 1987 to work for the Fetzer family, and her shop is the first place locals point anyone who's looking for a basic education in local wines. She describes it as "a vehicle to promote and showcase the best of Mendocino County."

The retail selection usually includes about 150 labels, all either locally produced or with a Mendocino appellation on the label. Stock rotates regularly throughout the year. On any given day eighteen wines are available to taste, organized into six flights with three wines in each. Anything on pour is also available by the glass. A big section is dedicated to organic and biodynamic wines, but proportionally it's not that much space. It "could be half my store," Byrne says. Guests sit around a big bar built out of river rock in the space that was formerly the Fetzer family's first tasting room. A small back patio is enlivened by riotous summer flowers, all of which Byrne planted herself.

LENA STAMP: Byrne is the Mendocino wine industry sage. And she's patient with games of twenty (or fifty) questions.

Gowan's Oak Tree
(128) 6600 Highway 128, Philo, (707) 895-3353, www.apples4sale.com; $; Open: Daily; Key: VEG, KIDS
It ain't just apples—it's everything from potatoes to peaches and plums, dried apples and sweet cherries, fresh apple cider and, for some bizarre reasons, a few slabs of smoked salmon in a refrigerator case. One of the best and most popular farm stands—since 1880! Though surrounded by vineyards and hills in every direction, it's not hard to find. When you begin to drive past orchards, start looking for the turnout.

ACCOMMODATIONS

Stanford Inn by the Sea
(HW1) Coast Highway and Comptche Ukiah Road, Mendocino, (800) 331-8884, www.stanfordinn.com; $$$; Key: VEG, PETS, DS, GAY
Owned by one of Mendocino County's most passionate small farmers and ecoadvocates, this property is sizable for the area and easy to spot when you're driving into town from the redwood half-light. The property is defined by its magnificent organic gardens, from which the Raven Restaurant sources all its key ingredients. The spa is another big draw. The focus is on getting back to nature and spirituality through yoga, massage, and outdoor explorations. Not exactly conducive to a glamorous wine country getaway—but if you want to mix wine up with

a little ecotourism, you'll find the property's canoes, bicycles, and backcountry itineraries quite appealing.

Living Light Inn
(HW1) 533 E. Fir Street, Fort Bragg, (707) 964-1384, www.livinglightinn.com; $$; Key: VEG
The lodging arm of the Living Light raw food center, this residential retreat offers a lot more creature comforts than the typical ecogetaway. The bed linens might be organic, but they're luxurious all the same—and the comfortable living room has a fireplace and small lending library. It's not lavish, but it's better than a cabin . . . or a tent.

TOUR PROVIDERS

Mendo Wine Tours & Limousine Service
(ALL) 45020 Albion Street, Mendocino, (707) 937-6700, www.mendowinetours.com; Fee: Y; Open: Daily by reservation
There aren't many limo tour companies in the county, but this one is reliable. It works with MacAllum House and the Mendocino Chamber of Commerce.

SUGGESTED TWO-DAY ITINERARIES

{THE ARTISTIC PALATE}

DAY ONE

From Highway 101 North

Morning: Taste at Maple Creek.

Mid-morning: Stop in downtown Boonville, pick up a picnic at a local market.

Late morning: Taste and see art at Scharffenberger.

Afternoon: Wine and food pairing at Goldeneye *or* sparkling wine and picnic at Roederer for lunch.

Mid-afternoon: Taste at Handley Cellars, then drive to Mendocino.

Evening: Have cocktails and dinner at MacCallum House.

DAY TWO

From Mendocino

Morning: Have breakfast at hotel.

Mid-morning: Explore historic village of Mendocino *or* visit Mendocino Art Center.

Late morning: Drive to Fort Bragg.

Afternoon: Go to Mendo Bistro for lunch.

Mid-afternoon: Visit North Coast Artist Collective, Triangle Tattoo Gallery.

Late afternoon: Taste at Pacific Star (call first) . . . try for sunset views.

Evening: Dinner at North Coast Brewing in Fort Bragg.

{GREEN TASTING}

DAY ONE

From Highway 101 North

Morning: Visit the Solar Living Center.

Mid-morning: Taste at Jeriko.

Early afternoon: Stop by SIP Mendocino *or* visit Parducci.

Afternoon: Taste and picnic at Navarro Vineyards.

Overnight: Stay at Philo Apple Farm.

DAY TWO

From Philo

Early morning: Take a Hendy Woods hike.

Afternoon: Have lunch at Boont Berry Farm.

Mid-afternoon: Taste at Toulouse.

Late afternoon: Arrive at Stanford Inn; get massage, go to the beach, explore Mendocino historic village.

Evening: Have dinner at Raven's Restaurant.

CALENDAR OF EVENTS

JUNE
- Taste of Chocolate, Wine & Ale

AUGUST
- Pure Mendocino
  www.puremendocino.com
- Yorkville Highlands Wine Festival

SEPTEMBER
- Winesong
  www.winesong.org

OCTOBER
- Hopland Passport
  www.hoplandpassport.com

RESOURCES

www.avwines.com
www.mcfarm.org (lists farmers' markets in Mendocino)
www.mendocinocoast.com
www.gomendo.com
www.yorkvillehighlands.org

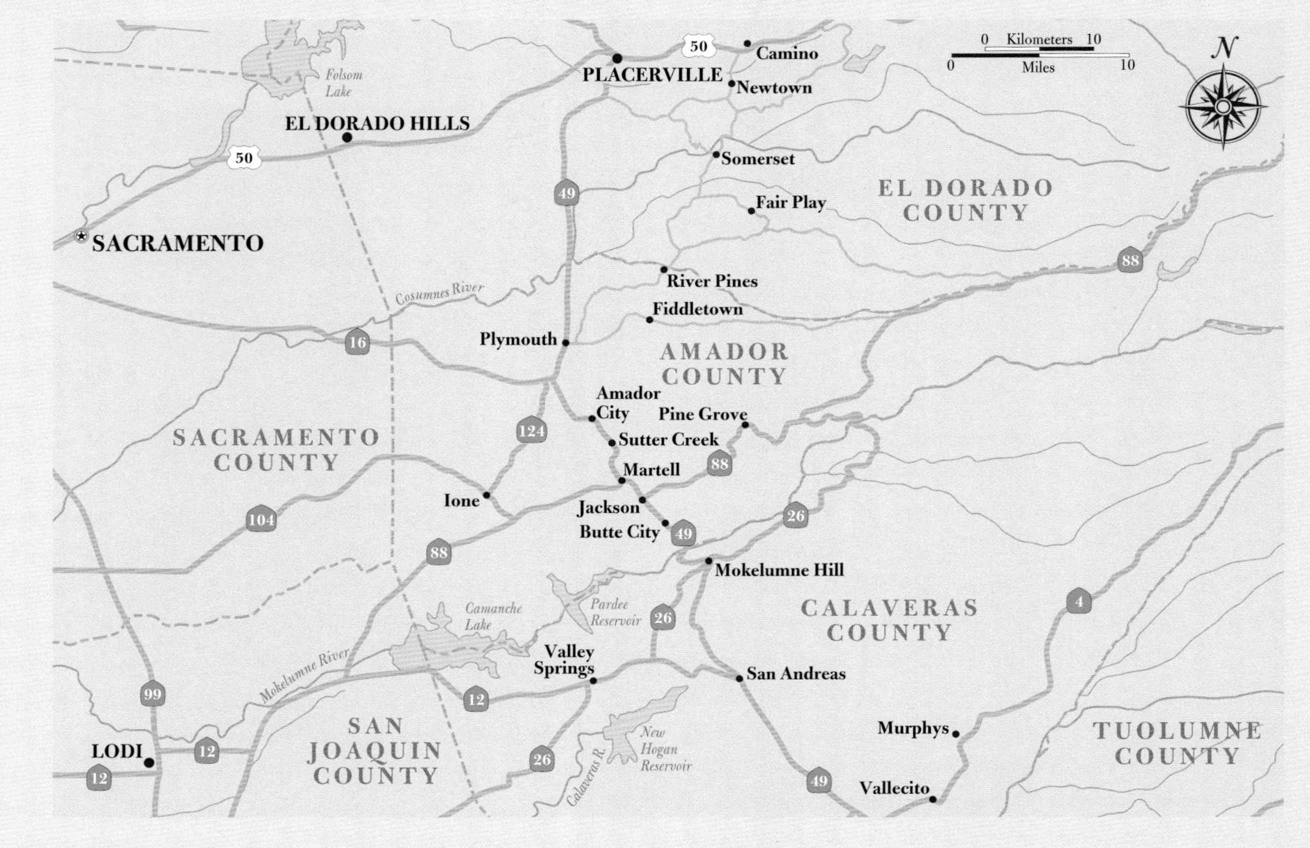
0 Kilometers 10
0 Miles 10
N
PLACERVILLE
Camino
Newtown
EL DORADO HILLS
Folsom Lake
SACRAMENTO
Somerset
Fair Play
EL DORADO COUNTY
River Pines
Fiddletown
Cosumnes River
Plymouth
AMADOR COUNTY
Amador City
Pine Grove
Sutter Creek
Martell
Jackson
Butte City
Ione
SACRAMENTO COUNTY
Mokelumne Hill
Pardee Reservoir
Camanche Lake
CALAVERAS COUNTY
Valley Springs
San Andreas
Mokelumne River
New Hogan Reservoir
Calaveras R.
Murphys
Vallecito
TUOLUMNE COUNTY
SAN JOAQUIN COUNTY
LODI
50
49
88
16
124
104
26
12
99
4

LIVERMORE/LODI/ SIERRA FOOTHILLS

First off, an admission:

It is downright unjust to put three areas as large, diverse, and historically significant as Livermore, Lodi, and Sierra Foothills into one chapter. However, since this is above all a travel book, we must squeeze regions. None of the three are tourism hot spots, but all have a place on the wine stage, particularly for those who have visited Napa and/or Sonoma and want something new.

Livermore is a pleasant San Francisco Bay community surrounded by vineyards that date back as far as a century. Some of the oldest vineyards in the West are located here. Farther east and up a wee bit is Lodi, one of the most polarizing wine regions in the state. Old vine Zin is Lodi's claim to fame. However, other connotations are not as positive. Formerly known for its vast acreage of low-priced Tokay grapes (used to make a sweet, inexpensive dessert wine), Lodi's had to fight its way back into the connoisseur's market.

Then there are the Sierra Foothills. This is a massive appellation; the acreage is bigger than some states, let alone most wine-growing regions. And it's truly the wine wilds. Little has been discovered, thousands of acres have gone unplanted, and with such diversity of elevation (Amador is at 1,000 feet; El Dorado peaks at 3,500), weather, and soil, anything might happen. Only the boldest winemakers venture out here. From the mountain soils spring South African, Portuguese, and Spanish varieties rarely planted before in the United States. Wine tasting is a fun and informal activity that's often mixed with horseback riding, kayaking, or a little bit of spelunking.

Since none of these regions have the name recognition that commands high prices on wines, you can rest assured that winemakers are in this lifestyle for the love of it. Whether they've come because they're bored with the red tape and formalities of the more populated places, or whether they're fifth-generation growers looking to transition into the winery side of things, they're enthusiastic about what they do and very proud to show it to visitors.

Getting Here

Oakland Airport is the closest to Livermore, although San Francisco International is about a ninety minutes' drive away (with light traffic). For Lodi or Amador, the Sacramento Airport is the most convenient.

In the Foothills, there's no telling what might be in this barrel.

Weather

Summer and fall temperatures in Livermore and Lodi can be intensely hot, with daily highs ranging from the mid-80s to more than 100°F, but Bay Area fog rolls in at night, bringing sweet relief to grapes and humans alike. Winters are mild in both places; the temperature rarely hits freezing, and rainfall is usually under three inches a month from December through March.

The Foothills AVA is the land of many microclimates, due to different elevations, mountainous terrain, and breezes coming off the Sierra Nevadas. As a general guideline, lower elevations tend to be hotter, and the highest parts of El Dorado get snow in the winter.

Recommended Transportation

A car is a necessity. So is a good map, if you (or someone in your group) are driving. However, there are a few tour companies, offering both vans and limos, in certain areas.

Style

Blue-jeans casual. In Lodi or the Sierras, you probably will want to bring a pair of hiking boots, a swimsuit, and a change of clothes. The natural attractions are stunning—and the winemakers strongly encourage visitors to experience them.

Fees
Some wineries are free to taste; others charge between $3 and $10.

Bird's-eye View
At the outermost eastern limits of the San Francisco Bay Area, Livermore is the obvious day-trip destination for people from the city or East Bay. Most of the wineries are on Tesla, although many new ones are opening along intersecting Greenville Road. The historic downtown area is north of the wineries, about two miles off the freeway.

Lodi is about fifty miles northeast of Livermore and thirty miles from Sacramento. Comprised of seven sub-appellations, Lodi grows more than 100,000 acres of wine grapes, including 40 percent of California's Zinfandel. However, the tasting rooms are situated within geographical grids or clusters to create easily accessible wine routes for would-be tasters. Lodi's picturesque downtown area has restaurants, wine bars, and shops, as well as public art and many scheduled events. The new-ish Lodi Wine & Visitor Center is about three miles away.

The Sierra Foothills appellation spans nine counties in California. Within it, notable sub-appellations include Amador, El Dorado, and Calaveras. Though it's spread out, there are some navigable wine trails, particularly Murphy's in Calaveras and Amador/Shenandoah.

Area Key:
LI = Livermore, Pleasanton
LO = Lodi, Acampo
HS = High Sierra Foothills including El Dorado and Amador Counties; Fair Play, Shenandoah Valley; Sutter Creek, Plymouth, Fiddletown
LS = Lower Sierra Foothills, Tuolomne and Calaveras counties; Murphys, Angels Camp, Highway 4, Sonora

The Panel

Tom Albanese, certified sommelier and owner, Campo di Bocce

Mark Chandler, executive director, Lodi-Woodbridge Wine Grape Commission

Jim Concannon, owner, Concannon Vineyards

Bill Easton, president and winemaker, Terre Rouge and Easton Estate

G. M. "Pooch" Pucilowski, chief judge and consultant, California State Fair Wine Competition; wine columnist at *Sacramento Magazine* www.universityofwine.com

Livermore: The Bay Area's Backyard

It's rather shocking how few Bay Area residents know about the Livermore AVA, given how serious San Francisco is about its food and wine. One reason for this is obvious: The East Bay is overshadowed by the famous regions to the north. The other main reason may be that Highway 580 doesn't cut through historic Livermore or the vineyard region. It's a blessing and a curse: These scenic areas are saved from traffic, smog emissions, and noise. However, people can (and do) drive right past this wine region for years without knowing it exists.

The Livermore wine landscape is actually suburban. The wine trail leads through vineyards, then through pleasant residential neighborhoods, and then into vineyards again. The wineries themselves are easily accessible and visitor friendly. Though they're not tourist hot spots, they're close to the big city and know how to make its denizens feel at home.

WINERIES

Wente
(LI) 5050 Arroyo Road, Livermore, (925) 456-2400 (Vineyard tasting room)
(LI) 5565 Tesla Road, Livermore, (925) 456-2300 (Estate winery and tasting room), www.wentevineyards.com; Fee: N; Open: Daily; KEY: TH

The oldest continually operated winery in the United States, Wente literally put Livermore on the map as a wine-making region. It opened in 1883 and is still family owned and operated, with fifth-generation descendant Karl Wente as the new winemaker. Historians credit Wente with spearheading the creation of the San Francisco Bay AVA, of which Livermore is a sub-appellation. (Though San Francisco is not much of a wine production region, its name is widely recognized.)

Wente has always been an integral part of the local community and social scene—perhaps now more than ever. Its main public facility on Arroyo Road consists of a tasting room, a white-tablecloth restaurant, a golf course, and an events center with a huge outdoor lawn for summertime concerts.

Tom Albanese says: "What they've done for Livermore is astronomical. Karl is a world-class winemaker. His Nth Degree small lot is phenomenal."

Concannon Vineyard
(LI) 4590 Tesla Road, Livermore, (800) 258-9866, www.concannonvineyard.com; Fee: Y; Open: Daily; Key: SF

Neck and neck with Wente for the title of oldest winery in the region, Concannon celebrated its 125th year of continuous operations in 2008. Like all of the other wineries that survived during Prohibition, this one also hung on by producing sacramental wine. (Forgive me if this is blasphemous, but I see similarities to the whole "medical marijuana–permitting thing going on in California right now.) Today the Concannon family home is a designated historic landmark—which is appropriate, since the first-ever vintage (1884) was made in the basement. On display is the first grape press from 1882, restored to gleaming mint condition. Jim Concannon recently struck a deal with the local conservancy, selling a good chunk of his surrounding lands with the stipulation that they be vineyard-allocated in perpetuity.

The historic Concannon estate.

Concannon has championed Petite Sirah since the early twentieth century, and to this day they're one of the top producers of the obscure red varietal, though they also make Merlot, Cab, and a portfolio of other wines. The "Captain Joe" (named after Jim's father) heritage wine is a collectors' item. Only 400 to 500 cases are produced annually, and it's only available at the winery, with a limit of one case per customer.

La Rochelle/Steven Kent
(LI) 5443 Tesla Road, Livermore, (925) 243-6442, www.lrwine.com, www.stevenkent.com; Fee: Y; Open: Daily; Key: XP

Pinot Noir nuts unite! Then divide, immediately: With four Pinots to taste and probably more than a dozen for sale, La Rochelle really encourages customers to have a defined personal taste, even over the most subtle differences. (This is, of course, something that Pinot people are already inclined to do.) The winery releases single-barrel Pinot labels several times a year—usually only to club members. Often, however, one club wine is on the tasting menu, just to lure in potential compulsives.

Livermore's Not-So-Little Legacy

Jim Concannon, Owner, Concannon Vineyards

Livermore's wine history is integrally tied in with Petite Sirah—and with Concannon Vineyards. So who better than the third-generation owner Jim Concannon to give us the big scoop on the little grape?

- Back in France, this grape was originally named Durif, after the plant pathologist who cross-propagated Syrah together with a grape called Peloursin, in the hopes of creating a mold-resistant grape.
- Durif didn't live up to expectations: It couldn't withstand mold, and it also created a rather weak wine.
- The first cuttings came in from France around 1909, and Livermore was the first region in the United States to begin planting them.
- When the Californians saw the cutting, with its tight clusters and small berries, they said, "Let's call it Petite!"—which is how it got its current name.
- The grape did better here because of the warm Mediterranean climate and lack of rainfall all the way through October.
- Petite Sirah was the most-planted grape in Napa in the 1890s because it was so versatile and such a good blending grape.
- Because their color is so vivid, Petite grapes are kept as a variety to blend into weaker-colored wines.
- The first time Concannon Vineyard bottled Petite Sirah separately was in 1961. It was released in 1964 with the trademark, "America's first Petite Sirah."
- Captain Joe Concannon (Jim's father) served under Pershing in World War I, and every year thereafter he would send Pershing a case of Petite Sirah and would receive a thank you note in return.
- Petit Syrah has tremendous longevity: Regular lots are released at three years old and can be drunk immediately or cellared for up to ten years, while reserve wines will live twenty to thirty years in the bottle.

Pinot madness aside, this is a fun winery to taste at, because it does sit-down flights with food pairings. Two flights of four wines are available—one all Pinot Noir, one a range—and flights typically change at least once a month. Accompanying nibbles include tapenade, cheese, and truffle mousse. (No, you cannot taste single wines or skip the food portion.)

Note: The adjacent winery, Steven Kent, opened in 1999 and is primarily known for its small-production premium reds: Cabernet, Merlot, Barbera, Sangiovese. It offers complimentary tastings.

Tom Albanese says: "Steven comes from the Mirassou family [one of the oldest West Coast wine-making families]. He grows some of the best Cab fruit around. His attention to detail is impeccable, the quality amazing. I also love his Sauvignon Blanc."

Wood Family Vineyards
(LI) 7702 Cedar Mountain Drive, Livermore, (925) 606-7411, www.woodfamilyvineyards.com; Fee: N; Open: By appt.; Key: FO
Former commercial pilot Rhonda Wood operates a tasting room out of her garage and has an aviation tower in her front yard. Her wine label features a watercolor-style graphic of a Woody station wagon.

Tom Albanese says: "Cab and Chardonnay are recommended. Her 'Para Mas Amigas' series is handcrafted from all Livermore fruit."

Mountain views from a Sierra Foothills winery.

Ruby Hill Winery
(LI) 400 Vineyard Avenue, Pleasanton, (925) 931-9463, www.rubyhillwinery.net; Fee: N; Open: Thu–Sun
There is good buzz on this place, which is one of the newest wineries in town . . . and one of the oldest, too! It was founded in the 1800s but was out of commission for decades; only in February 2008 did it open to the public again. Small-lot wines are by Chris Graves, who is the former winemaker for Tamás Estates (a Wente brand).

Tom Albanese says: "I sell three of his labels: Chardonnay, Cabernet, and Sangiovese. The style is Old World, as opposed to jammy and overloaded."

Garré Winery
(LI) 7986 Tesla Road, Livermore, (925) 371-8200, www.garrewinery.com; Fee: N; Open: Sat–Sun; Key: KIDS
Stop here if you're hungry and don't feel like picnicking: it has one of the only on-site restaurants in the wine region. Friday's Italian dinner nights are a fan favorite.

ATTRACTIONS

Wente Event Center & Golf Course
(LI) 5050 Arroyo Road, Livermore, (925) 456-2475 (golf course), (925) 456-2450 (restaurant), www.wentegolf.com; Fee: Y; Open: Hours vary; Key: KIDS, RR (golf), LN, SF
This place packs in people on a scale most wineries would never aspire to. During one of the summer concerts, the gates become a barricaded fortress, while the line of cars waiting to move forward starts to resemble rush hour traffic. The appeal's understandable, though: With its gourmet white-tablecloth dinner packages, lawn setting, and star-studded oldies/soft rock/jazz lineup, Wente's concert setup is far more pleasant for a certain demographic than any concert venue in San Francisco. It also offers twilight movie-dinner packages twice a month in summer, and music in the much more intimate restaurant setting on Thursdays.

The golf course is its own entity and staff advise you to reserve fourteen days in advance. Designed by Greg Norman, it used to be a PGA tour stop and is still a championship course. The clubhouse grill provides a halfway point between formal dining in the main restaurant and going home to make yourself a sandwich.

Blacksmith Square
(LI) Livermore Avenue and Railroad Avenue, Livermore, www.blacksmith-square.com; Fee: Varies; Open: Hours vary
This mixed-use retail destination in a historic downtown Livermore site is currently home to half a dozen tasting rooms that pour more than forty different wine labels. A few retailers have also opened their doors, and there's a chance of more to follow—the complex only debuted in 2006. Live music, harvest festivals, and art events are part of the planned entertainment offering.

RESTAURANTS

Campo di Bocce
(LI) 175 E. Vineyard Avenue, Livermore, (925) 249-9800, www.campodibocce.com; $; Open: L, D and bocce daily; Key: KIDS, SCENE
It doesn't quite do this venue justice to list it under restaurants, because it's much more of an all-around hangout spot. Food, drink, games, conversation . . . everything sort of blurs together and loses its time stamp, in a relaxed way that recalls the Mediterranean. Even the quietest midweek afternoon hours are pleasant: late afternoon sun warming the outdoor courts; a few businesspeople wrapping up a boozy, three-hour lunch; and a hand-in-hand duo at the bar, taking their time choosing a chilled white wine. The main hall, with its four regulation-size bocce courts, gets filled up in the evenings. (If you want to play on Friday or Saturday night, make reservations one week in advance.)

Regular diners can watch or ignore the games from either the dining room or the covered patio. Players can deposit their plates at side tables that rest up against the court rails and snatch bites standing up in between turns. The gourmet pizzas (wild boar sausage and roast red potatoes; shrimp and pesto) lend themselves to utensil-free eating, though the pastas are a bit tougher to manage. Owner Tom Albanese introduced the dining/bocce/bar concept to the East Bay diner (however, it must be said that the boozy bocce picnic is a summer tradition among

Italian-descended wine country families). He's dedicated to promoting the game of bocce within the United States. A Level II sommelier, Albanese is also a knowledgeable proponent of Livermore wines and wine education in general. He holds private trainings weekly for his staff.

Zephyr

(LI) 1736 First Street, Livermore, (925) 961-1000, www.zephyrgrill.com; $$; Open: L and D daily; Key: DS

Old-timers and hipsters alike give this restaurant high marks. Classic American dishes made with artisan ingredients range from California inspired to soul-kitchen staples. Signatures include fried chicken and "Texas Funeral" seven-layer fudge cake. The staff is able to speak knowledgeably about the wide selection of local wines.

ENTERTAINMENT AND NIGHTLIFE

Blue Agave Club

(LI) 625 Main Street, Pleasanton, (925) 417-1224, www.blueagaveclub.com; $$; Open: L and D daily; Key: PU

The expansive outdoor patio and colorful decor hint at happy hour hijinks and lazy summer suppers, complete with top-shelf margaritas and modern-leaning gourmet Mexican cuisine. Housed in a recently renovated historic building, this downtown favorite is equally popular with dinner and cocktail crowds.

Pleasanton Hotel

(LI) 855 Main Street, Pleasanton, (925) 846-8106, www.pleasantonhotel.com; $$; Open: L and D daily, B Sun, events Thu–Sat; Key: SF, CHEESE

No hotel here—just a restaurant that's actually more of a local hangout spot. The saloon-style bar is a reliable watering hole that attracts all different ages. The ever-changing event schedule includes stand-up comedy, murder-mystery dinners, winemaker dinners, and more. Live jazz Friday and Saturday; blues on the patio Thursday night starting at 5:30 p.m.

SHOPPING

The Wine Steward
(LI) 641 Main Street, Pleasanton, (925) 600-9463, www.thewine steward.com; Open: Tue–Sun
Sometimes this retailer seems like it's so busy, nobody knows which end is up. Nonetheless the locals love it for its wine-educated staff, wide selection, and focus on local wines. The on-site wine bar is open weekends only and closes along with the retail store.

Vino Cellars & Accessories
(LI) 2241 First Street, Livermore, (877) 447-8700, www.vino-cellars .com; Open: Tue–Sat or by appt.
It isn't too often that you find a bricks-and-mortar store within such a specialized niche. However, it seems logical that serious customers wouldn't consider the merchandise unless they'd seen it firsthand. Vino sells wine cabinets, coolers, modular racks, and other mid- to large-size wine storage systems. Even the smallest pieces are not cheap: Climate-control technology is an expensive addition to an already pricey piece of furniture. Custom-designed cellars are another side of the business. In this category, the showroom only provides some displays designed to inspire prospective buyers. Though the company has an online store, its recent move into downtown Livermore bodes well for the local wine industry—demand for its oh-so-specialized product may be increasing among local homeowners.

ACCOMMODATIONS

Rose Hotel
(LI) 807 Main Street, Pleasanton, (800) 843-9540, (925) 846-8802, www.rosehotel.net; $$; Key: DS, SF
Genteel, highly polished, and gracefully aged, with local politicians in the lobby and perhaps a resident ghost or two. This is the sort of boutique hotel you'd expect to find in the South, not suburban East Bay. And the plot thickens! It's owned by John Madden's son, Mike, who apparently is rather a player in the local lodging scene. (Who knew?) Mike has good taste: The bouquets in the foyer are gorgeous and no doubt expensive, the furnishings are antique, the in-room coffee packets are Peet's, and the electronics are Bose. Wonderful design touches include a curved lobby staircase with banisters polished to a high gleam. According to the front desk manager, this hotel is often booked midweek with business travelers who want to bring their spouses for a little R&R in a noncorporate setting.

LENA STAMP: When Sarah Jessica Parker stayed in the Grand Suite, the hotel installed a full-length mirror at her request. Smart move, SJP! Thanks, on behalf of future female guests of the Rose.

Purple Orchid Inn, Resort & Spa
(LI) 4549 Cross Road, Livermore, (925) 606-8855, www.purpleorchid.com; $-$$; Key: DS, SF
In truth, this is not a resort but only a B&B, with rooms that are slightly themed and slightly prefab . . . however, it's the only unique "wine country" accommodation in Livermore. The olive grove bordering the drive is a nice touch, and the lobby/living room is pleasant and intimate. However, the real magnet is the recently redone backyard, featuring two hot tubs, a snazzy outdoor kitchen, and a free-form pool with its own waterfall. The spa treatment rooms are in tiny individual outbuildings tucked around the pool area.

Lodi: Old Vines, New Developments

You can always spot Zinfandel lovers by the way they respond to the mention of Lodi. If their eyes light up and they say, "Old vines! Yum!" you've got a live one. If they stare blankly, they're probably Pinot or Cab fans. This area is the largest producer of Zinfandel in the world.

There are 800 wine-grape growers in Lodi, and most of them have been there for four to five generations. By contrast, there are only seventy-five wineries—and that number's probably five times what it was in 1998. The appeal of owning a winery, as opposed to farming massive quantities of grapes, is just now becoming evident.

WINERIES

Vino con Brio Winery
(LO) 7889 E. Harney Lane, Lodi, (888) 410-8466, (209) 369-5392, www.vinoconbrio.com; Fee: Y; Open: Thu–Mon or by appt.; Key: DS, PETS

Though wine critics associate this winery with its big reds, the 2007 Passionate Rosé is an award winner in its own right. The redesigned tasting room features a tasting bar that the vintner's daughter, Anne Matson, made out of barrel staves. The patio and front yard, featuring a pond with weeping willow trees, is a popular wedding site. Amarosa Garden B&B is on the property.

Pooch Pucilowski says: "Double gold at Cal State Fair for Pinotage, double gold for Sangiovese."

Mark Chandler says: "Very unique wine varieties."

LENA STAMP: This winery makes a late-harvest Viognier, which is a wine I rarely see and love beyond all reason.

Borra Winery
(LO) 1301 E. Armstrong Road, Lodi, (209) 368-2446, www.borrawinery.com; Fee: Y; Open: Daily

Housed in an old stone building, this charming little tasting room does double duty as a gift shop/boutique, thanks to the enthusiastic free-form buying of the Borra daughters. It's a favorite of local women, who often pop in just to see what's new in knickknacks, jewelry, and clothes.

On a viticultural note, Borra's 2005 Red Fusion blend is widely awarded and was named best red blend in the region at the 2008 California State Fair.

Van Ruiten
(LO) 340 W. Highway 12, Lodi, (209) 334-5722, www.vrwinery.com; Fee: N; Open: Daily; Key: TH, SCENE

One of the big Lodi grape growers for a few generations, this is now a "big" local winemaker as well (though the latter is a relative term). It's only been a winery since 2000. Locally it's known for its Cabernet-Shiraz; however the premium flagship wine is the Zinfandella. A new value-positioned series called "Glory Days" is getting good buzz, and the Pinot Gris is a winner on price and quality fronts (it won a gold medal at the Cal State Wine Competition). The friendly, inviting tasting room is right at the front of the winery.

Current and Future Forecasts

G. M. "Pooch" Pucilowski, Chief Judge and Consultant, California State Fair Wine Competition and Wine Columnist, *Sacramento Magazine*

You want to know about Sierra Foothills wineries? Ask Pooch. You want to know the entire history of Lodi? Ask Pooch. You want to know what's winning medals at the Cal State Fair, what may win medals next year, and where the hottest competitions will be? Ask Pooch. Over the decades he's had his hands in every aspect of the California wine industry, but the northern counties are his area of expertise. Clearly, we need a peek at his crystal ball . . .

"Most Napa and Sonoma wineries have been getting grapes from Lodi for years, but with rare exceptions, none would admit it. Now with the proliferation of Lodi wines, the region is getting recognized for Zinfandel, Petite Sirah, and some really nice Cabs. At the California State Wine Competition, some of them were showing *really* well.

"Amador and El Dorado have been around for a long time and are always fun to watch. But Placer wasn't doing anything, and then suddenly a dozen wineries have come up within the last ten years. So that's an area to keep an eye on.

"In Clarksburg and Lodi you'll see Petite Sirah, Zinfandel, and the Spanish variety Tempranillo. Without a doubt Clarksburg is producing some of the best Chenin Blanc as well. In the Foothills, you'll find Petite Sirah. In El Dorado, look for Cab Franc. I also predict a growth in Barbera.

"Though these areas are known for Zin, winemakers aren't afraid to grow things besides Zinfandel. They're bold. They're pioneers. Plus, the overall popularity of blends is growing."

Michael David

(LO) 4580 W. Highway 12, Lodi, (888) 707-9463, (209) 368-7384, www.lodivineyards.com; Fee: Reserve Only; Open: Daily; Key: KIDS, XP, TH

This is probably the most-visited winery in the area and the first to charge $60 for a Zinfandel bottle—the "Lust" Zinfandel, which was part of the signature "Seven Deadly Zins" series. The owners are a sixth-generation farm family. On any given day a handwritten sign on the winery's front door might read, "Baby chicks for sale!" Baby goats and miniature ponies wander the grounds. The pumpkin patch supplies a lot of local Halloweens, and the on-site cafe does a good breakfast and lunch.

Macchia

(LO) 7099 E. Peltier Road, Acampo, (209) 333-2600, www.macchiawines.com; Fee: N; Open: Thu-Mon

The new kid on the block, this husband-and-wife team is quickly garnering a reputation as *the* place to go if you like red wines. Tim Holdener calls himself a Zinfanatic. His "Outrageous" Zin was named "Best of State" at the California State Fair.

Pooch Pucilowski says: "Their wines are showing really well."

Heritage Oak Winery

(LO) 10112 E. Woodbridge Road, Acampo, (209) 986-2763, www.heritageoakwinery.com; Fee: N; Open: Mon-Fri (p.m. only), Sat-Sun

Owner Tom Hoffman is perhaps not quite what you'd expect of a fifth-generation farmer. A concert-level pianist, he's passionate about wine making as well as the land. This property is located along the Mokelumne River, and visitors are invited to picnic on the riverbanks (BYO supplies). Tom and his wife/business partner Carmel are working with Sierra Adventure Outfitters to offer wine and kayaking tours; in the meantime, hiking and birdwatching are encouraged. Open afternoons only on the weekdays.

LENA STAMP: Local sources tell me that Tom Hoffman is known for building some of the most beautiful handcrafted birdhouses in the land. Quite the iconoclast, eh?

St. Amant

(LO) 1 Winemaster Way, Lodi, (209) 367-0646, www.stamantwine.com; Fee: N; Open: By appt.

One of the first local wineries to institute sustainable practices and denote it on the label, this family-owned operation is a local industry leader and fan favorite. The old vine Zin wins a lot of awards, as does its Tempranillo produced from Amador grapes. Port is also highly praised. This is a winery first, vineyard second. The tasting experience is not fancy: It's by appointment, often straight from the barrel. However, the wine's some of the best in the area. Highly recommended.

ATTRACTIONS

Jessie's Grove Winery
(LO) 1973 West Turner Road, Lodi, (209) 368-0880, www.jgwinery.com; Fee: Y; Open: Daily
This winery doubles as a historic attraction. Its vines are the oldest in the region, dating back 120 years, and its grounds include the thirty-acre Valley Oak preserve, with a very interesting collection of farm equipment dating back to the 1850s. Owner Wanda Woock Bechtold wrote and published the book *Jessie's Grove—100 Years in the San Joaquin Valley,* which features old photos shot by her great-uncle.

Mark Chandler says: "If visitors are lucky, or call ahead, they can arrange a tour with Wanda Woock Bechtold, Jessie Spenker's granddaughter, who has written a magnificent book covering her family history in the area from 1850 to 1950. It just so happens her great-uncle was an amateur photographer, and she found a treasure trove of his images. Many of the photos show the same pieces of equipment that are now displayed in the restored barn. A very personalized experience, especially with a glass of old vine Zin in hand."

Lodi Wine & Visitor Center
(LO) 2545 W. Turner Road, Lodi, (209) 367-4727, www.lodiwine.com; Fee: Y; Open: Daily
Operated by the Lodi-Woodbridge

Winegrape Commission, this is a smart place to start a wine exploration. The tasting bar pours a rotation selection of nine local wines. In the little demonstration vineyard, guests can see and taste different grape varieties, as well as check out growing methods like the trellising system. Another exhibit shows the different types of soil in Lodi's seven sub-appellations. Knowledgeable staff advise guests about which local wineries to visit and provide trail maps and driving directions. It's adjacent to the Wine & Roses inn.

RESTAURANTS

Rosewood Bar & Grill
(LO) 28 S. School Street, Lodi, (209) 369-0470, www.rosewoodbarandgrill.com; $$; Open: D daily; Key: SCENE, PU
Owned by Wine & Roses, this restaurant is located in downtown Lodi. Locals say it's the hot place to go on a Friday or Saturday night for great specialty martinis, bacon-wrapped prawns, and cocktail chatter. Indoor and outdoor seating.

Mark Chandler says: "Great bistro-style menu."

Woodbridge Crossing
(LO) 18939 Lower Sacramento Road, Woodbridge, (209) 366-1800, www.woodbridgecrossing.net; $$; Open: L and D daily, B Sun; Key: FO
Probably because it's the only thing going in the one-horse town of Woodbridge, this place aims to play two roles: dive saloon and rustic-elegant steakhouse. Big-city sophisticated it ain't—but professional service, well-prepared prime cuts, and white-tablecloth-meets-Old-West atmosphere add up to a memorable evening. Maybe a bit more memorable if you adjourn to the bar after dinner for bourbon and bar chatter.

Mark Chandler says: "Historic Western-style restaurant with authentic art and bronzes from the 1800s."

ENTERTAINMENT AND NIGHTLIFE

Cellar Door
(LO) 21 N. School Street, Lodi, (209) 339-4394, www.lodicellardoor.com; $; Open: Tue–Sun; Key: SCENE
This tasting room, wine bar, and once-a-week live music lounge is a collaboration between the owners of Jessie's Grove, Van Ruiten, and Michael David—and unsurprisingly, one of the favorite hangouts in town Thursday through Saturday, when it stays open till 9 p.m. "Don't miss it on Friday night," advise locals. "Casual and comfortable—you don't have to worry about some weirdo trying to pick you up."

SHOPPING

Sierra Adventure Outfitters
(LO) 120 N. School Street, Lodi, (209) 368-3461, www.sierraadventureoutfitters.com; Open: Mon–Sat
For the year-round adventurer or the spontaneous visitor, this downtown Lodi store provides outdoor equipment to buy or rent. Kayaking is a summertime mainstay—outfit yourself here with everything necessary for a day on the river.

Stogies Cigar Lounge
(LO) 230 W. Pine Street, Lodi, (209) 334-5764, www.stogiesoflodi.com; Open: Tue-Sat AM/PM
A smallish space dedicated to wine, tobacco, and company. In addition to a range of hard-to-find cigars, the store sells small-production, mostly local wines,

ACCOMMODATIONS

Wine & Roses
(LO) 2505 W. Turner Road, Lodi, (209) 334-6988, www.winerose.com; $$; Key: DS
This picturesque old farmhouse inn started as a tiny B&B with chickens and rabbits underfoot even during the elegant weekend brunches, which would swiftly become a tradition. Its reputation grew fast as a preferred wedding site and atmospheric overnight accommodation. The opening of the official Lodi tasting room next door helped. "Women come to taste, and they fall in love with the look of the place," says a tasting room employee. By now it's probably Lodi's best-known lodging option, but Sunday mornings in spring remain as tranquil as one could wish.

Amarosa Inn & Gardens
(LO) 7889 E. Harney Lane, Lodi, (888) 410-8466, (209) 369-5392, www.vinoconbrio.com; $; Open: Tasting room Thu-Mon or by appt.; Key: SF, DS
Breakfasts are incredible at this small country B&B on the Vino con Brio winery grounds. The vineyard setting is enhanced by a tree-shaded lake.

Mark Chandler says: "Elegant ranch-style home converted to a relaxing B&B."

Sierra Foothills: The Wild Red Yonder

An eclectic and worldly group of go-getters make up the wine industry here. They prefer the tiny Gold Rush–era towns, rugged mountains, and diverse soils to California's more established wine regions. The fruit they eke out of the land is distinctive and noteworthy—not just because of the *terroir,* but also because the varieties themselves are so unusual that no other regions have taken a chance on them. Already acknowledged as a place to discover great red wines, the Sierra Foothills are on tastemakers' radar and predicted to be the "next big region" a decade from now. However, we don't recommend waiting. Already, the Sierra Foothills landscape surprises you with its beauty, and the wineries with their unique charm.

WINERIES

Ironstone Vineyards

(LS) 1894 Six Mile Road, Murphys, (209) 728-1251, www.ironstonevineyards.com; Fee: N; Open: Daily; Key: TH, SC

Have you been to Ironstone? Have you been to Ironstone? Have you have you *have you*? If you mention the Sierra Foothills and wine tasting in the same sentence to anyone familiar with the area, this is what you'll hear back. Even though, if we're being honest, Ironstone doesn't necessarily have the best wine in the region. What this iconic property *does* have is ambience to beat the pants off anything in Sonoma or Monterey, 10,000 square feet of wine caves, and the biggest crystalline gold leaf nugget in the world. A museum has been built around it, with many other smaller gold pieces playing supporting roles. Gold panning sluice and waterwheel are also on the grounds.

Overall, the thing people (locals and visitors alike) love about this winery is that it's authentic to the Gold Country. With stalactites in the wine caves and a tasting room that looks like an old stamp mill—even a gigantic 1927 pipe organ in a dedicated theater—Ironstone feels like a winery of the Sierra Nevadas, not a wannabe villa that might as well be in Napa or Tuscany. Daffodils carpet the grounds in March, miners instruct would-be gold panners on weekends, and Gold Rush spirit prevails, even in the twenty-first century.

Stevenot Winery

(LS) 2690 San Domingo Road, Murphys, (209) 728-0638, www.stevenotwinery.com; Fee: N; Open: Daily; Key: DS

458 Main Street, Murphys (209) 728-0148; Fee: N; Open: Wed-Mon in season, Thu-Mon off-season

An oldie, a goodie, and a local pick to boot, this winery puts out a pretty broad portfolio but is known for its warm weather reds. Offerings change year by year, but include everything from the Spanish varietal Tempranillo (which sells out) to the much-disparaged but indubitably Californian Merlot (on the winery's sassy sister label Red Rover). Taste either in the dedicated tasting room in downtown Murphys or out on the historic ranch. In summer the latter property hosts live music and theater.

Ironstone: the ultimate Mother Lode Winery.

Milliaire

(LS) 276 Main Street, Murphys, (209) 728-1658, www.milliaire winery.com; Fee: N; Open: Daily

One of the oldest wineries in the area, this multi-generational family operation produces 2,500 cases annually, and is proud of its traditional methods. Though they own no vineyards, the Millers work closely with all their growers over the year, and vineyard-designate every bottling. They taste out of a former gas station in downtown Murphys. Note: Tasting fee applied to groups of six or more.

Easton/Terre Rouge

(HS) 10801 Dickson Road (just off Shenandoah Road), Plymouth, (209) 245-3117, www.terre rougewines.com; Fee: N; Open: Fri-Mon

Terre Rouge and Easton Wines are two separate brands that founder Bill Easton started concurrently. Both brands operate out of his Amador County winery. Terre Rouge is his Northern Rhône program; Easton produces the traditional California lineup of Cabernet, Zinfandel, and Sauvignon Blanc. A liberal arts major, Easton entered the wine business on the bottom rung, working in a cellar in Sonoma County. He

The Essence of Amador: Key Points on the Land

Bill Easton, President and Winemaker, Terre Rouge and Easton Estate

Prickly at first but passionate once you get him started, the erudite Mr. Easton epitomizes the Sierra Foothills winemaker. Wine geeks love him but can't always get him to talk. We, however, had no such problem . . . just mention the word "*terroir*" and it's all systems go. Below, Easton's nutshell overview of the Sierra Foothills, the sub-appellation of Amador, and why some consider its *terroir* to hold winemaking gold.

- The Sierra Foothills appellation is 250 miles long and 40 miles wide, encompassing 2.4 million acres in 9 counties.
- It runs from Lassen in the north to Mariposa in the south; the sub-appellation of Amador is in the middle.
- Amador is at 1,000 to 2,500 feet in elevation, with minerally mountain soils that are volcanic and granite-based.
- The soil of Amador is similar to the decomposed granite soil of Hermitage in the Northern Rhône.
- Also similar to the Northern Rhône is the cooler climate, which is created by the mountain location: Vineyards get cooling breezes not only from the Bay Area but from air rushing down the mountain.
- The less fertile mountain soils produce grapes with a lot of flavor and intensity, but not large crops.
- When the taste of the soil pulls through into the wine because of devigorated rocky soils, it creates what the French call *Gout de terrroir*—taste of the earth.
- Amador wines are regarded to have *Gout de terroir* and to be similar to European wines: more acidity and structure, as opposed to "fruity" flavors.
- Historically the Amador region is known for Zin, but that is now being surpassed by Syrah (the main Rhône variety) and Barbera.
- Even though some Amador Rhônes have proven themselves, the bigger red wines should probably be cellared five years after vintage to reach full potential.

gradually worked his way up to owning a retail wine store in the Bay Area. The store sustained him financially during the early days of the Easton winery. In 1994 his winery got profitable enough to sustain itself, and he's been one of the most visible and best-respected Amador County producers ever since. Easton is intense about wines and about his adopted region, which he calls "a diamond in the rough."

Vino Noceto

(HS) 11011 Shenandoah Road, Plymouth, (877) 466-2386, (209) 245-6556, www.noceto.com; Fee: N; Open: Daily

Sangiovese is the specialty here, and eight different labels are available—including a couple of Sangiovese-based red blends. This husband-and-wife winery also does a rosato, a couple of light dessert wines, and a grappa. Tours are by appointment. This is Terre Rouge's neighbor, and the two wineries sometimes cohost events.

Cooper Vineyards

(HS) 21365 Shenandoah School Road, Plymouth, (209) 245-6181, www.cooperwines.com; Fee: N; Open: Fri–Sun

This is a new winery by a respected longtime vintner and his family. Out of their diverse and extensive portfolio, Barbera is the grape from which experts predict great things.

Pooch Pucilowski says: "Crissy Cooper's dad [Dick Cooper, owner] has been growing grapes for years, for about a dozen known labels. The winery's keeping his daughter busy."

C. G. Di Arie Winery

(HS) 19919 Shenandoah School Road, Plymouth, (209) 245-4700, www.cgdiarie.com; Open: Thu–Mon

The husband-and-wife owners of this winery are, improbably, a breakfast food inventor and a fine artist/ballerina. Right out of the starting gates, husband Chaim Gur-Arieh started releasing critically acclaimed red wines—in very limited production at first, but increasing as more of the fifty-acre estate vineyard tract is cultivated.

Pooch Pucilowski says: "His nickname is 'Captain Crunch.' They're doing amazing wines."

Perry Creek

(HS) 7400 Perry Creek Road, Fair Play, (530) 620-5175, www.perrycreek.com, Fee: N; Open: Daily

Though known for the Zinfandels that it does so well, this winery is starting to produce some noteworthy Rhône wines. It has an active hospitality program with lots of cool events on the schedule during summer and harvest.

Pooch Pucilowski says: "At the 2008 California State Fair, their Petit Sirah was named best in California."

Mt. Brow Winery
(LS) 10850 Mt. Brow Road, Sonora, (209) 532-8491, www.mtbrowwinery.com; Fee: N; Open: Fri-Sun; Key: DS
Panoramic vineyard views span outward in front of the shady picnic area at this picturesque winery. The charming tasting room has its own little gift store. This small mom 'n' pop venture exemplifies everything that's endearing about Sierra Foothills wineries.

La Bella Rosa
(LS) 17990 Old Wards Ferry Road, Sonora, (209) 533-8668, www.labellarosavineyards.com; Fee: N; Open: Sat-Sun
This new winery only had their second crush in 2008, but already they've started a great red program. Also a beautiful tasting room and gift shop, for those who factor aesthetics into the equation.

ATTRACTIONS

Horse & Barrel
(LS) 2000 Nickerson Lane, Murphys, (209) 728-9333, www.horseandbarrel.com; Open: Daily
Bikes, Segways, limos . . . pshaw. Who needs 'em when you're in the Mother Lode? This new company takes people wine tasting through Calaveras County on horseback. Trot through the vineyards and up the hills, hitch your reins to a post, and get yourself boots 'n all into the tasting room. Of course not all wineries in the county are quite rustic enough to support the whole rancher-on-the-range fantasy, but Calaveras is certainly rural enough to lend itself to such adventures. Tours vary in length, and advance reservations are strongly recommended though not required.

LENA STAMP: This was new at press time so I didn't get to do it, but it sounds awesome. As long as no trotting is involved—especially late in the game.

California Cavern
(LS) 9565 Cave City Road, Mountain Ranch, (866) 762-2837, www.caverntours.com; Fee: Y; Open: Daily mid-May through mid-Sept,

walking tours mid-Sept through mid-May weekends; Key: FO
Take a sightseeing tour through the center of the earth at this state historic landmark. The horizontally oriented caverns allow for walking tours through their underground passageways and larger chambers. Walking tours are quick and easy, with electric lighting installed along the route. For people who want the real McCave, the Mammoth Cave Expedition is a two-hour small-group journey into the caverns. This adventure goes into places that are not open to the public. It's an introduction to the sport of caving; equipment provided. For daredevils and experienced spelunkers only, there's the four-hour Middle Earth Expedition. Expeditions require advance reservations, and you must take a quick claustrophobia test in the "Womb Room" before you can join one.

Expeditions are offered July through January, weather permitting. Walking tours cost about $15 for adults, cave expeditions about $130. Located approximately forty minutes from Sutter Creek.

RESTAURANTS

Taste
(HS) 9402 Main Street, Plymouth, (209) 245-3463, www.restauranttaste.com; $$; Open: Thu–Mon; Key: DS
Sacramento foodies make their way out to Amador to dine in this renowned contemporary American bistro. Located on the main drag of the small town of Plymouth, Taste features seasonal cuisine of the region. It tends to be on the rich side: Sonoma foie gras, filet mignon, hearty root vegetables, and fresh-made sauces. Charcuterie and desserts are made in house. Monday night prix-fixe suppers are always a bargain and a culinary surprise.

Bill Easton says: "Fairly casual—a good place for two people to enjoy dinner and a bottle of wine. Good wine list, with lots of European and domestic labels."

Andrae's Bakery and Cheese Shop
(HS) 14141 Historic Highway 49, Amador City, (209) 267-1352, www.andraesbakery.com; $; Open: Thu–Sun
A legend to all who know it, this place has been located in

Amador City for years but is constantly dogged by rumors of an imminent move to Sutter Creek. As yet, it hasn't happened, and visitors to Amador's mountain wineries can stop by en route and pick up imported charcuterie, gourmet box lunches, and fresh-baked cookies and pastries.

Bill Easton says: "Incredible sandwiches like the Kobe beef pastrami. A great selection of cheeses and really nice baked goods."

The Dining Room at the Groveland Hotel

(HS) 18767 Main Street, Groveland, (209) 962-4000, www.groveland.com; $$$; Open: Nightly in summer, Oct-March, Tue-Sun; Key: DS, SF, FO

Though a name change is in the works, this surprising restaurant in the historic Groveland Hotel is one of the best in several counties, no matter what its name is. It's located in a historic hotel, one of the only businesses in the tiny ridgetop town of Groveland. Known primarily as a launch point for whitewater rafting, Groveland draws foodies only because of this restaurant's fabulous California seasonal cuisine. Everything is made from scratch. The menu changes in its entirety weekly, but features a little something different every day. Most notably, this place has the best wine list in the Sierra; it is industry-awarded, extensive, and mostly California-focused. There's a full bar as well, but for after-dinner drinks, pop over to neighboring Iron Door, the oldest bar in California.

Though there are 50 seats in the dining room, it's surprisingly cozy and charming. Cozy leather club chairs, mood lighting and cheery art lend to the self-described "mountain elegant" feel, which does have a bit of the "mountain living room" about it. During the warmer season, an expansive outdoor patio seats 80. Dining room closed the last part of January for two weeks.

Mineral

(LS) 419 Main Street, Murphys, (209) 728-9743, www.mineralrestaurant.com; $$; Open: Thu-Mon; KEY: VEG, SCENE

The notion of vegetarian dining in mining territory—a place historically populated by the super-macho—is so odd, it almost feels sacrilegious. However, this is one of the swankier and more modern of downtown Murphys restaurant offerings. (Note: Though typically the provenance of '50s diners, big red round booths can indeed be surprisingly swanky when teamed with rough-hewn walls and white tablecloths.)

Salad eaters from all around converge to enjoy gourmet wraps, fresh-baked pastries, beautifully presented pâtes, and inventive salads. Wood-fired pizzas are also on the menu. Though this restaurant is primarily vegetarian, Spanish sausage, eggs, and other omnivorous offerings sneak their way onto the menu.

ENTERTAINMENT AND NIGHTLIFE

Gold Rush Saloon at the National Hotel
(LS) 18183 Main Street, Jamestown, (800) 894-3446, (209) 984-3446, www.national-hotel.com; $; Key: PETS
Wine seekers may indeed feel like they've struck gold at this little hotel on Main Street. All the wines on the award-winning list are from the Sierra Foothills gold country, and most are so boutique-like, the average American consumer might never discover them. Live music on the weekends lends a festive touch.

Alchemy Market and Wine Bar
(LS) 191 Main Street, Murphys (209) 728-0700, www.alchemymarket.com; $$; Open: AM daily, PM Tue and Thu-Sun
Though probably more of a gourmet deli by day and restaurant by night than a bar, this breezy, modern, foodie hangout in downtown Murphys has a great by-the-bottle wine list and an even better beer selection. Approximately 50 bottled brews are available, most of them imported, obscure, or both. The wines are primarily from Calaveras county, and are quite reasonably priced.

SHOPPING

Fine Eye Gallery
(HS) 71 Main Street, Sutter Creek, (209) 267-0571, www.fineeye.com; Open: Daily
There are more shops lining the funky wood-planked main drag of Sutter Creek than you might imagine, but this one is a local favorite. Featuring everything from contemporary wall art to jewelry and handcrafted ceramics, it's a feast for the eyes and a threat to the pocketbook.

Old Vines

(LS) 1252 S. Main Street, Angels Camp, (209) 736-9912; $$; Open: Tue-Sat

Everything's for sale in this wine bar and antique shop in a historic Angels Camp building—even the chair you sit on, and the definitely-not-Macys-Home wineglass from which you drink. And the vintage you're drinking even has an unopened counterpart that's ready for retail. Even without the unusual wine bar/antique store/ wireless Internet hub mix of offerings, this would still be an interesting place to visit. Its stone walls, old-fashioned checkerboard, and eclectic merchandise are eye-catching, and very appropriate to the offbeat locale. Nice selection of local wines, chocolates, odd mulled drinks, and other sweets that make you go *hmm*.

LENA STAMP: This is one of those stores that could never exist in a city because it follows no rule. You can check e-mail, have a glass of port at 11 a.m., buy some random East Indian wall-hanging, listen to opera . . . whatever. I don't own a smoking jacket, but if I did, I would wear it here.

ACCOMMODATIONS

Hanford House

(HS) 61 Hanford Street, Highway 49, Sutter Creek, (209) 267-0747, www.hanfordhouse.com; $

Here's one story for the *What Color Is Your Parachute?* textbooks: Ambitious young duo quit their big-city careers, buy a historic property in a pioneer town, and open a ten-room gold country B&B with "tastemaker" appeal. Their next step: open an on-site restaurant and bar, which will surely redefine Sutter Creek's meager nighttime scene.

Bill Easton says: "The hippest place in Amador County."

Sutter Creek Inn

(LS) 75 Main Street, Sutter Creek, (209) 267-5606, www.suttercreekinn.com; $; Key: SF

Geographically and atmospherically, this longtime lodging standby is halfway between wine country and gold country. Its claim to be "the first bed 'n breakfast in the West" is debatable, but it's definitely the oldest one still in operation. The main house dates back to the early 1800s; adjunct buildings are newer, and guests say they lack the charm of the original.

Fitzpatrick Winery & Lodge
(HS) 7740 Fair Play Road, Fair Play, (800) 245-9166, www.fitzpatrickwinery.com; Fee: N; Hotel cost: $; Key: CHEESE
It's a B&B! It's a winery! It's a bit of the old Blarney! Guests enjoy Celtic traditions as well as American ones (like an indoor hot tub). Though this place is whimsical in its Irish theme, the proprieters take winemaking quite seriously, using organically grown grapes and hand-pruning techniques.

TOUR PROVIDERS

Aloha Transportation (Livermore)
(LI) Dublin, (925) 640-1600, www.alohatrans.com; Fee: Y
Knowledgeable about East Bay wineries and attractions, this company offers reasonably priced wine-country tour packages in a van, limo, or town car.

Limousine Club (Sierra Foothills)
(ALL FOOTHILLS) 2945 Ramona Avenue A2, Sacramento, (800) 757-6093, www.limoclub.com; Fee: Y
One of the first companies to offer wine tours of the Sierra Foothills, this limo company has more than twenty years in the business It's recommended by the Amador Vintners' Association and offers customized trips to the Amador and Fairplay/El Dorado regions.

SUGGESTED TWO-DAY ITINERARIES

{LIVERMORE: THE BAY AREA'S BACKYARD}

DAY ONE

From Livermore

Morning: Taste at Concannon Vineyards.

Mid-morning: Taste at Steven Kent, La Rochelle with food pairings.

Afternoon: Visit Blacksmith Square for shopping, tasting, snacking.

Late afternoon: Drinks and games at Campo di Bocce.

Evening: Dinner at Campo di Bocce *or* Zephyr in downtown Livermore.

DAY TWO

From Livermore

Morning: Visit Ruby Hill.

Mid-morning: Taste at Wente, followed by lunch.

Afternoon: Golf at Wente *or* taste at Wood Family Vineyards (advance booking required for both).

Late-afternoon: Cocktails and jazz on the patio of Pleasanton Hotel *or* Blue Agave Club.

Evening: Dinner at Pleasanton Hotel *or* Blue Agave Club.

{LODI: OLD VINES, NEW DEVELOPMENTS}

DAY ONE

From Lodi

Morning: Visit Lodi Wine & Visitor Center.

Mid-morning: Taste at Michael David.

Afternoon: Have lunch at Michael David.

Mid-afternoon: Visit a family-owned winery—either Macchia or St. Amant.

Late afternoon: Have drinks at Cellar Door *or* Wine & Roses.

Evening: Have dinner at Wine & Roses.

DAY TWO

From Lodi

Morning: Pick up rental kayak equipment at Sierra Adventure Outfitters and pick up lunch at Old Town retailer.

Mid-morning: Taste and tour at Jessie's Grove.

Afternoon: Taste at Heritage Oak and then picnic on the riverbank Heritage Oak for lunch.

Mid-afternoon: Go kayaking *or* taste at Borra.

Evening: Have dinner at Woodbridge Crossing.

{SIERRA FOOTHILLS: THE WILD RED YONDER}

DAY ONE

From Sutter Creek

Morning: Pick up picnic at Andrea's Bakery.

Mid-morning: Taste the wines of Shenandoah Valley: Easton, Vino Noceto, Cooper.

Afternoon: Have a picnic at a winery.

(continued)

Early evening: Have dinner at Taste.
Evening: Sightsee in downtown Sutter Creek.

DAY TWO
From Murphys
Morning: Visit California Caverns.
Afternoon: Have lunch at Mineral.
Mid-Afternoon: Taste at wineries in Murphys, along Highway 4.
Evening: Have drinks and dinner at Alchemy (mid-range) or Groveland (special occasion).

CALENDAR OF EVENTS

MARCH
- Passport Weekend El Dorado
- Lodi International Wine Awards www.lodiwineawards.com

MAY
- Lodi ZinFest www.zinfest.com

JUNE
- Fair Play Festival
- Passport Weekend, Calaveras

JULY
- California State Wine Competition www.thebestcaliforniawine.com

SEPTEMBER
- Annual Harvest Wine Celebration, Livermore (Labor Day)

OCTOBER
- Amador Big Crush Harvest Festival
- Calaveras Grape Stomp

DECEMBER
- Holidays in the Vineyards, Livermore

RESOURCES

www.amadorwine.com
www.amadorwinegrapes.com
www.calaveraswines.org
www.eldoradowines.org
www.fairplaywine.com
www.familywinemakers.org
www.foothillwine.com
www.lodiwine.com
www.lodirules.com
www.lvwine.org
www.nswinecountry.com
www.zinfandel.org

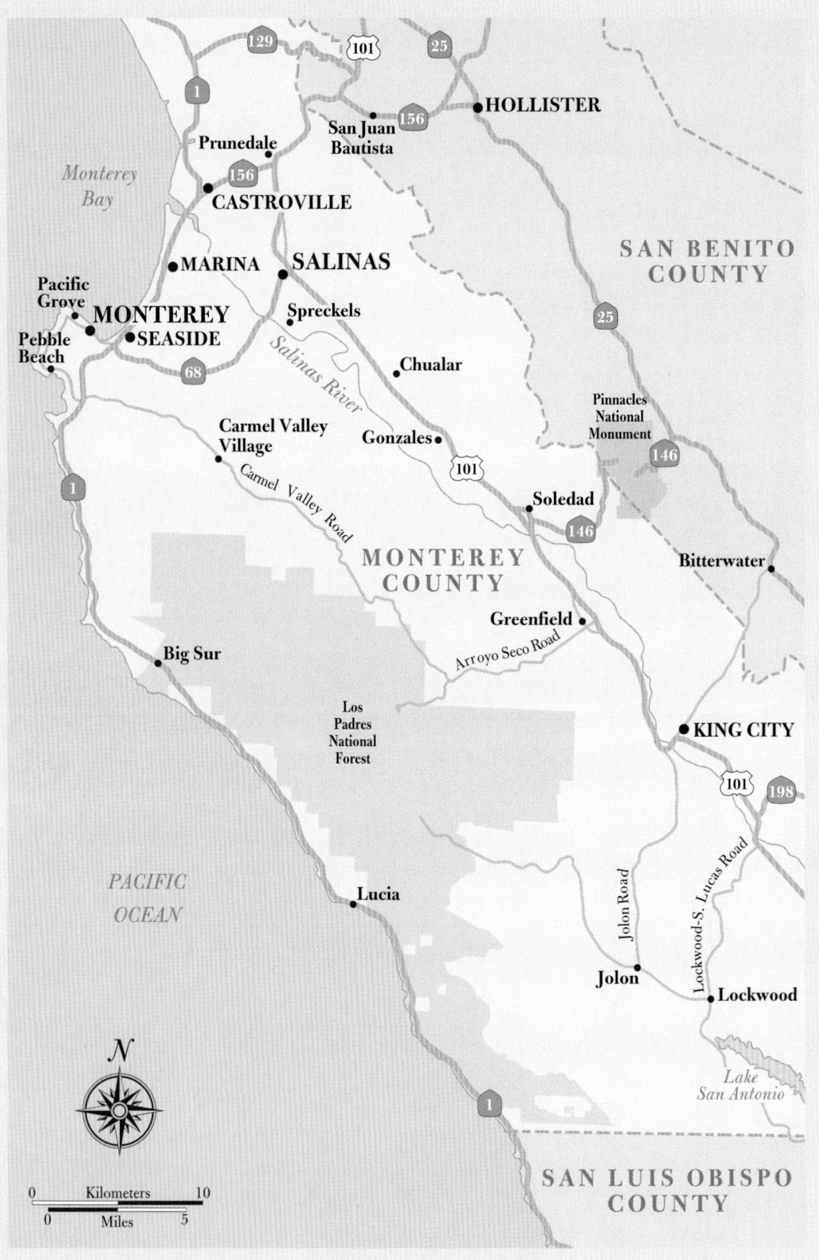

129
101
25
1
HOLLISTER
156
San Juan
Bautista
Prunedale
Monterey
Bay
156
CASTROVILLE
SAN BENITO
COUNTY
MARINA
SALINAS
Pacific
Grove
MONTEREY
Spreckels
25
Pebble
Beach
SEASIDE
68
Salinas River
Chualar
Pinnacles
National
Monument
Carmel Valley
Village
Gonzales
146
101
1
Carmel Valley Road
Soledad
146
MONTEREY
COUNTY
Bitterwater
Greenfield
Arroyo Seco Road
Big Sur
Los
Padres
National
Forest
KING CITY
101
198
Jolon Road
Lockwood-S. Lucas Road
PACIFIC
OCEAN
Lucia
Jolon
Lockwood
N
Lake
San Antonio
1
SAN LUIS OBISPO
COUNTY
0
Kilometers
10
0
Miles
5

3

MONTEREY

Monterey is a county where dramatic contrasts abound . . .

Lonely cliffs and bustling resort villages; sleepy, far-out farmlands and glossy championship fairways; Steinbeck and sea otters, and fittingly, its biggest industries are large-scale agriculture and hospitality. You might think this would lead to a booming wine tourism trade, but in fact, that isn't the case. Grapes are only a minority percentage of Monterey County's crop output. Thus vintners here have traditionally viewed themselves as farmers first, operating on a large scale by desire and necessity. Wine making is an expensive, time-consuming luxury they have only recently afforded themselves. Significantly, successful brands from neighboring regions have opened new wineries here, finding the Santa Lucia Highlands AVA impressive enough to merit buying into permanently. Following their lead, a number of artisan winemakers have moved into the compact, visually appealing Carmel Highlands.

In the past decade Monterey labels have gained a presence in the glamorous dining rooms of Carmel and Pebble Beach. More recently, tasting rooms have cropped up in downtown Monterey and Carmel. While wine is not the main attraction in Monterey, it's becoming a necessary component in a golf/beach/gallery getaway.

Note: We struggle with how to put this politely, but the age range here skews old, or toward families, or both. This is a perennially popular spot for multi-generational reunions. In Monterey prepare for dances with strollers; in Carmel, you'll see a disproportionate number of silver foxes in Bentleys.

Getting Here

Nearest major airports are San Jose and San Francisco International. If there's a route that doesn't involve a stint on the traffic-packed Highway 101, followed by a long, confusing drive around twisty mountain roads, we haven't found it.

Weather
By the ocean the morning fog lifts around 10 a.m. in the summer and fall, and slightly later in the winter. The temperature doesn't go much higher than the low 70s, or much lower than 60°F. Inland it can get up to twenty degrees hotter, with intimidating winds.

Recommended Transportation
All downtown areas are pedestrian friendly in the extreme. For River Road wine tasting or to get from one town to the other, driving is your best bet.

Style
Of all the places in California, Carmel is probably where you'd feel most comfortable in a sport jacket. (Silver foxes, *hello*!) Monterey and Salinas are way more dressed down.

Fees
The minimal fee of $3 to $5 is typical for tastings in town. Salinas tasting rooms are often free.

Bird's-eye View
Out of this whole sprawling, environmentally diverse region, there are only three spots that figure onto the wine map in any significant way: Carmel Valley Village is where the most in-town tasting rooms are. It's basically within a one-mile stretch, either right on or just off Carmel Valley Road. In Monterey there are currently a handful of tasting rooms either on Cannery Row or just off of it. The Santa Lucia Highlands area is the best-known wine-growing region in Monterey County, and it's here that winemakers are creating their own mini-wine trail, right on River Road. Currently, wineries number around a dozen, but that number could grow. (Many wineries are also accessible off Highway 101, but it's an unpicturesque, high-speed way to tour.) Compared to the picturesque tourist zones of Cannery Row and Carmel Valley, Salinas wine country is a dusty, unglamorous ramble—but many of the real finds are hidden way out here.

Area Key:
CA = Carmel, Carmel Valley
MT = Monterey, Pacific Grove
RR = Salinas, Soledad, River Road

The Panel

Wendy Brodie, chef, *Art of Food* on PBS

Mark Buzan, wine director, Highlands Inn

Mark Jensen, wine director, Bernardus Lodge

Richard Smith, owner, Paraiso Vineyards and Valley Farm Management

The Chic Epicurean

Whether you do it for love of the grape or to show the world that you (and your AMEX) have arrived, wine collecting is something of a snobby hobby. And ironically, considering how inexpensive most Monterey wines are, the Carmel Valley tasting rooms are very chi-chi indeed. If you've got the tastes and the budget for it, though, the experience can be stunning.

WINERIES

Bernardus Tasting Room
(CA) 5 West Carmel Valley Road, Carmel, (800) 223-2533, (831) 659-1900, www.bernardus.com; Fee: Y; Open: Daily; Key: SCENE, AT
Adjacent to the Lodge and therefore a couple miles apart from the rest of the Carmel Valley Village, this tasting room looks out onto the Marinus vineyard, where Bernardus grows the grapes for its estate reds. In addition to the regular and reserve wines, some small-production wines are for sale here and nowhere else.

Joullian
(CA) 2 Village Drive, Carmel Valley, (831) 659-8100, www.joullian.com; Fee: Y; Open: Daily; Key: AT, SF, DS
Housed in an immaculately restored historic stone building that looks like a teacup-sized church, this tasting room is richly furnished with antiques and Oriental rugs. In spite of the imposing looks of the place, wines are affordable and the portfolio wide-ranging. Though the winery does have holdings in the nearby Carmel Mountains, the vineyard-designated wines actually come from the Santa Lucia Highlands.

Talbott/Georis Tasting Room
(CA) 53 W. Carmel Valley Road, Carmel, (831) 659-3500, www.talbottvineyards.com; Fee: Y; Open: Daily; Key: AT
Two well-known local food and wine figures operate under one shingle in the "Mouth of the Valley"—literally a few feet from the Carmel Valley Village welcome sign.

Mark Buzan says: "Robert Talbott Winery is one of the best producers of the Burgundian varieties of Chard and Pinot."

Wendy Brodie says: "Rob Talbott has been a dedicated community member, producing outstanding wines that we are all so proud of and covet. . . . Georis is a landmark family in the restaurant business, and is known for its art and photography in addition to its award-winning wine."

Parsonage Village Vineyard
(CA) 19 East Carmel Valley Road, Carmel, (831) 659-2215, www.parsonagewine.com; Fee: Y; Open: Thu–Mon; Key: AT
Looking as much like a gallery as a tasting room, this little space has paintings in the front windows and very limited-

Building a World-Class Wine Cellar: An Interview with Mark Jensen, Wine Director, Bernardus Lodge

There are collectors, and then there are curators—and Mark Jensen is the latter. With 1,900 labels in the Bernardus cellar, his challenge is to anticipate and satisfy his customers' tastes while constantly surprising and challenging them with new discoveries.

TT: With basically all the great wines of the world within your buying power, how do you know where to begin?
MJ: I think the cuisine somewhat dictates the nature of the wines on the list. We have incredible local ingredients—everything is fresh—and I look for wines that work well with that.

TT: Do you mainly focus on a certain area or varietal?
MJ: My main focus is on classical wines and small family-owned wineries from around the world.

TT: Why?
MJ: We're a special-occasion restaurant in many regards. People are celebrating anniversaries or birthdays and tend to look toward classical wines with history or a boutique nature.

TT: How do you keep abreast of all of the boutique labels entering the market?
MJ: I'm not trying to be on the crest of the wave—to go out and buy everything that's new. Sometimes it takes a couple of times trying the wine before you understand what they're trying to do and get a sense of where they're going.

TT: How long is the discovery process for you?
MJ: Sometimes you don't get it at first, but over the years a winemaker's style evolves and your palate evolves, and you come together.

TT: How could you have so much patience with a "missed connection" that's been going for several years?
MJ: It's a relationship whenever you buy wine. You have to think about what you carry on your list. You want to represent them with style. You want them to work for you, and you want to believe in the wines and the wineries.

production estate-grown wines on pour. Parsonage is a family operation; the vineyards and winery are located just a few miles outside Carmel Valley Village. Blending seminars are offered by appointment.

ATTRACTIONS

Art of Food cooking classes
(CA) P.O. Box 221940, Carmel, (831) 626-9000, www.wendybrodie.com; Fee: Y; Open: Daily and by appt.; Key: SF, VEG
"California Cuisine to me is all about using fresh organic and sustainable products in ways that magnify their flavors and rich textures without overcooking or masking their beauty. California agriculture, aquaculture, and viticulture are an inspired bounty," says Chef Wendy Brodie of the PBS show *Art of Food.* "California cuisine is influenced by the many cultures that exist here: Hispanic, Italian, and Chinese. It almost could be considered a form of fusion."

Chef Wendy calls her cooking classes "a cocreative experience" and encourages her guests to come up with their own ideal program, including a menu. Sometimes everything is hands-on, but if some group members want to participate while others want to sit back and have a glass of champagne, that's fine. She does try to get everyone to participate in at least one thing, though.

"I let people create their own salads, with edible flowers, different-colored tomatoes, many dressings, and basil oil made in front of them. We give a prize for the best-looking salad," she says.

This food experience takes place in an open show kitchen in Chef Wendy's house (which is also where her show is filmed). It's set on 4 acres overlooking the Pacific Ocean, around 500 feet elevation, with a 180-degree view of the ocean. There is a minimum of six persons per class, with a maximum of twenty (demo-style classes only).

The Crossroads Shopping Village
(CA) 243 Crossroads Boulevard, Carmel, (831) 625-4106, www.crossroadsshoppingvillage.com; Fee: N; Open: Daily; Key: PETS, KIDS, SF
Though technically an upscale mall, this Carmel destination also

has a fish market, an Internet cafe, and even a tasting room (for Morgan and Lee Family wines)—making it slightly more appealing for the foodie or wine-tasting tourist. It is also less pretentious than Carmel-by-the-Sea. Note that while restaurants may stay open for dinner, retail mostly closes by 6 p.m.

RESTAURANTS

Marinus
(CA) 415 Carmel Valley Road (at Bernardus), Carmel Valley, (888) 648-9463, (831) 658-3400, www.bernardus.com; $$$$; Open: D nightly; Key: XP, SCENE, DS
Cuisine of the local land and wines of the world . . . it seems an unlikely match, but it in fact works perfectly at this gourmet landmark. Chef Cal Stamenov seeks out ingredients that best express the local *terroir* (earth), and showcases them when they're at their freshest, ripest, and best. Meanwhile, Mark Jensen seeks out boutique discoveries and classic (often French) bottles that take the experience to new peaks. Sumptuous decor and stunning views round out an exquisite experience. (Note: This place is so pricey, even the silver fox set saves it for special occasion spots.)

Volcano Grill & Mai Tai Bar
(CA) 27 E. Carmel Valley Road, Carmel Valley, (800) 828-9463, (831) 659-1280, www.volcano-grill.com; $; Open: D, nightly; Key: KIDS
This place is just a couple of steps up from a quintessential neighborhood family restaurant and in self-consciously charming, überexpensive Carmel, that is a welcome change. The dining room's packed with a loud mixed crowd, and the menu features island-inspired small plates and grill fare, including sweet potato fries, Kobe sliders, and pepper-crusted duck. Tropical drinks are a bar specialty.

SHOPPING

Cheese Shop
(CA) Ocean and Junipero, Carmel, (831) 625-2272, www.cheeseshopcarmel.com; Open: Daily; Key: LN
Taste many cheeses and wines at this local foodie favorite.

Mark Jensen says: "An extensive wine department with great cheeses. They specialize in boutique local wines."

Nielsen Brothers Market
(CA) Seventh and San Carlos, Carmel, (831) 624-6441, www.nielsenmarket.com; Open: Daily; Key: SCENE, XP
This is the ultimate family-owned gourmet grocery store, complete with locally sourced, handpicked, and high-end meats, seafood, and produce. The on-premise wine shop has become a destination in itself, with a contingent of regulars that relies on it for education, standbys, and last-minute recommendations.

Mark Jensen says: "Pretty active in the local wine scene. That's where I started in my first wine industry job. They call it a 'non-supermarket,' with one of the best wine selections around. You can actually go and taste; they have a little tasting room."

Brinton's
(CA) 546 Carmel Rancho Shopping Center, Carmel, (866) 624-8541, (831) 624-8541, www.brintons.com; Open: Daily; Key: XP
The tag line of this store is "remarkable home and garden store," and local epicureans agree that its kitchen cookware and hardware live up to the billing. It offers brand-name appliances, cooking supplies, and cutlery, plus equally impressive departments for every other room in the house.

ACCOMMODATIONS

Carmel Valley Lodge
(CA) Carmel Valley Road at Ford Road, Carmel Valley, (800) 641-4646, (831) 659-2261, www.valleylodge.com; $$; Key: PETS, DS
Lily ponds, trellises, ivy, and lush flowering plants create a bucolic country scenescape one hundred yards off the main road. A tiny bridge arches over a pond; steps lead down to a small, cozy lobby. Rooms are comfortable and reasonably priced, with fireplaces in the cottages. However, this hotel's chief attraction for the weekend young(ish) professional set can be summed up in two words, according to the manager: "Dog friendly." Pooches are allowed in rooms, wandering the property on leash, and even by the pool. The hotel is across from a dog-friendly park and within walking distance to the village, so an early morning park visit followed by a leisurely wine-tasting stroll is the obvious itinerary.

Tickle Pink Inn
(CA) 155 Highlands Drive, Carmel, (831) 624-1244, www.ticklepinkinn.com; $$$; Key: DS
Everyone's charmed by this honeymooner hot spot, which combines contemporary luxury with boutique comfort and charm. You get the best of both worlds: plasma TVs and wood-burning fireplaces; room service and evening wine and cheese. And you pay for it all, but not nearly as much as you would at the marquee-name hotels.

Getting Beyond "Wrath"

When you think of Salinas, you think of Steinbeck. Actually, whoever thinks about Salinas? *scratches head* Well, anyway. At last, it's time to give this wide-open West Coast salad platter its due. It is growing some *tres bien* wine grapes, and whether you consider it from an agricultural perspective, a historic one, or a leisurely (and lengthy) cruise down River Road, it deserves a closer look than you gave it during eleventh-grade English.

WINERIES

Ventana Vineyards
(MT) 2999 Monterey-Salinas Highway, #10, Monterey, (831) 372-7415, www.ventanawines.com; Fee: N; Open: Daily; Key: FO
(RR) 38740 Los Coches Road, Soledad, Fee: N; Open: Fri–Sat; Key: LN
Just as you're driving away from Cannery Row, this tasting room appears, looking slightly out of place in the boxy downtown streetscape. Inside, guests taste some of the most decorated Chardonnay and red Bordeaux wines grown in California, before picnicking with a bottle on the picturesque patio. "Substance over strategic location" is the motto when it comes to marketing. In addition to its Monterey tasting room, Ventana just opened another (listed above) in dusty, far-out Soledad.

Morgan Winery at the Crossroads
(CA) 204 Crossroads Boulevard (Carmel Crossroads Shopping Village), Carmel, (831) 626-3700, www.morganwinery.com; Fee: Y; Open: Thu–Mon
Taste single-vineyard Chardonnays and Pinots from organically farmed Double L Vineyard, or from other equally acclaimed Monterey grapes. Nominal per-person fee is applied against individual's bottle purchase.

Marilyn Remark
(RR) 645 River Road, Salinas, (831) 455-9310, www.remarkwines.com; Fee: N; Open: Sat-Sun; Key: FO
This winery has a few love stories attached to it: the love between founders Joel Burnstein and Marilyn Remark, the love of wine making, the love of Rhône grapes, and so on. Production is very limited: Each grape variety only pours out to a few hundred cases. However, local aficionados rave over it.

Mark Buzan says: "It's a couple who have fallen in love with the Rhône, and that's what they specialize in: Grenache, Syrah, Viogner, Marsanne. You'll get a thrill comparing these wines with what you've tried before. They're very elegant."

Paraiso
(RR) 38060 Foothill Road, Soledad, (831) 678-0300, www.paraisovineyards.com; Fee: N; Open: Daily; Key: FO
One of the first wineries founded in the Santa Lucia Highlands, this facility tastes Chardonnay and

Getting to Know Monterey Wines: An Interview with Mark Buzan, Wine Director, Highlands Inn

When he came to California in 2006 to take over the Highlands Inn's 30,000-botttle cellar, Mark Buzan also faced a second challenge: familiarize himself with all the winegrowers of Monterey—their specialties and labels, and what differentiates them from the other winemakers of Northern California. This he has done admirably . . . as you can see, since we're passing all his best tips on to you.

TT: You've got quite a cellar over there. What do you see moving the fastest out of it?

MB: We go through more Monterey Chardonnay and Pinot than any other category on the wine list. More than Spanish or French Burgundy or French Bordeaux.

TT:How would you describe Monterey wines?

MB: The forward and very ripe nature of the wines from Monterey used to catch me off-guard. We have such a long, cool growing season here that the wines are very ripe. Look for abundance of fruit and richness.

TT: Why would that catch you off-guard? It sounds great.

MB: Coming from a European wine background, it took me a while to get used to it. Those wines are balanced toward acidity and earth, linear construction. Monterey wines are very round.

TT: What are your favorite Monterey wines?

MB: There are actually three varietals. First would be Pinot. And I think those Pinots have really put the Santa Lucia Highland appellation on the map. It's now considered a rival to more established regions like the Russian River Valley. It's a different style—a rich hedonistic style—but it really works.

TT: Second?

MB: Chardonnay does quite well here. Once again, the wines are lavish, rich. They have good acidity to them. They're not over the top. They've been not quite as highly regarded as Pinot, but they're holding their own.

TT: Third?

MB: The surprise for me has been Syrah. Most Syrah that comes out of Monterey has more cool-climate characteristics to it. The wines really do well with food. They're ripe and forward, but they're not big, rich, saturated low-acid wines. They tend to retain their crisp acidity, with some earthy aromatics.

Monterey bounty in the Wine Room at Pacific's Edge.

Riesling on the white side, Syrah and Pinot on the red. Don't miss their Souzao Port—you can only buy it direct from the winery. Founder Richard Smith describes the tasting room as "a pleasant rural farm stand experience—like going to a farm stand on Highway 101 to buy strawberries or cherries."

Pessagno
(RR) 1645 River Road, Salinas, (831) 675-9463, www.pessagnowines.com; Fee: N; Open: Fri–Sun
This winery offers many single-vineyard wines, of which the "Intrinity Chardonnay" and "Four Boys Pinot Noir" come highly recommended by local connoisseurs. They also have lots of dessert wines and ports.

Wendy Brodie says: "A relatively new winery with awards and ratings in the nineties. Owned and created by Steve Pessagno, the former winemaker at Lockwood."

Pelerin
(RR) 150 Katherine Avenue, Salinas, (831) 320-0146, www.pelerinwines.com; Fee: N; Open: By appt.; Key: RR
Formerly of local giant Morgan, winemaker Chris Weidemann now runs his own little mom-and-pop shop. If the name, which is French for "pilgrim," is any indicator, the Weidemanns are in this for the long haul.

Mark Buzan says: "Pinots and Syrahs are fantastic. Super-small production."

Pisoni Vineyards
(RR) P.O. Box 908, Gonzales, (800) 270-2525, www.pisonivineyards.com; Open: By appt. (limited); Key: LN
The pie-in-the-sky vineyard for the serious taster, this family-operated winery does only one wine—an epic Pinot Noir—that has a tremendous following.

Mark Buzan says: "Considered the crown jewel vineyard within the Santa Lucia appellation. Tough to get into—by invitation only. Pisoni used to be a grower but started his own label in 1998 and has become a cult producer."

ATTRACTIONS

Taste of Monterey
(MT) 700 Cannery Row, Monterey, (831) 646-5446, www.tastemonterey.com; Fee: Y; Open: Daily; KEY: TH, KIDS, LN
You call this a tasting room? Pshh.

"I Am the Ag Man"

Richard Smith, Owner, Paraiso Vineyards and Valley Farm Management

As owner of Paraiso Vineyards and Valley Farm Management, Richard Smith is one of the founding vintners and first winemakers in the Santa Lucia Highlands. He's also one of the agricultural players who first put Monterey grapes on the map.

"By 1975 we had 35,000 acres of wine grapes in Monterey County—all premium varietals farmed on a fairly industrial scale—and we shipped virtually all the grapes out of the region," he remembers. "As farmers do, we managed to way oversupply . . . and by 1985, we were down to 22,000 acres. People began to reevaluate, and diversify."

This ultimately wound up being a positive thing, since it inspired some local vintners to found their own wineries, with labels sporting the Santa Lucia Highlands AVA that the industry had already come to know and respect.

"We knew we had good grapes," Smith says. "We had to find the resources to put together small wineries and build small facilities for artisan wines."

In an area dominated by large-scale farming, this wasn't an easy task. Smith estimates only 20 percent of Monterey County's farm acreage is planted to vineyards.

"Ag in general is one of the most significant parts of the local economy, but wineries are a very small part," he says.

Nor were local wine brands significant to the hospitality business: "When we started selling Paraiso in 1992 or 1993, there were virtually no Monterey wines in Monterey restaurants," he says. "If you go today, more than one-third have a Monterey section on list, and another one-third have Monterey wines mixed in with other wines."

Many are from the artisan winemakers who have recently moved into the Carmel Mountains and set up tasting rooms in the mouth of the valley. "There's lots of recreational appeal there," Smith says. While these wineries are a tiny fraction of the size of the Salinas/Soledad vineyards, the artisans have stirred up excitement where there was little before—while the large-scale producers continue to turn out inexpensive, high-quality wines that are distributed on a mass scale. Their Sustainability in Practice (SIP) Program dates back to 1994.

"A group of Central Coast growers started detailing and specifying a sustainable farming protocol. It was all about doing a better job farming, and it was a grower-managed group," he says. "Because of our size, we have a lot of technical people who are well qualified to make changes. We're always going to be technically a step ahead of the rest of the industry, and promotionally a step behind."

(continued)

At last, though, the Santa Lucia Highlands is developing a wine route of its own. It's loosely knit, since each vineyard stretches for over one hundred acres—but along River Road, Smith notes, there's starting to be a "critical mass" of wineries open to the public. "In the valley, you don't take a number, you don't stand in line," he says. "It's all very personal and low-key."

And yes, it slowly but inevitably is becoming part of the tourism/hospitality platform. "There's a strong alliance between agriculture and hospitality at the moment," says Smith. "And wine is the agricultural contribution to tourism—there's just not much sizzle in Brussels sprout production."

Try: the equivalent of all Monterey tasting rooms, in one big, cheerful, ocean-facing space. From Marilyn Remark rose to Pessano port, all Monterey County's premier vintages are here—and so are all the new releases, obscurities, and standards. Approximately 200 wines are in stock, representing the majority of local producers. There are a couple random bottles as well—such as Coppola's "Sofia,"—but for the most part, Monterey County is the common theme. Each week, fifteen wines are on pour in the tasting room, and the same wines are available by the glass.

The tasting bar occupies a relatively small chunk of real estate; instead, there are a dozen tables where guests can sit and drink while enjoying Pacific views through wall-to-wall glass. The large, well-stocked gift area has all kinds of tchotchkes, plus yummy snacks from Monterey Chocolate. Although this store isn't affiliated with the local vintners' association, individual winemakers say it's the biggest retail support for their wines and AVAs. Note: This facility is located in a cute, busy complex on Cannery Row, surrounded by all the touristy sightseeing you can handle.

National Steinbeck Center
(RR) One Main Street, Salinas, (831) 775-4721, www.steinbeck.org; Fee: Y; Open: Daily; Key: KIDS

Want a little culture with your Chardonnay? Kick off a day of Salinas exploration with a visit to John Steinbeck's memoriam. This is definitely the biggest visitor attraction in Salinas: It's comprised of a museum devoted to the author and his works; the Valley of the World agricultural center; and an art exhibition space that shows everything from *Sunset* magazine retrospectives to traveling Smithsonian installations. There's a gift shop on-site. Steinbeck's historic home is two blocks away and is open limited hours.

RESTAURANTS

Passionfish
(MT) 701 Lighthouse Avenue, Pacific Grove, (831) 655-3311, www.passionfish.net; $$$; Open: D Wed–Mon; Key: DS, VEG
It's a bit out of the way, but foodies make the pilgrimage without complaint. Unique, artistic sustainable seafood creations are beautifully paired with rare—but not prohibitively priced—wines. On the decadent side: slow-cooked meat and house-made desserts. Though the place gets packed, service remains attentive. Also a bonus: Pacific Grove itself has the kind of authentic beach-town charm that its glossy neighbors simply can't duplicate.

Hula's Island Grill and Tiki Room
(MT) 622 Lighthouse Avenue, Monterey, (831) 655-4852, www.hulastiki.com; $; Open: L Tue–Sat, D nightly; Key: VEG, SCENE
Just off Cannery Row, this restaurant gets a thumbs-up from locals for its healthy, vegetarian-friendly menu and friendly service. Choices range from a Cajun burger to veggie tofu stir-fry.

ENTERTAINMENT AND NIGHTLIFE

Crown & Anchor
(MT) 150 W. Franklin Street, Monterey, (831) 646-6496, www.crownandanchor.net; $; Open: AM/PM/OWL; Key: LN, PU, TH
Everybody knows about this place, either as a stalwart for good fish-and-chips and other British pub grub, or as a landmark watering hole that's surprisingly authentic in spite of its Old Monterey locale. It offers more than twenty beers on tap and an impressive whiskey selection (also including single malt Scotch and Kentucky bourbon).

SHOPPING

Monterey Wine Market
(MT) 192 Country Club Gate Center, Pacific Grove, (831) 646-0107, www.montereywinemarket.com; Open: Daily
This is another pleasant Pacific Grove surprise, owned by George Edwards. The former wine director for Pebble Beach Resorts, he's unpretentious, enthusiastic, and voluble—check out his regularly updated blog for proof (and picks). Note that though this shop's open daily, it closes mid-afternoon on Sunday but stays open until the evening every other day.

Wendy Brodie says: "He has arranged the wines so that it is easy to match a menu and select wines that will pair well."

ACCOMMODATIONS

The Clement Intercontinental
(MT) 750 Cannery Row, Monterey, (831) 375-4500, www.ichotelsgroup.com; $$$$; Key: DS, SF, LN
Making excellent use of a former abandoned cannery site, this new hotel sits right across from the center wherein Taste of Monterey is located. Subtlety of design and cheerful, professional service are the Clement's strengths. After an overdose of manufactured Cannery Row charm and jollity, this hotel's quiet, grown-up demeanor envelops you in a happy Zen glow and lets you breathe again. It's a sleek, contemporary property done up in sandstone hues and warm gold lighting. Sweeping ocean views through oversize windows soothe the soul, particularly with the window cracked to allow in the sound of the waves. A minibar stocked with premium wine splits, oversize bathtubs for soaking, and a miniature Japanese rock garden on the mantle . . . ahhh . . . peace at last—and with all Monterey's wines just one hundred feet from the hotel door.

LENA STAMP: Caymus "Conundrum" in the minibar? I could probably live here very happily. Splurge for a suite with French doors leading out to a private ocean-view balcony.

Highlands Inn
(CA) 120 Highlands Drive, Carmel, (831) 620-1234, www.highlandsinn.hyatt.com; $$$; Key: DS, XP, SF

Family owned for decades, this distinctive property is now under the Hyatt umbrella, and some subtle changes are evident, including a "sleek, user-friendly" revamp of the storied 30,000-bottle wine cellar. Mega-awarded Pacific's Edge Restaurant offers inspired California-French cuisine from premium local sources. Panoramic ocean views are a distinguishing design feature, not just in the restaurant but in most of the rooms.

LENA STAMP: Wine director Mark Buzan hasn't been in California for long, but he knows his Monterey wines better than anyone else I've ever met. Pick his brain if you're planning to tour and taste.

TOUR PROVIDERS

The Wine Trolley
(MT) 527 Hartnell Street, Monterey, (831) 624-1700, www.toursmonterey.com; Fee: Y; Open: By appt. Fri-Sun and some weekdays; Key: CHEESE, TH

Kinda silly, but you know what? This is kinda fun: A biodiesel-powered trolley transports people from downtown Monterey to Ventana, and from there to the vineyards of Carmel Valley. In total, it's a five-hour tour. The trolley seats twenty-four, and typically sells out Friday through Sunday; however, other days are subject to season and demand. Reserve in advance. Rates are very low compared to limo service—starting around $49 per individual, and becoming a better deal if you book as a twosome, a four-person group, and so on.

SUGGESTED TWO-DAY ITINERARIES

{THE CHIC EPICUREAN}

DAY ONE

From Carmel

Morning: Have breakfast in hotel.

Mid-morning: Carmel Valley wineries walking tour: Joullian, Talbott/Georis, Parsonage Village.

Afternoon: Crossroads Shopping Village for lunch, shopping, and tasting.

Mid-afternoon: Have a sumptuous dinner at Marinus (book table in advance) *or* casual snack at Volcano Grill.

DAY TWO

From Carmel

Early moring: Plan tonight's menu over coffee.

Mid-morning: Go to Nielsen Brothers for gourmet supplies and a carry-away snack.

Afternoon: Visit Brinton's for high-end kitchen tools.

Mid-afternoon: Go to Wendy Brodie's for an afternoon cooking class using the ingredients you just bought.

Evening: Go back to the hotel for wine and cheese, sunset drinks, hot tub soak.

{GETTING BEYOND "WRATH"}

DAY ONE

From Monterey

Morning: Visit Taste of Monterey.

Afternoon: Have lunch at Hula's.

Mid-afternoon: Taste at Ventana Vineyards.

Evening: Have a sunset dinner at Highlands (expensive) *or* fun pub-grub dinner at Crown & Anchor and then early to bed . . .

DAY TWO

From Monterey

Morning: Depart for Salinas.

Mid-morning: Visit the National Steinbeck Center.

Afternoon: Hit the River Road wineries (check Resources for online maps); lunch at one of the taco trucks or farm stands along the route!

Mid-afternoon: Return to the hotel.

Early evening: Hot tub soak and room service *or* dinner at Passionfish (book ahead).

Evening: Take in ocean views—either from your hotel terrace or a beach path.

CALENDAR OF EVENTS

APRIL

- Pebble Beach Food & Wine
  www.pebblebeachfoodandwine.com

SEPTEMBER

- TomatoFest
  www.tomatofest.com

OCTOBER–NOVEMBER

- The Wine Business (eight-week course)
  extended.csumb.edu/wine

NOVEMBER

- Great Wine Escape Weekend

RESOURCES

www.montereywines.org
www.gomonterey.com
www.carmelcalifornia.org
www.riverroadwinetrail.com

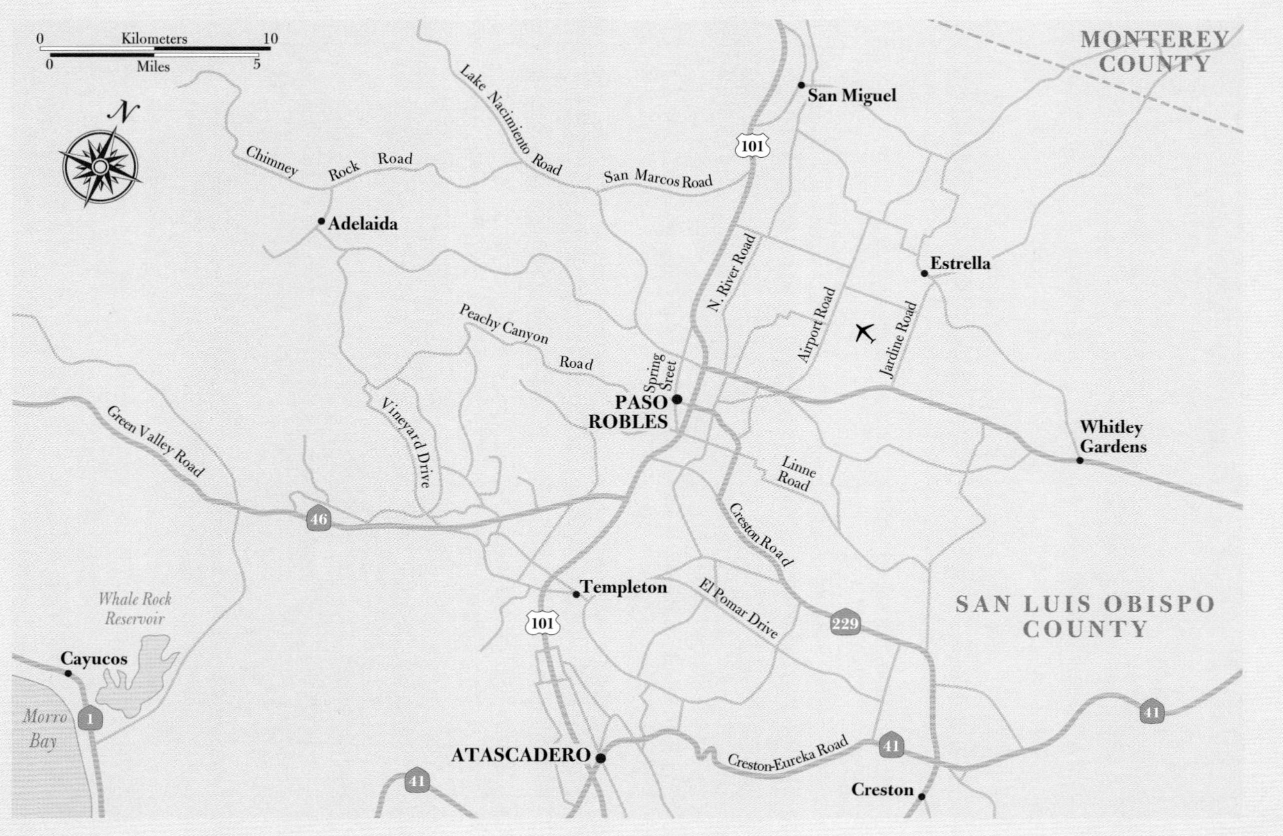
0 Kilometers 10
0 Miles 5
N
MONTEREY COUNTY
San Miguel
101
Lake Nacimiento Road
Chimney Rock Road
San Marcos Road
Adelaida
Estrella
N. River Road
Airport Road
Jardine Road
Peachy Canyon Road
Spring Sreet
PASO ROBLES
Whitley Gardens
Green Valley Road
Vineyard Drive
Linne Road
46
Creston Road
Templeton
El Pomar Drive
SAN LUIS OBISPO COUNTY
Whale Rock Reservoir
101
229
Cayucos
Morro Bay
1
41
ATASCADERO
Creston-Eureka Road
41
41
Creston

PASO ROBLES

It's hot, it's hilly, and it's half an hour from the ocean, but this region's star is rising nonetheless.

Finally. Even though grapes were first planted here more than a century ago, Paso fell victim to a common pattern: People didn't know what to plant, they put in varieties haphazardly, and they end up with inferior grapes. Not that all of them were bad—they just weren't as dazzling as those from other places. Thus, they were shipped off to other areas to be bottled under other AVAs. Paso became known as an agricultural region with Wild West rancher-style and reliable vineyards.

The introduction of pure Rhône clones in the 1980s and 1990s changed Paso's fortunes forever. Suddenly the area went from a so-so region for bulk grape growing to the likely successor of France's fabled Chateauneuf-du-Pape region. Over the ensuing ten years, Rhône vineyards sprang up all over the area—planted by people who either couldn't pay Northern California land prices, or didn't feel like it. As the vines mature, young maverick wine-makers have started releasing wines that follow no one's rules but their own. Curious European and East Coast connoisseurs are dropping into town to see what's going on . . . and sometimes they decide to stay. The town of Paso Robles has gone from frumpy-dumpy to charming, while the surrounding countryside has started to see enough tourist traffic to sustain tasting rooms and shops. After many false starts, the Paso wine region has a buzz and an identity of its own.

Getting Here

San Luis Obispo County Regional Airport, located half an hour south, and San Jose, which is two hours north, offer mostly regional service (although San Jose is technically an international airport). Most people fly into San Luis Obispo, which is a three-hour trek. Do not—repeat, *do not*—make this into a one-day jaunt from San Francisco. It deserves at least three or four days.

Weather

In early spring pack in layers. It's cold in the morning and evening, though it can get as warm as 80°F in the day. Midday temperatures may start to climb past 90°F by the middle of June. Summer is extremely hot in the day, but comfortable in the mornings and evenings. Blissful, cooling breezes come in from the ocean. Indian summer lasts into October. Winter (November through February) is mild, though sometimes rainy.

Recommended Transportation

If you're a couple or a small group, it's probably easier to rent a car and designate a driver. Tour companies are still set up for ten-person groups, with very few exceptions.

Style

Shorts and T-shirts with a warm pullover, particularly in spring, to protect from early morning or mid-evening temperature drops. This is one of the most casual regions—and one of the hottest.

Fees

Some wineries only charge when they're getting low on a certain vintage, and some don't charge at all—but most of the established tasting rooms now ask about $5 per person.

Bird's-eye View

Paso Robles is actually part of San Luis Obispo County. There are vineyards and wineries scattered throughout San Luis Obispo; however, they're spread out, often obscure, and usually secondary to other attractions. Hence, with great regret, we've decided to skip over them (though we've included many informative area Web sites in the Resources section).

Paso Robles got the vote not just because it's going through a growth spurt, but because it's easy to tour if you stay near the main artery (Highway 46). Wineries are dotted along Highway 46 West and clustered around the intersecting roads. Highway 101 takes you straight to downtown Paso, where most of the restaurants and shops are. Highway 46 East starts at the Highway 101 intersection and leads out to some famous large-production wine estates.

The farther you venture from Highway 46, the more you enter Wild West territory. It's all narrow roads, canyons, ranches, and boutique wineries that might not even have proper signage—very exciting for the "discovery" wine connoisseur. Note: Not everyone is cut out for backcountry winery adventures. Be sensitive, or you may wind up spending hours in a small vehicle with a carsick person who has to pee and really hates you.

Area Key:
46W = Highway 46 West, from Highway 101 intersection to Willow Creek Road
WP = Western Paso (including Vineyard Drive and Adelaida Road)
TG = Templeton Gap
46E = Highway 46 East from the Highway 101 intersection
PR = Paso Robles proper
NC = North County: San Miguel, San Marcos Road, Highway 101 North
SP = South Paso

The Panel

Coy Barnes, owner, the Wine Wrangler

Allie Rush Carscaden, certified sommelier and owner, 15 Degrees C Wine Shop

Tony Domingos, vineyard manager, Villa San Juliette

Jason Haas, Tablas Creek Vineyard

Stacie Jacob, executive director, Paso Robles Wine Country Alliance

Jan Manni, certified sommelier and owner, the Wine Attic

Christian Tietje, partner/winemaker, Four Vines Winery

Wild West Wine Tasting

The title of this section refers to many things. For one, there's the history of the region. For another, there's the look of the countryside: endless rolling hills, cattle, no buildings. Then, there's the fact that so many winery owners are recent settlers—fifteen years ago they were basically homesteading. And finally, there's the huntin', fishin', ridin', and ropin' cowboy lifestyle, which hasn't even begun to go away. If you want to mix up your wine tasting with a few hours at the shooting range, there's a man in muddy boots who can point your rifle in the right direction.

WINERIES

Wild Horse
(TG) 1437 Wild Horse Winery Court, Templeton, (805) 434-2541, www.wildhorsewinery.com; Fee: N; Open: Daily; Key: FO
Wild by name, nature, and neighborhood, and coming up on its quarter-century birthday, this pioneering winery was founded right before Paso got its own official AVA designation. It's named in honor of the county's few surviving wild mustangs. While case production now hovers around 150,000 per year—not small, in other words—the estate keeps its Old West flavor because it's so far out in the Templeton Gap that civilization hasn't managed to find it. Known for its Pinot Noir, this winery sources grapes from many regions in addition to its own estate

Bella Luna
(TG) 1850 Templeton Road, Templeton, (805) 434-5477, www.bellalunawine.com; Fee: N; Open: Fri–Sun; Key: FO
This winery is even older than its neighbor, Wild Horse, but has about 1 percent of the annual production. Bold, unfiltered wines make Old World connoisseurs sit up and take note. The portfolio includes Barbera, Tempranillo, estate Sangiovese, and the flagship "Fighter Pilot Red" organic Zinfandel. The winery sells through its limited stock each year.

Turley
(TG) 2900 Vineyard Drive, Templeton, (805) 434-1030, www.turleywinecellars.com; Fee: Y; Open: Daily; Key: FO
Based out of Napa, this brand is new to the area but not to the game. It's opening this property to expand its Zinfandel program, which had already been sourcing grapes from Paso. According to rumor, vineyard managers will be using old-fashioned cultivation techniques, including draft horse farming.

Pipestone
(46W) 2040 Niderer Road, Paso Robles, (805) 227-6385, www.pipestonevineyards.com; Fee: Y; Open: Thur–Mon
Former environmental engineer Jeff Pipes got way up close and personal to toxic waste in his "former" life; as a result, he does everything at Pipestone sustainably and responsibly, according to small farm traditions. Vineyard labor is done by hand or with the help of horses; the garden

is organic; the wines are handmade. Domestic/business partner Florence Wong oversees the organic garden and the feng shui of the entire operation. (If this doesn't seem very Wild West to you, think about San Francisco's population during the Gold Rush era.) Rhône blends are currently the focus, but Zinfandel is a staple.

Paso vineyards: big, but not always glamorous.

L'Aventure

(46W) 2816 Live Oak Road, Paso Robles, (805) 227-1588, www.laventurewinery.com; Fee: Y; Open: Thur–Sun; Key: SCENE, LN

In every classic Western, there's the dapper European dandy who seemingly has no business being in a frontier town, yet survives because he's a quicker draw and a sharper shooter than all the other roustabouts. L'Aventure's owner Stephan Asseo is the winemaker version of that guy. He majored in oenology in Burgundy, opened several acclaimed châteaux in France, and finally arrived in Paso Robles by way of Chile and South Africa, attracted by the area's pioneer spirit. His first vintage was in 1998. His portfolio changes every year, from Bordeaux classics to blends to single-varietal Rhônes to rosés. Nonetheless, he sells through everything within a couple years of release. His "tasting salon" is actually a small, cheerful room in a big metal building that looks like a barn. French visitors chatter away at the tasting bar, while New Yorkers drink rosé on the front lawn.

LENA STAMP: Long, bumpy, dusty access road from hell. But worth it—you'll want to hang out for a while.

A Ten-Point Paso History Lesson

Stacie Jacob, Director, Paso Robles Wine Country Alliance (and Paso Vintners)

It roared onto the wine stage a few years back, but unlike many overnight successes, Paso Robles wine country had a long climb toward fortune and fame. Here are a few historic high points from its 160-year journey.

- Jesse James's uncle, Drury James, was one of the founding fathers of Paso Robles. Jesse James used to come here to hide out.
- The first grapes were planted in the 1850s. Commercial wine making began in 1882, with the first varieties being Zinfandel and Muscat.
- Throughout the early 1900s, this was an agriculture area known for nut orchards and dry farming of grasses, wheat, and barley.
- In the 1920s, larger vineyards were introduced by Italian immigrants. Some of these vineyards still exist today, producing highly regarded Zinfandel grapes.
- Much like Calistoga to the north, the town's first tourist draw was its position smack-dab on a volcanic fault; the volcanic hot springs and their purported healing powers drew everyone from members of Spanish missions to international luminaries.
- Paso Robles Zinfandel was first championed by the Polish statesman and concert pianist Ignace Paderewski, who came to town in the 1930s hoping the hot springs would soothe his degenerative arthritis. He wound up staying, buying a 2,000-acre ranch, and planting various vines including Zinfandel.
- Paso Robles became a designated wine region in 1983. It started out with only seventeen wineries.
- Gary Eberle introduced the modern plantings of Syrah to the "New World" in the 1980s through cuttings he spirited in from the Rhône.
- Robert Haas of Tablas Creek eventually went through the whole legal process of importing pure southern Rhône clones into the United States through the U.S. Food and Drug Administration.
- In 2004 Paso had a major earthquake that opened a fissure in the city hall parking lot—which remains open to this day. When you drive through town on a still day, you can smell the sulfur.

ATTRACTIONS

WineYard at Steinbeck Vineyards
(46E) 5410 Union Road, Paso Robles, (805) 238-1854, www.thewineyard.com; Fee: Y; Open: By appt.; Key: KIDS, CHEESE, FO
While plans to become a working winery are still in development, this property offers educational vineyard jeep tours, which can include a vineyard picnic or dinner with the winemakers. It seems like you get all of the schooling and none of the tasting . . . but insiders swear it's fun anyway. And it's kid friendly, which is relatively rare among Paso wineries. Packages start at $50 per person ($20 for sixteen years and under), advance reservations required.

Harris Stage Line
(NC) 5995 N. River Road, Paso Robles, (805) 237-1860, www.harrisstagelines.com; Fee: Y; Open: By appt.; Key: Cheese, FO, KIDS
Immaculately refurbished old stagecoaches and buggies aren't merely decorative; they're also the preferred method of transportation inside this ranch. Owner Tom Harris used to be a stunt coordinator and animal wrangler, so he's skilled at training people to ride and drive.

RESTAURANTS

Vic's
(PR) 841 13th Street, Paso Robles, (805) 238-3988; $; Open: B and L daily, D Mon-Sat; Key: SF
If you want to rub shoulders with winemakers at dawn (as per your instructions at the beginning of this chapter), locals say you've got to have breakfast at this downtown diner. It opens at 6 a.m., with fresh homemade cinnamon rolls and biscuits and gravy for one and all. An old-school greasy spoon: red leather booths, counter seating, friendly servers, and a gang of ancients that show up at 5 p.m., for early-bird supper.

McPhee's Grill
(TG) 416 S. Main Street, Templeton, (805) 434-3204, www.mcphees.com; $$$; Open: L and D daily; Key: DS
Texans might not know what to make of this cow-town steak-

house with wine country flair, but Northern California denizens say, "Mmmm." Oak-grilled meats are teamed with house-made sauces, seasonal vegetables, and downright snooty potatoes (Yukon gold, garlic mashed, sweet potato fries). The place has an old-school saloon setting and nice service—it's a standby, though not a local secret.

Loading Chute
(SP) 6350 Webster Road, Creston, (805) 237-1259; $; Open: L and D daily, B Sun; Key: FO
If McPhee's is too highfalutin' for you, check out this totally unpretentious steakhouse/grill/bar. As Creston's de facto cultural center, it hosts everything from fund-raisers to wine-tasting events to barn dances.

Tony Domingos says: "Some of the best steaks, in this little hick ranch town fifteen miles east of Paso."

ENTERTAINMENT AND NIGHTLIFE

Elkhorn Bar
(NC) 1263 Mission, San Miguel, (805) 467-3909; $; Open: B, L, D daily, OWL Fri–Sat; Key: PU, SKETCH
The mustaches, cowboy hats, and spurs in this landmark dive saloon are not to be believed. As for the people attached to them—well, personalities range from taciturn to friendly to over-friendly to spoilin' for a fight. (The last one is hearsay; barroom brawls typically happen after smart girls have called it a night.) On the walls are deer heads, elk heads, longhorns, several rifles, and a wild boar's head. Posted newspaper clippings date back to World War II. A jukebox in front, pool tables in back, live music on weekends, and a pump-and-power supply store next door.

Tony Domingos says: "Best place to have a beer and play pool."

LENA STAMP: Beat-up in the looks department, completely cowboy and cool as hell.

SHOPPING

Boot Barn

(PR) 1340 Spring Street, Paso Robles, (805) 238-3453, www.bootbarn.com; Open: Daily; Key: CHEESE

Authentic Western apparel and gear, from Wranglers to hats to boot polish. You will know it by the parking lot full of four-by-four trucks and the huge sign promoting a sale on lariats. Note: This is actually a decent-size California/Nevada chain, but most branches are not in places that anyone wants to visit.

LENA STAMP: Paso's one of the only places where it's cool to be a redneck; I personally recommend you get into the spirit.

ACCOMMODATIONS

Paso Robles Inn
(PR) 1103 Spring Street, Paso Robles, (800) 676-1713, (805) 238-2660, www.pasoroblesinn.com; $$; KEY: TH, SF, KIDS, LN
Meh. This is the oldest game in town, luxury lodging-wise, but it still thinks it's the only one. Because of that, service has gotten lax, while the decor in the outbuildings is more motor inn than historic hotel. Nonetheless it's in here because it's centrally located, a landmark, a reliable watering hole (in the upstairs lounge), and has private mineral spas in select suites.

Chanticleer
(46W) Off Highway 46 West, Paso Robles, (805) 226-0600, www.chanticleervineyardbb.com; $$–$$$; Key: DS
There are only three rooms in this elegant little B&B, which gets a thumbs-up from locals even though it does little advertising. It's set on a vineyard, with rosebushes in front, a pool in back, and kitties sleeping in the sunshine. However, children are strongly discouraged, and there's no smoking on the property.

Way Out in Santa Margarita

Located smack-dab in the middle of nowhere, this tiny town is inexplicably the site of a famous antiquing spot: the Santa Margarita Auction Barn. Once-a-month auctions are among the best antiques in California—and probably the whole West Coast. Also worth the drive, depending where your interests lie: Lake Santa Margarita, known for bass and striper, and Ancient Peaks Winery, which is ironically one of Paso's newer wineries and still not regularly open to the public. Wind up your visit with dinner at the Range, a new-ish but classic steakhouse that recently inspired *Los Angeles Times* food critic Irene Virbila to wax rapturous (with a twang, no less).

American Rhône Redux

Paso Robles transformed from cow country to chic European-flavored village in less than a decade, and all because of a few lil' acres of Rhône grapes. Of course it's going through growing pains and arguments over who and what came first . . . but regardless, its identity right now is the Rhône of the New World.

At some point it'll probably all become very pretentious, but for now it's pleasant and quaint if you're new to the area—and downright miraculous if you know what the town looked like in 2000.

WINERIES

Tablas Creek Vineyard
(WP) 9339 Adelaida Road, Paso Robles, (805) 237-1231, www.tablascreek.com; Fee: Y; Open: Daily; Key: FO, TH

Tablas Creek's mass-scale import and propagation of Rhône grapes started it all, and in return, the winery was granted legendary status overnight. Walking in, though, you wouldn't immediately know that. The tasting room is informal, casual, low ceilinged, and busy. It's also beautifully laid out: Four tasting bars are spread throughout several rooms, diffusing any potential traffic jams before they start. A fifth bar in the barrel room is set up to handle overflow traffic, especially large groups. Gifts and books are invitingly displayed, and a sign at the front bar reads, REAL MEN DRINK ROSÉ. Which is true . . . in the Rhône.

Allie Rush Carscaden says: "Classic, pure, beautiful. As close to Chateauneuf-du-Pape wines as you can get without going to France. The tour includes a great education portion and vineyard visit."

Denner Vineyards
(WP) 5414 Vineyard Drive, Paso Robles, (805) 239-4287, www.dennervineyards.com; Fee: Y; Open: Fri–Sun or by appt.; Key: AT, SCENE

Owner Ron Denner will lead spontaneous private tours of the barrel room and gravity-flow winemaking system if asked by a repeat customer. Otherwise he mostly hangs out behind the bar with a glass of wine. Happily, there are plenty of staff on-hand—both behind the tasting bar and out in the working winery, where technological and aesthetic improvements seem to be nonstop. Denner makes Rhône wines, and its signature is the "Ditch Digger."

Allie Carscaden says: "The architecture is beautiful. I really like their Syrahs. I just had the Viognier yesterday. The '07 has amazing acidity, which is rare in California Viognier. They have Tablas Creek clones."

LENA STAMP: Probably the snootiest of the Paso wineries, but the building is amazing.

The Short but Exciting Modern History of Rhône Grapes in Paso Robles

Jason Haas, Tablas Creek Vineyard

"Paso Robles used to be seen as an economical place to grow decent grapes," says Jason Haas, heir apparent to Tablas Creek cofounder Robert Haas and current overseer of the winery. "Now, the area's transforming into a world-class place to grow Syrah and other Rhône varieties." In between day-to-day business, Jason gave us the story of the Rhône takeover—with dates included.

Prologue—1800s through Prohibition Various Rhône varietals are brought in at random by Spanish colonizers, immigrant families, and early ranchers—until Prohibition halts wine production and, by extension, wine country development.

1933 After Prohibition is repealed, strict new Food and Drug Administration rules come into place, prohibiting the casual transport of vines. The impure Rhône vines already planted in Paso continue to grow, producing inferior-quality grapes.

1960s to 1970s Napa's success with Cabernet inspires massive Cabernet plantings in all regions. Paso proves an adequate—though not stellar—Cabernet growing region and sinks into a state of comfortable obscurity as a mediocre high-volume vineyard region. There are some exceptions, such as J. Lohr Vineyards and Eberle, both of which produce award-winning Cabernet.

Mid-1970s Gary Eberle plants a Northern Rhône Syrah clone at Estrella River. Within a few years, wineries statewide clamor after the fruit and the plant material.

1983 Paso gets two of its own AVAs. Gary Eberle is instrumental.

1987 Wine importer Robert Haas partners with the Perrin brothers, who own the great Chateau de Beaucastel in Chateauneuf-du-Pape. Noting California's climatic similarities to the Southern Rhône, the men decide if they can find similar calcareous soil (decayed limestone from ancient seabeds), and then plant pure Chateauneuf-du-Pape clones, they may be able to duplicate Chateau de Beaucastel in California.

1987 to 1989 The hopefuls follow the tracks of CalTrans all through California, examining road cuts for calcareous soil. Unfortunately most of California is comprised of volcanic soil, with only a few caches of calcareous soil in cool coastal regions inappropriate for Southern Rhône grapes.

1989 After two years they discover perfect conditions near Paso Robles: pure, chalky limestone in a hot, dry area sheltered from the ocean. Though they have no ties to the region, the partners buy land and found Tablas Creek Winery based on their findings.

1989 to 1992 Robert Haas brings nine pure Rhône clones out of France, going through the United States Department of Agriculture in spite of mandatory three-year quarantine laws. The red varieties are Movedre, Syrah, Grenache, and Counoise; the whites are Rousanne, Marsanne, Viognier, Grenache Blanc, and Picpoul Blanc. Three are brand-new to the United States.

1992 The pure clones come out of quarantine. However, Tablas Creek is only allowed to bring in six cuttings of each clone. The next two years are spent propagating vines in the nursery.

1994 The first vines are planted at Tablas Creek.

1997 Tablas Creek's first harvest, bottling, and labeling occurs.

1998 The first Tablas Creek white is released.

1999 The first Tablas Creek red is released.

2000-ish Tablas Creek begins to sell its Rhône vines to other winemakers in Paso Robles, having determined that the "best thing we could do for ourselves would be to improve the whole category" of area wines. They sell 3 million vines to their neighbors, thus beginning a legacy.

2008 Though only 10 percent of Paso Robles acres are planted to Syrah, almost all of it is produced, labeled, and sold under a Paso AVA. The county also plants more Viognier and Rousanne than anywhere else in California. Boutique wineries are cropping up everywhere—most of them specializing in Rhône wines.

Summerwood Winery & Inn
(46W) 2175 Arbor Road, Paso Robles, (805) 227-1365, www.summerwoodwine.com; Fee: Y; Open: Daily; Key: DS
Pretty, relaxed, sunny, and sophisticated, with a sassy but friendly staff. A broad front lawn is bordered with flowers and a wide brick sidewalk. The building looks like a Southern McMansion, but in a good way. The flagship wines are a "Sentio" Bordeaux blend and a "Diosa" Rhône blend. Most tastings are at the bar, but a sit-down flight with food pairings is available on weekends for $35. Picnic supplies are sold on-site, and there a few seats outdoors under shade.

Jan Manni says: "Sells all products out of tasting room, including special wines you won't find anywhere else."

Eberle Winery
(46E) 3810 East Highway 46, Paso Robles, (805) 238-9607, www.eberlewinery.com; Fee: N; Open: Daily; Key: SCENE, TH, SF
If you're a Syrah drinker and you visit Tablas Creek but not Eberle, the spirit of Estrella River will come to haunt you. Okay, this is overly dramatic—but in fact, Estrella River is no more, and this is where you'll find the whole Gary Eberle portfolio, from the Cabs to the storied cool-climate Syrah. The winery also produces

Paso's annual Autumn Wine Festival.

about a zillion other things, including an estate Muscat and several red blends.

The grounds are over-the-top, with a scenic lookout spot, bocce courts, a fountain featuring a life-size wild boar sculpture, and wine caves. The latter are the highlight of the free tour, of course. The tasting room is a sophisticated, high-ceilinged three-ring circus. The foyer setup leads one to wonder whether admission is guest-list only, but in fact the gatekeepers are friendly.

LENA STAMP: Makes a Syrah rosé—you don't see that often. Rosés are back, by the way.

Robert Hall Winery

(46E) 3443 Mill Road, Paso Robles, (805) 239-1616, www.roberthallwinery.com; Fee: Y; Open: Daily; KEY: TH, SCENE

Massive, massive, massive . . . imposing, imposing . . . and finally, geometric. From the palatial front steps to the severely modern fountain to the ten smaller archways flanking the central one (yes, I counted), this is a supersize study in mathematically precise architecture. Were it not set among vineyards, it could pass for an avant-garde governor's palace or a museum.

As for the wines . . . they show, score, and sell well. Hall isn't an artisan, per se—but he's a smart businessman and an overachiever. He spends a lot of time out in the vineyards and an equally significant chunk of time promoting the brand. Most of the wines are affordable Rhône varieties, though there is a $50 Cab in the portfolio.

Jan Manni says: "'Blanc de Robles' is a flagship Rhône blend. Winemaker Don Brady is award winning."

ATTRACTIONS

Pasolivo Olive Oil

(WP) 8530 Vineyard Drive, Paso Robles, (805) 227-0186, www.pasolivo.com; Fee: N; Open: Thu-Mon, Jack Creek Winery Fri-Sun; Key: SF, KIDS

Some of the countryside isn't yet ready to go under vine—just look at forty-five-acre Willow Creek Olive Ranch, which continues to supply the olives for the coveted Pasolivo label. Olive oils are infused with citrus: lemon-lime, tangerine, and orange. The country store/tasting room stocks a variety of stuffed olives and tapenade, vinegars, and spreads. Little of it is set out to taste (probably to discourage people from treating the place like a buffet). However, one thing that's usually open and that I highly recommend is the coarse-ground "Dukkah" seasoning salt.

Visiting this facility counts as a two-fer, since Jack Creek Winery has a tasting bar in back. The property is bright and sunny, with fantastic impressionist art on the walls and tall trees shading the parking lot and front lawn.

RESTAURANTS

Cowgirl Café

(PR) 1316 Pine Street, Paso Robles, (805) 238-6403, www.cowgirlcafe.net; $; Open: B and L daily; Key: CHEESE, KIDS

They slather on the aw-shucks charm with a butter knife at this downtown restaurant, but not to the point where it detracts from your appetite. An antique cast-iron stove ornaments the entry; saddles and Western gear ornament the dining room. The menu is standard American diner fare: sandwiches, burgers, omelets, and oversize pancakes. This is a Central Coast franchise with a few other locations.

Villa Creek Restaurant

(PR) 1144 Pine Street, Paso Robles, (805) 238-3000, www.villacreek.com; $$$; Open: D daily; Key: DS

Walking out of the 100°F summer heat and into this restaurant has approximately the same effect as taking a long slug of a chilled, crisp white wine: You sigh in relief, feel instantly 50 percent less sweaty, and yearn to press your cheek against the nearest cold surface (which would be the host stand; don't do it). The lights are pitched low, the long dining room is cool but not fridge-like, and the furniture is smooth wood. It's Tuscan modern meets Southwest, with Mediterranean-influenced wine country cuisine to match. Ingredients are locally sourced, sustainable, organic, and all other desirable labels. The mouthwatering aroma of the signature brick-roasted chicken permeates the whole space. Along with macadamia-crusted goat cheese salad, it's the only item that's permanently on the menu.

This is also the tasting facility for Villa Creek wines: They're on pour by the flight or glass throughout the bar and restaurant. The winery also has a tasting room, but it doesn't have the chicken, so it really can't compare.

Bistro Laurent

(PR) 1202 Pine Street, Paso Robles, (805) 226-8191, www.bistrolaurent.com; $$$; Open: Tue–Sat; Key: DS, SF

Prepare for French Provençal charm overload: exposed brick, banquette seating, cream tablecloths, colored tiles at the entry, art and flowers placed just so. It's exquisite in every detail, in a way that can usually only be achieved by set designers or magical elves. The cuisine is classic French bistro with contemporary preparations. It changes regularly, but roast chicken, rack of lamb, and crispy tarts are standbys. Four- and five-course tasting menus are always available. The wine list is half Central Coast, half French. The adjacent wine shop opens at 10 a.m.

ENTERTAINMENT AND NIGHTLIFE

Level Four

(PR) 1216 Park Street, Paso Robles, (805) 237-2111, www.level4speakeasy.com; $$$; Open: PM/OWL; Key: DS, SCENE, PU

The swankiest underground speakeasy west of Chicago—you almost expect to see Jessica Rabbit slink onto the stage in a bombshell red dress. Several booths are all down one side of the bar; tables hug the railing on the other. The front of the room holds several couches that are primarily open to bar patrons. The barrel room offers a quiet, well-lit atmosphere completely separate of the lounge scene. The "Social Club" can go either way: Bare but for a stunning prism chandelier, it can become a private banquet area or a champagne party room. Upscale contemporary American cuisine (flank steak, lobster pot pie) and a bar menu until midnight. Sweet, enthusiastic service with zero attitude—you've got to love it.

SHOPPING

Wine Attic
(PR) 1305 Thirteenth Street Alley, Paso Robles, (805) 227-4107, www.wineattic.com; Open: Wed–Mon or Tue by appt.; Key: SF
This contemporary first-floor retailer (names can be so misleading sometimes) is sophisticated and European flavored, pouring over fifty wines by the glass. There are between 250 and 300 bottles available for retail. The selection rotates all the time, but Central Coast wines make up half the stock. All the marquee Paso Rhônes are represented, plus a few cult labels like Jacob Toft and Austin Hope. Customized flights are a fun option—we think of it as "discovery, with direction." The all-day menu offers up charcuterie, *panini,* and Cal-Med small plates. The pretty courtyard holds about ten tables and is shared with We Olives and Kaya. Approximately twenty beers (mostly imported) round out the sipable selection.

Martin & Weyrich Gift Shop
(46E) 2610 Buena Vista Drive, Paso Robles, (805) 238-2520, www.martinweyrich.com; Fee: Y (to taste); KEY: TH, CHEESE, KIDS
The wine is negligible, and the tasting experience contrived and artificial . . . but somehow, Andrea Bocelli soundtrack and all, the gift shop puts you in a spendy mood. It's huge and full of so very many kitchen goodies, glossy gifts, coffee-table books, and two-foot-tall modern art jars full of colored vinegar—it wakes up your inner Fine Living Network freaky alt-personality in two seconds flat. Scented soaps, gourmet chocolates, and other irresistible little dangers are all over the front cash wrap.

ACCOMMODATIONS

Villa Toscana
(46E) 4230 Buena Vista, Paso Robles, (805) 238-5600, www.myvillatoscana.com; $$$$; Key: CHEESE, DS
Exterior shots of this place suggest that an entire Medici retinue might come riding down the driveway on horseback at any moment . . . but inside, it happily leans a bit more toward "upscale B&B" than "intimidating Ital-

ian summer palace." It's on the grounds of Martin & Weyrich Winery, who showed both foresight and optimism when they opened it back in 2002. Though small—only nine suites plus a winemaker guesthouse—it's one of the most luxurious places in town, with vineyard views and oversize Jacuzzi tubs in the guest suites.

Summerwood Inn
(46W) 2175 Arbor Road, Paso Robles, (805) 227-1365, www.summerwoodwine.com; $$$; Key: SF

A graceful, elaborately landscaped property across the road from Summerwood Winery. It was built to be an inn and feels rather new inside, but the focus is not there—it's outside in the vineyards and gardens. There are nine guest rooms, each with its own private balcony. Culinary service includes sumptuous breakfasts, afternoon hors d' oeuvres and nighttime desserts; however, dinner service is only on Saturday. The staff chef may do a midweek dinner by special arrangement.

The New Frontier

At the crossroads of the Old West and the New Rhône, wine critics pontificate and founding fathers fight over who deserves more credit. Manhattanites want to know if this is where *Sideways* was filmed, Napa-philes declare that Syrah isn't as elegant as Cabernet, and Sonoma folks want to know if they can skinny-dip in the hot springs . . . and no matter how loud the hubbub, a core group of feisty, passionate winemakers really doesn't give an eff about any of it. They're busy doing their thing—whether it be Rhône blends or Spanish, Italian standalones or organics. Some of them are new to the industry; others come from old wine-making families. Whatever their background, they're here to have fun with juice, end of story.

WINERIES

Four Vines
(46W) 3750 Highway 46 West, Templeton, (805) 237-0055, www.fourvines.com; Fee: Y; Open: Daily; Key: SCENE
This winery is dedicated to the study of Zinfandel. The name refers to California's four best Zinfandel AVAs: Paso, Sonoma, Lodi, and an ever-changing fourth (Napa originally, but the vineyards have gone all Cab, winemaker Christian Tietje explains). However, recently it's garnering attention for the "Freak Show" 2006 *tete de cuvee* (winemaker's best) collection: three red blends and a Petite Sirah. Tietje does it to showcase the Rhône and under-the-radar Spanish varieties that may be Paso's next claim to fame. The tasting room is small and friendly, with down-to-earth staff and a little bakery right next door.

Lone Madrone
(46W) 2485 Highway 46 West, Paso Robles, (805) 238-0845, www.lonemadrone.com; Fee: Y; Open: Daily; Key: DS
Judged purely on the basis of creativity and heart (rather than big-budget design), this property might take the prize for best atmosphere. Its herb gardens, recycled junk sculptures, rabbit hutches, and flower beds are beyond picturesque. The piece de resistance is the perfect miniature reproduction of the tasting room, perched in a tree across from the actual tasting room. (It serves no purpose whatsoever.) The tasting room itself is airy, open, and casual. Young staffers look like they could have come straight out of Berkeley or Santa Cruz.

Winemakers have a lot of fun naming the wines and writing the tasting notes. For the 2006 Barbera, they declare, "Spicy watermelon peppercorns rain down for a week after" you taste.

Lone Madrone: the cutest little winery in the West.

Way Out on Spring Mountain
Portrait of a New Frontiersman

You can pick out Christian Tietje in a Paso parking lot—even if you've never met him—by the anarchy sign on the back of his truck. There's an identical one on the label of his 2006 "Anarchy" blend—a Rhône blend mixed with some old vine Zinfandel.

Tietje, the co-owner/winemaker at Four Vines, is the new school ambassador of old vine Zin and some new vines, too. He has dynamic, ever-evolving relationships with Sonoma's refined "James Bond" vines, and the underappreciated "maverick" wines of Amador. He's the quintessential young Paso winemaker: an East Coast kid who spent every summer from age fifteen on working in restaurants, did the New York punk-rock thing in his early twenties, moved to California to surf, and wound up buying land in Paso Robles and appointing himself the official "Zin Bitch."

"Ten years ago, people were able to get in and play the game for a lot less if they were doing the right varietals," he says. "The region has just found out what it grows well."

The 2004 Cabernet has an "everlasting finish." Special blends include the "Old Hat" (Zinfandel/Petite Sirah) and the "Barfandel" ("Never mind the name," urge the notes. It's a Barbera blend.) This is a good stop for white wine drinkers, as it has a full spectrum of whites ranging from obscure Alvarinho to "Sweet Cheeks" Viognier to a Spanish blend.

Allie Rush Carscaden says: "Old Bonny Doon tasting room; an amazing picnic spot. The winemaker does some unusual varietals, as well as blends. The owner of Lone Madrone is the winemaker at Tablas Creek."

Adelaida Cellars

(WP) 5805 Adelaida Road, Paso Robles, (800) 676-1232, www.adelaida.com; Fee: Y; Open: Daily; Key: FO

Some things about this winery seem Old Guard in the extreme—and in fact, it's one of the area's oldest—but it has a long-standing practice of marching to its own tune—or flavor, as the case may be. It's one of the only wineries in the county to make Pinot

Noir; it's able to do this because it acquired a precious parcel of Pinot-growing vineyard in an obscure Paso microclimate decades ago. Wines in the main portfolio start at $25—which is not cheap—but an entire "Schoolhouse" series is priced at $15 a bottle or less. This is described as "the winemaker's little side project." Another of his side projects is an ice wine *hommage.* He's Canadian, so this last one makes sense.

LENA STAMP: A wine geek's winery: If you have either intellectual or scientific interests in wine making, you'll find like-minded souls, special events, and some very in-depth literature here.

Villa Creek

(WP) 5995 Peachy Canyon Road, Paso Robles, (805) 238-7145, www.villacreek.com; Fee: Y; Open: By appt. weekends only

Spanish grapes get as much attention as Rhônes at this buzz-garnering boutique winery. Though production is small—max output thus far has been 3,000 cases—ambitions seem rather large. In addition to this tasting room, the husband-and-wife owners have a gorgeous restaurant in downtown Paso (see separate entry). While currently sourcing grapes from the neighbors, they've acquired their own seventy-acre estate, which they'll be planting in 2009.

Allie Rush Carscaden says: "Up and coming, small, but cult-like, getting great scores. Winemaker Cris Cherry makes a 100 percent Grenache wine but labels it *Garnacha*—as they call it in Spain. Mostly he does Rhône and Spanish blends—or he'll do a Rhône blend and put in Tempranillo."

Villa San Juliette

(NC) 6385 Cross Canyon Road, San Miguel, (805) 550-0522, www.villasanjuliette.com; Fee: N; Open: Thu-Sun

Tony Domingos is the vineyard manager at this quirky, clever new brand with a Tuscan theme and 165 planted acres. Any grapes that aren't estate-grown are purchased from neighborhing vineyards. The owners are entertainment big shots (one's a producer of *American Idol*, the other is the producer of *So You Think You Can Dance*), but the young team running the winery seems to have plenty of leeway. Winery manager Jamie Glenn was formerly with Garretson Wine Company, also of Paso Robles, and winemaker Adam LaZare is as proficient with blending as he is with the Bordeaux varietals that make up the bulk of estate growth. Opening in early 2009 with the 2007 releases, but the 2006 releases have been available online. Tasting bar in the barrel room to start, with a dedicated tasting room open in May.

ATTRACTIONS

Green Acres Lavender
(SP) 8865 San Gabriel Road, Atascadero, (805) 466-0837, www.greenacreslavenderfarm.com; Fee: N; Open: Daily; Key: FO
A small family farm growing 12,000 lavender plants on four acres. Lavender oil distilled onsite every day. Vacation rentals and private Pilates classes also offered.

Coy Barnes says: "She's the original lavender farm in the area. She presses it into oils and waters, creates soap out of it, puts it in cookies, and makes lavender lemonade that you would not believe."

Jack Creek Farms
(46W) 5000 Highway 46 West, Paso Robles, (805) 238-3799, www.jackcreekfarms.com; Fee: N; Open: Seasonal; Key: KIDS
Styled after a frontier main street, this "Mercantile, Sheriff, Livery Stable" actually turns out to be a funky family farm stand. The farm grows everything from corn to pumpkins and offers u-pick for all crops as they're in season (except for apples—the trees are too much of a liability). With antique farm equipment on display and a haystack for kids to roll around in, the property really can feel like a time-warp back to the 1800s if you sit on the porch long enough. The store has all kinds of little indulgences: Nubian goat milk lotion, homemade fudge, and blackberry jam. Cider and fresh-fruit granitas are usually available to sample.

Franklin Hot Springs
(SP) 3085 Creston Road, Paso Robles, (805) 712-5373, www.franklinhotsprings.com; Fee: Y; Open: Daily; Key: FO, KIDS
Soak in healing hot spring waters for $7 at this bizarre, funky, and obscure natural bath. Either submerge in an artesian well, or sit in the communal human-made pool. There are also individual hot tubs. The water spills out into a stocked pond in which people are encouraged to fish or sail model boats. Paintball tourneys take place out in the field.

RESTAURANTS

Jose's (San Paso Truck & Auto)
(NC) 81 Wellsona Road, Paso Robles, (805) 467-2971; $; Open: Daily; Key: KIDS

This dinky little diner has the most fantastically meaty, chunky gravy, perfectly baked biscuits, and butter-fried eggs ever. You could pay $14 for eggs in a hotel and they wouldn't compare. Of course the food is cheap as can be: Friday brings all-you-can-eat fish-and-chips for about $14. Guests range from tattooed guys with the thousand-mile stare to local mothers and daughters. The service is so good, it's awe-inspiring: The waitress will plead, sweet-talk, and cajole the cook into making up special requests for her regulars. She'll also ask for your first name—and then remember it. The down side is totally unflattering lighting—but hey, this isn't a place to be vain.

LENA STAMP: From now on whenever I want a perfect greasy-spoon breakfast, I'm going where the truckers go.

Artisan
(PR) 1401 Park Street, Paso Robles, (805) 237-8084, www.artisanpasorobles.com; $$; Open: L and D daily, B Sun; Key: SCENE

Owned and operated by two brothers, one of who was formerly in the entertainment business in LA and is pleased as anything to have escaped the Southern California circus. Cosmopolitan-design sensibilities are in evidence: sleek lines, dark and cream color scheme, an open kitchen, and a contemporary bar at the front. The seasonal wine country cuisine changes "with no rhyme or reason" according to owner Michael Kobayashi. Flatiron steak, Cayucos red abalone, and seared yellowfin tuna make regular appearances, however. Central Coast wines, microbrews are on on tap.

Ristorante Da Gaetano
(PR) 1646 Spring Street, Paso Robles, (805) 239-1070, www.ristorantedagaetano.com; $$; Open: L and D daily, B Sun; Key: SF

Inside a small green cottage on a suburban Paso street, a mixed crowd dines on classic Italian dishes, from stuffed chicken to homemade lobster ravioli. The dining room is cozy and charming, with red carpet, red-velvet curtains, and plaid accents. And just when you're about to overload on cutesy, out comes the host—tattooed, ripped, wearing a T-shirt—and the chef: also ripped, in pinstripe pants, and wearing Crocs.

ENTERTAINMENT AND NIGHTLIFE

Bernick's

(PR) 835 Thirteenth Street, Paso Robles, (805) 226-9400, www.bernicks.net; $$$; Open: D daily, L Fri-Sun; Key: SCENE, PU

This is the American steakhouse gone modern, with exposed brick walls, high ceilings, and flat screen TVs behind the bar. Opened in mid-2008, this has already become a gathering place for thirtysomething yupsters who order their top-shelf spirits by brand name. The menu offers gorgonzola-topped filets, bone-in hangar steak, and waffle fries.

Pony Club

(PR) 1021 Pine Street, Paso Robles, (866) 522-6999, www.hotelcheval.com; $; Open: Daily; Key: SCENE, SF, DS

This cocktail spot in the exquisite Hotel Cheval offers ambience to the max and a prime downtown location. Though you could get away with drinking chilled rosé, the sophisticated setting practically begs for a good bottle of bubbly . . . and a long-stemmed cigarette holder . . . and perhaps a vintage Chanel suit. Chic nibbles served from 3 p.m. to 10 p.m. on weekdays and until 11 p.m. on Friday and Saturday.

SHOPPING

15 Degrees C

(NC) 1121 Rossi Road, Suite A, Templeton, (805) 434-1554, www.15degreescwines.com; Open: Daily

Owner Allie Rush Carscaden has a lot of support in the local wine industry, which is important in a place as tight-knit as Paso: She worked in many of the Paso Robles restaurants before opening this gourmet food and wine retail spot. If you want to learn about young, up-and-coming winemakers, she's a good person to talk with.

ACCOMMODATIONS

Hotel Cheval
(PR) 1021 Pine Street, Paso Robles, (866) 522-6999, www.hotelcheval.com; $$$$; Key: SCENE, SF, DS, XP

Tiny but perfectly formed, this hotel sets the gold standard for Paso Robles. Residents have a serious crush on it ("It's beautiful, it's downtown, it's horse themed . . . "), while guests seem to have come from an alternate universe where everyone drives Bentleys (perhaps Beverly Hills?). Inexplicably, it's not pretentious: The service is warm, the patio bar charming, and the horse-and-carriage service a quaint village-y touch.

La Bellaserra
(46E) 206 Alexa Court, Paso Robles, (805) 238-2834, www.labellasera.com; $$$; Key: DS

Whoever outfitted this hotel has obviously stayed in a lot of places and taken a lot of notes, because the amenities are off the charts. Every time you need something, it's exactly where you'd like it to be. There's an extra fridge, a Jacuzzi tub built for two, wired *or* wireless Internet, and eye makeup remover and facial soap in the toiletry basket. Most impressive, though, is the thin-screen, Internet-wired computer provided free of charge in each room.

This hotel is a one-off, but it feels like it either is a chain or has a lot of potential to be one. The decor is glossy and a wee bit prefab, the service is very professional, and the full-service restaurant/lounge/spa/gift shop facilities are done beautifully. The gift shop is even open twenty-four hours, in case you need batteries at 5 a.m. See? This place thinks of everything.

LENA STAMP: I was amazed at how well the developers of this independent hotel had thought things through. The freebie toiletries are endless and there are great wines in the honor bar.

TOUR PROVIDERS

The Wine Wrangler
(ALL) 800 Pine Street, Paso Robles, (866) 238-6400, (805) 238-5700, www.thewine wrangler.com; Fee: Y; Open: By appt.
This tour provider offers van tours with a focus on customizable cultural experiences. Though you can choose to do nothing but visit wineries, the company's recently added other tours, including a great agricultural/culinary one that visits places like the red abalone farm out on the coast and Windrose Farms, an organic farm that sells to many local chefs. With advance notice, they can help set up participatory farm stays or other special experiences.

California Limousine
(ALL) P.O. Box 12214 San Luis Obispo, (805) 544-2233, www.bookcalifornialimo.com; Fee: Y; Open: By appt.
The easygoing young owner runs a limo tour operation that's luxe, but not stuffy. They have new cars, good relationships with the wineries on their route, and drivers who balance the tightrope between good service and camaraderie.

SUGGESTED TWO-DAY ITINERARIES

{WILD WEST WINE TASTING}
DAY ONE
From Paso
Early morning: Have breakfast at Vic's.
Mid-morning: Get boots and wranglers at Boot Barn.
Afternoon: Taste in Templeton Gap: Turley, Bella Luna, Wild Horse.
Late afternoon: Have a few beers, followed by early dinner at McPhee's Grill.
Evening: Head back to Paso.

DAY TWO
From Paso
Early morning: Learn to drive cattle at Harris Stage Line (prebook).
Afternoon: Visit Harris Stage Line.
Mid-afternoon: Taste at Pipestone and L'Aventure.
Early evening: Drive to Loading Chute for a down-home steak dinner.

{AMERICAN RHÔNE REDUX}
DAY ONE
From Paso
Early morning: Have breakfast at Cowgirl Café.
Mid-morning: Taste at Summerwood, Denner; buy picnic supplies at Summerwood.
Afternoon: Taste olive oil and buy more snacks at Pasolivo and picnic on the grounds *or* picnic and taste wines at Tablas Creek.
Mid-afternoon: Escape the heat at Wine Attic *or* Villa Creek Restaurant in Paso with wines by the glass and snacks . . .
Evening: Have dinner at Villa Creek.

DAY TWO
From Paso
Early morning: Taste and take in dramatic settings at Hall.
Mid-morning: Take a cave tour at Eberle, taste and relax on back porch.
Afternoon: Buy gifts, picnic supplies, and bubbly at Martin & Weyrich; picnic on grounds.
Mid-afternoon: Visit Wine Attic if you haven't yet *or* have afternoon cheese and wine at the hotel.
Evening: Have dinner at Bistro Laurent and cocktails at Level Four.

{THE NEW FRONTIER}
DAY ONE
From Paso
Early morning: Have breakfast in the hotel.
Late morning: Taste at Four Vines, Lone Madrone.
Afternoon: Buy picnic supplies at the bakery adjacent to Four Vines and picnic at Lone Madrone.
Mid-afteroon: Go to Jack Creek Farms for granitas or cider and u-pick fruit *or* taste Adelaida and other "far out" wineries as recommended.
Late afternoon: Head back to town.
Evening: Have dinner at Artisan.

DAY TWO

From Paso

Morning: Have breakfast at Jose's.

Mid-morning: Go to 15 Degrees and get recommendations for the newest wineries around Templeton, Highway 46 East.

Afternoon: Soak in the Franklin Hot Springs.

Mid-afternoon: Have drinks at the Pony Club.

Evening: Have dinner and cocktails at Bernick's *or* Ristorante Da Gaetano.

CALENDAR OF EVENTS

MARCH

- Zinfandel Festival

MAY

- Hospice du Rhône
- Annual Paso Robles Wine Festival www.pasowine.com/events/winefestival.php

JUNE

- Annual Atascadero Wine Festival www.atascaderowinefestival.com

JULY

- Central Coast Wine Classic www.centralcoastwineclassic.org

AUGUST-SEPTEMBER

- Annual Paso Robles Olive Festival www.pasoolivefestival.com

SEPTEMBER

- Annual Donati Family Vineyard Harvest Party

OCTOBER

- Harvest Wine Weekend

RESOURCES

www.faroutwineries.com
www.pasorobleswine.com
www.pasowine.com
www.prcity.com
www.pasorobleschamber.com
www.rhonerangers.org

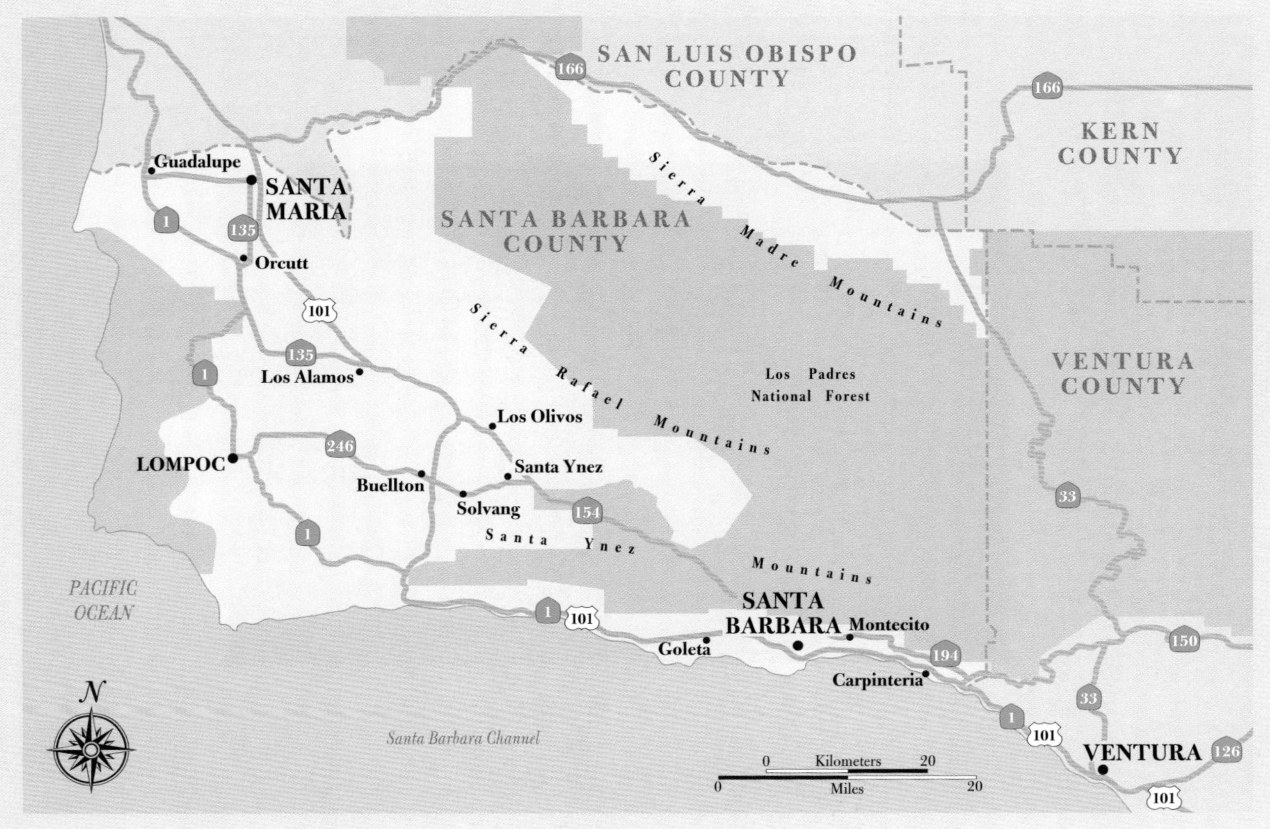
SAN LUIS OBISPO COUNTY
KERN COUNTY
SANTA BARBARA COUNTY
VENTURA COUNTY
Guadalupe
SANTA MARIA
Orcutt
Los Alamos
LOMPOC
Buellton
Solvang
Los Olivos
Santa Ynez
SANTA BARBARA
Montecito
Goleta
Carpinteria
VENTURA
Sierra Madre Mountains
Sierra Rafael Mountains
Santa Ynez Mountains
Los Padres National Forest
PACIFIC OCEAN
Santa Barbara Channel
N
0 Kilometers 20
0 Miles 20
166
166
1
135
101
135
1
246
1
154
1
101
194
1
101
33
33
150
126
101

SANTA BARBARA

This region is right behind Napa and Sonoma in terms of tourist traffic, reputation, and hype . . .

thanks to Los Angeles's proximity and the awe-inspiring marketing mojo of the movie *Sideways*. Its land has always been in high demand, with huge wine-making conglomerates, diversified corporations, and old Southern California fortunes playing tug-of-war over the choicest bits and pieces. However, no matter what corporate interest might rule from afar, most of the denizens still keep their rebel-artist spark. They're a diverse mixture of Hollywood escapees and retired billionaires, cowboys and surfers, dot-com brats and nutty professors.

The first thing to understand about Santa Barbara wine country is that the actual growing region is forty miles north and inland of the city. And it's rural! Santa Ynez is all hills and hidden lakes. Santa Maria is made up of country roads running through pastures. The tasting rooms of Los Olivos and Solvang offer an easily accessible, centralized wine-tasting experience, albeit with nary a vine nor cluster to be found. The newly designated Santa Barbara Wine Trail leads tourists along HIghway 101, from Summerland to downtown Santa Barbara, where wineries hide away within warehouse blocks or next door to surf shops.

Getting Here

There is an airport in Santa Barbara, but it only services a dozen domestic cities, the farthest being Dallas-Ft Worth. Most people fly into Los Angeles and take Highway 101 up the coast, which is about a two-hour drive, depending on traffic.

Weather

Santa Barbara has possibly the best weather in Southern California. An almost-perfect Mediterranean climate, with an approximate average of 300 days of sun per year. Inland is ten degrees hotter than the coast by day and ten degrees cooler by night.

Recommended Transportation

If you're tasting in Los Olivos or Solvang, your feet will work just fine to get around. For the wineries on Highways 101 and 246, you'll be fine with a rental car and a designated driver. If you're hunting out obscure little places in the canyons, use a tour guide or car service whenever feasible.

Style

The style here is Southern California–casual chic. Blue jeans are fine, particularly out in the country. But a designer label and/or funky piece of jewelry wouldn't go amiss.

Fees

Tastings are usually between $5 and $10.

Bird's-eye View

There are three main wine-growing regions in Santa Barbara County.

Santa Rita is between Highway 101 and the ocean. It is a small, cool-climate appellation that has historically specialized in Pinot Noir and Chardonnay. Santa Ynez is an east-west corridor of land that's recently become known for its Syrah and other Rhône varietals. Local winemakers grow and produce everything from obscure Italian grapes to Merlot and Cab. Though it's sometimes portrayed on screen as a wine snob's mecca, Santa Ynez is actually earthy, rustic, and full of cowboys.

Santa Maria is where the wine industry started and has remained largely untouched over the centuries. "It's worth the drive up Santa Rosa Road," says Jim Fiolek of the local vintner's association, "to see California the way it was 200 years ago." The drive all the way up to Santa

Maria's north end, however, is formidable enough that we (with regret) could not include it. If you decide to visit, check the wine trail resource at www.sbcountywines.com.

The town of Los Olivos is in the Santa Ynez Valley, but it retains its own identity—which, ever since 2004, has been "the town you saw in *Sideways*." Then there's the Danish village of Solvang, where two dozen tasting rooms are scattered among bakeries, pancake houses, and antiques shops. Solvang's about fifteen minutes away from Los Olivos on Highway 101.

The towns of Santa Barbara and Montecito aren't growing grapes, but they're dotted with tasting rooms, gourmet delis, and restaurants. The Santa Barbara Urban Wine Trail traces a path down Highway 101 and through town, hitting every tasting room along the way.

Area Key:
101 = Santa Barbara proper, Montecito, Summerland
SY = Santa Ynez Valley, Los Olivos
SR = Santa Rita Hills, Solvang, Buellton, Santa Rosa Road
FC = Foxen Canyon, Santa Maria's southern border

The Panel

Ian Blackburn, owner and chief wine educator, Learn About Wine

Jim Fiolek, executive director, Santa Barbara Vintner's Association

David Hopkins, winemaker, Bridlewood Estate

Bob Lindquist, founder, Qupé

Sam Marmorstein, owner, Los Olivos Wine Merchant & Cafe

Jill Tweedie, owner/chief executive officer, Breakaway Tours

David Yates, tasting room manager, Jaffurs organizer, Santa Barbara Urban Wine Trail

Wine (on the) 101

Santa Barbara County is a glamorous place, always ready for its close-up. Just up Hightway 101 from Los Angeles, it gets plenty of entertainment-industry types—some visiting for the weekend, others settling in for good. Many of the wineries along Highways 101, 154, and 246 are owned by conglomerates or retired business bigwigs, and they offer a pleasant, picturesque tasting experience that's easy to navigate, though sometimes a bit crowded.

WINERIES

Jaffurs
(101) 819 E. Montecito Street, Santa Barbara, (805) 962-7003, www.jaffurswine.com; Fee: Y; Open: Fri–Sun; Key: LN

Locals refer to this down-to-earth little place as "the surfer winery" because that's what most of the staff are doing during their off hours. The tasting room consists of a few tables set up in the barrel room on weekends. "You can take a tour without even moving your feet," jokes tasting room manager David Yates. Though it doesn't sit on a lush estate, the founders make a convincing argument for its oceanside locale: The humidity from the ocean keeps the barrel room damp and cool, so unlike the valley wineries, air-conditioners and humidifiers aren't necessary. It's a more enviro-friendly winemaking method—or at least one that generates a lower electric bill. Grapes are sourced from nine Santa Barbara County blocks and used to make limited-production handcrafted Grenache, Syrah, Viognier, and several other Santa Barbara Rhônes.

Summerland Winery
(101) 2330 Lillie Avenue, Summerland, (805) 565-WINE (9463), www.summerlandwine.com; Fee: Y; Open: Tue–Sun; Key: DS, CHEESE

This is a picturesque tasting room across from the ocean—almost within walking distance of Summerland Beach. They offer Cal-Bordeaux varietals and some Rhônes, plus a single-vineyard reserve collection. Gift baskets seem to be a booming business.

Santa Barbara Winery
(101) 202 Anacapa Street, Santa Barbara, (805) 963-3633, www.SBWinery.com; Fee: Y; Open: Daily; Key: LN

This is a downtown fixture and the first of the in-town wineries, founded by Pierre Lafond in 1962 before Santa Barbara was even considered wine country. Though downtown's "Funk Zone" has sprung up around it, the spacious, modern tasting room remains unfunked. Guests sit around a big square bar with a view of the barrel room. Santa Barbara and LaFond wines are on pour.

Firestone
(FC) 5000 Zaca Station Road, Los Olivos, (805) 688-3940, www.firestonewine.com; Fee: Y; Open: Daily; Key: TH, KIDS

The Urban Wine Trail

David Yates, Jaffurs Tasting Room Manager,
Organizer of the Santa Barbara Urban Wine Trail

"People don't necessarily have a whole day to spend going up to the Valley—or a whole group that wants to commit to it," says David Yates, one of the organizers of the newly anointed Santa Barbara Urban Wine Trail. Comprised of six actual wineries and four tasting rooms, it caters to those hapless visitors who think Santa Barbara wine country is located down the block from their in-town hotel. It's not quite walkable, but the farthest-afield winery is probably ten to fifteen minutes away instead of a couple of hours.

The wineries offer a variety of different experiences (although a vineyard tour is not one of them). From Oreana, which provides a fun experience for young people learning about wine; to Jaffurs, where Yates himself will take you through the limited production Rhône experience; to Whitcraft's shrine to "unfined, unfiltered" wines—every place has its own niche.

"We're not competing with each other; we're finding that each addition makes it a better overall draw to visitors," says Yates.

In-town crush, on the Urban Wine Trail.

If you're new to the world of wine, this large, crowd-friendly facility is a good first stop. It starts with an informative but fun tour and winds up with a tasting of wines you've seen in the grocery store. Most critics think that Firestone beer surpasses its wine these days—sample both and judge for yourself. (A word for all you *The Bachelor* fans: Foley acquired Firestone in 2008, which means *US Weekly* cover boy Andrew Firestone is no longer going to be hanging about the winery looking all gorgeous. Not that he ever did anyway.)

Ian Blackburn says: "Their facility is built for tours. You can come in on a charter bus tour and be very comfortable or come as a solo visitor—either way, their arms are wide open. They specialize in consumer-related, value-driven wines."

Roblar

(SY) 3010 Roblar Avenue, Santa Ynez, (805) 686-2603, www.roblarwinery.com; Fee: Y; Open: Daily, L

This winery is a newcomer with a great visitor facility and hospitality program. It offers wine and food pairing demos and cooking classes in an on-site exhibition kitchen. As a winemaker, though, it hasn't quite hit its stride.

Gainey Vineyard

(SY) 3950 East Highway 246, Santa Ynez, (805) 688-0558, www.gaineyvineyard.com; Fee: Y; Open: Daily; Key: TH, KIDS, DS

This winery opened in the early 1970s and offers one of the most comprehensive and visitor-friendly experiences in the area—even if it does feel a wee bit Disney. Indoor and outdoor tasting rooms offer both affordable wines and reserves at different "stations" set up to accommodate crowds. Various spreads and snacks are sold on-site, and you can often taste them as well. There's a small courtyard bordered in vine arbors, with a lawn where tipsy guests often sprawl in the sun. It offers picnic facilities and a tour.

Ian Blackburn says: "Situated on a horse ranch, and owned by one of the main Santa Barbara landholding families. Only a couple hundred acres are under vine; most is still pasture. Sauv, Chard, and Merlot are their backbone varieties."

Artiste Winery

(SY) 3569 Sagunto Street Studio 102, Historic Old Santa Ynez, (805) 686-2626, www.artiste.com; Fee: Y; Open: Daily; Key: SCENE, TH

Founded by a son of the Sunstone family, this is a unique winery concept that pairs wine and art appreciation. The label only does blends, primarily red. Unique blending seminars pick a painting and blend a bottle of wine to "match" it. There's a second location in Dry Creek, Sonoma County.

Ian Blackburn says: "Fun and hip, with gorgeous packaging. A girl paints the wine labels using wine."

Fess Parker Winery
(FC) 6200 Foxen Canyon Road, Los Olivos, (800) 841-1104, (805) 688-1545, www.fessparker.com; Fee: Y; Open: Daily ; Key: TH, CHEESE
One of the most famous and stagey-feeling wineries in all of the county, this place is owned by a classic local personality and former TV star. In *Sideways*, this was "Frass Canyon," the winery where Miles drank out of the spit bucket (gaahhh!).

ATTRACTIONS

Zaca Lake Retreat
(FC) 8000 Foxen Canyon Road, Los Olivos, (805) 688-5699, www.zacalakeretreat.com; Fee: Y; Open: Daily; Key: FO, RR (for overnight cabin rental)
Located up (and up, and up) the road from Fess Parker, this is the kind of rustic, pastoral retreat that some people love—and some people find creepy. All kinds of wildlife: deer, birds, and occasional bears. There is fantastic hiking and a lake so deep, rumor has it no one's ever found the bottom. According to some locals, this is still a revered Native American site of worship. Also, rather notably, it's where *Friday the 13th* was filmed.

RESTAURANTS

Wine Cask
(101) 813 Anacapa Street, Santa Barbara, (805) 966-9463, www.winecask.com; $$$; Open: L Mon–Fri, D; Key: DS, VEG
The fabled and fabulous wine list is the main draw, but it would take about a year to *really* learn it. So don't try to pore through all sixty-plus pages. Stick with the forty by-the-glass selections, or get guidance from a resident

expert. The colorful, veggie-ful California menu has many light pastas and Asian inspirations, but the chef seriously knows his way around a New York strip. An undeniably handsome dining room, but the courtyard is more ambient on a summer night (possibly because it's not so brightly lit). Adjacent wine bar and (natch) fantastic wine shop.

Olio e Limone
(101) 11 West Victoria Street, Santa Barbara, (805) 899-2699, www.olioelimone.com; $$; Open: L Mon-Sat, D nightly; Key: VEG
A perennial favorite for all the right reasons: fresh ingredients, friendly owners, and consistently good Italian cuisine featuring house-made pastas and Sicilian-inspired seafood. The dining room is pretty but unassuming, with close-together tables that leave many first-timers wondering, "This is fine dining?" (Answer: No, it's a once-a-week standby for wealthy locals—and a splurge for everyone else.)

Hitching Post II
(SR) 406 E. Highway 246, Buellton, (805) 688-0676, www.hitchingpost2.com; $$$; Open: D daily; KEY: TH
The dining room is seriously dowdy, but the oak-grilled meats

could make a carnivore drool for joy. Smoked duck breast, grilled artichoke, and french fries are must-tries. Reasonably priced wines by the glass or bottle. Ian Blackburn says: "A bullet-proof tourist destination."

SHOPPING

Metropulous
(101) 216 E. Yanonali Street, Santa Barbara, (805) 899-2300, www.metrofinefoods.com; Open: B and L Mon–Sat
Cute little gourmet deli and wine and cheese shop owned by husband-and-wife team Craig and Ann Addis. They offer sandwiches and Italian-imported snacks.

C'est Cheese
(101) 825 Santa Barbara Street, Santa Barbara, (805) 965-0318, www.cestcheese.com; Open: Mon–Sat
Insiders give two enthusiastic thumbs-up to this family-run cheesemonger/gourmet store that has chocolate, oils, vinegars, salami, and other edibles . . . plus an ample selection of wines under $40.

ENTERTAINMENT AND NIGHTLIFE

Joe's Cafe
(101) 536 State Street, Santa Barbara, (805) 966-4638; $; Open: AM/PM; Key: LN
Possibly the ugliest bar in town, but it seems to be immortal nonetheless, thanks to cheap drinks that are strong enough to knock your head off. It's an excellent place to pre-drink before heading out to the trendy lounge of the moment. They have a full menu of so-so food. No cover.

Wildcat Lounge
(101) 15 W. Ortega Street, Santa Barbara, (805) 962-7970, www.wildcatlounge.com; $$; Open: PM/OWL; Key: SCENE, PU
An eclectic calendar and fairly inclusive door keep this clubby cocktail spot on the map. It helps

that the cover rarely exceeds $5. The nightly lineup could include everything from a rock band to a drag fashion show, so scope it out online before going if you're picky.

ACCOMMODATIONS

Canary Hotel
(101) 31 West Carrillo, Santa Barbara, (805) 884-0300, (877) 468-3515, www.canarysanta barbara.com; $$$; Key: SCENE, DS, PETS
Cheerful and yellow, you wonder? Perhaps a bit—but also hip, youthful, and Euro-chic, with a rooftop pool and in-room spa service. Moroccan/Moorish accents spice up the sunny Spanish decor that's become de rigueur for the area. Canaries tweedle hello from their home in the lobby. The restaurant has a bistro-style chalkboard menu, contemporary cuisine, and fun fancy-schmancy cocktails like the Tahitian pomegranate mojito. A newcomer with a pedigree: Its two sister hotels (Shutters and Casa del Mar) consistently top Santa Monica's "it" list.

The Presidio Motel
(101) 1620 State Street, Santa Barbara, (805) 963-1355, www.thepresidiomotel.com; $$
This is an artsy, contemporary little charmer of a motel, with sixteen individually styled guest rooms and an enthusiastic, friendly staff. Used to be a run-of-the-mill motor lodge, but it was revamped and reopened in July 2008. There is a complimentary continental breakfast, and guests can borrow beach cruisers.

San Ysidro Ranch
(101) 900 San Ysidro Lane, Santa Barbara, (805) 565-1700, www.sanysidroranch.com; $$$$; Key: XP, DS, SF
This ranch has picture-perfect grounds and graceful bungalows that have welcomed some of the world's legendary couples, including John and Jackie Kennedy. There are two fabulous restaurants. Historic, lovely, romantic, and so expensive it makes you choke.

The Tipsy Pedestrian

In-town tasting rooms have evolved into a convenient and convivial mainstay of Santa Barbara County wine tourism. For the local winemakers, it's a cheaper and easier way to do consumer outreach than running a tasting room on winery grounds. For visitors, it's a way to taste multiple wines from many places, without driving around or wasting time. The downsides are overcrowding, little to no winemaker interaction, and an atmosphere that can often lean toward tavern-like—particularly later in the afternoon on a weekend.

Some tasting rooms are just for one winery; some pour a number of different brands. They're mostly located either along the main drag in Los Olivos, or scattered around the kitsch-alicious Danish streets of downtown Solvang.

WINERIES

(TASTING ROOMS ONLY)

Los Olivos Tasting Room
(SY) 2905 Grand Avenue, Los Olivos, (805) 688-7406, www.losolivoswines.com; Fee: Y; Open: Daily; Key: LN, KIDS

This was one of the first tasting rooms in town, and a standby for favorite Central Coast wines produced far out in the sticks, usually in facilities that are closed to the public. They have lots of Au Bon Climat, Stephen Ross, and so on, as well as some Amador and San Luis Obispo AVAs.

Qupé
(SY) 2963 Grand Avenue, Suite B, Los Olivos, (805) 686-4200, www.qupe.com; Fee: Y; Open: Daily

After more than a quarter of a century of making renowned wines from a closed facility, Bob Lindquist pulled a half-Willy Wonka and opened a tasting room in Los Olivos—or rather, allowed his grown children to open one—in fall 2008. It pours most of the wines from Qupé's comprehensive Rhône portfolio: Marsanne, Viognier, Grenache, and of course that legendary Syrah. The Central Coast Syrah is by far the most popular (50 percent of Qupé's total output), but Syrah fans should try the cool-climate single-varietal from Bien Nacido Vineyards—it's the founder's fave. His tasting notes: "Spicy and peppery, with lavender and violet aspects in the aroma. In the mouth it tends to be rich, but with cool acidity, so it's very refreshing."

LENA STAMP: Did you know that Qupé is the Chumash Indian name for the California poppy? Lindquist found it in a book of California folklore. The poppy on the label is a pen-and-ink design from the Arts and Crafts era.

Carhartt Vineyard
(SY) 2990A Grand Avenue, Los Olivos, (805) 688-0685, www.carharttvineyard.com; Fee: Y; Open: Wed–Mon

Possibly the world's smallest tasting room—and definitely the only one with a frog petting zoo. Sam Marmorstein says: "A very small producer who makes a handful of wines and is usually pouring them himself. Small, handcrafted wines: a Merlot, a Syrah, and a Sauvignon Blanc."

Longoria Wines
(SY) 2935 Grand Avenue, Los Olivos, (866) 759-4637, (805) 688-0305, www.longoriawine.com; Fee: Y; Open: Daily; Key: LN
One of the first Los Olivos tasting rooms and still a must-visit, although no groups over eight people.

Sam Marmorstein says: "This has to be one of the premier winemakers in the area. He makes a really neat Pinot Grigio, and some obscure, different wines like [Spanish variety] Tempranillo."

Consilience
(SY) 2933 Grand Avenue, Los Olivos, (805) 691-1020, www.consiliencewines.com; Fee: Y; Open: Daily
Local wine geeks agree that the "wonderful" wines (their word—we're faithfully relaying it) here merit a visit. Of the diverse portfolio of wines produced, many of the grape varieties are French Rhône, but done in big opulent California style.

Epiphany Cellars
(SY) 2963 Grand Avenue, Los Olivos, (805) 686-2424; Fee: Y; Open: Thurs–Mon; Key: RR (for groups of six or more)
Owned by Eli Parker, son of Fess. Wines get the local stamp of approval.

Sam Marmorstein says: "Eli's in the tasting room sometimes, just like Fess is in the hotel."

Alisal Cellars
(SR) 448 Alisal Road, Solvang, (800) 630-9941, (805) 686-4329, www.alisalcellars.com; Fee: Y; Open: Daily, PM daily, OWL weekends; Key: PU
Located downstairs from street level, Solvang's original tasting room has hints of the rock club and basement rec room about it. The tasting bar/wine shop occupies the left side—it's a buzzing, convivial space with tables, display shelves, and an all-ages clientele. On the right is a second bar, which only pours at night, but is where the owner and his friends sometimes hang out and play darts by day. All the way to the back is a stage where live bands play every Friday and Saturday. The tasting room offers six wine flights daily; each flight includes five wines. Sake, beer, and sparkling wine flights are mixed in with Central Coast labels. No hard liquor. Burgers and other bar food served. There's a parking lot adjacent, and a more sophisticated sister venue, 5 Wine Bar, is upstairs. Flexible hours, but usually open until 11 p.m. weekdays and as late as 1 a.m. on weekends.

Wandering Dog
(SR) 1539 Mission Drive "C", Solvang, (805) 686-9126, www.wanderingdogwinebar.com; Fee: Y; Open: Daily; Key: PETS
Named in homage to the owner's parents' dog, this pup-friendly tasting room/wine bar is upbeat and casual, with a comfy couch near the entrance and a "Director de Vino" who saps off a microbrewed beer stashed behind the bar. Of 200 different wines, 50 are open at any time, poured by the taste or the glass. A cheese plate and a few other snacks are available. Stays open until 9 p.m. or later.

Honeywood & Old Mission Wine Co.
(SY) 1539 Mission Drive, Unit B, Solvang, (805) 686-9323, www.houseofhoneywood.com; Fee: Y; Open: Daily
Two tasting rooms in one: Old Mission, which promotes limited-production (under 500 cases) wines from the Central Coast, and Honeywood, which has the largest selection of sweet wines in Santa Barbara County. Altogether this funky, brightly lit storefront houses 300 labels from forty different wineries. Ten wines are on pour daily—five dry and five sweet.

Tastes of the Valleys—A *Sideways* Wine Bar
(SY) 1672 Mission Drive, Solvang, (877) 622-9463, www.tastesofthevalleys.com; Fee: Y; Open: Daily; KEY: TH, DS, KIDS
Life imitates art shamelessly at this wine bar/tasting room, which licensed its name and borrowed its concept from the titular film. Though some find the stagey atmosphere offputting, the upmarket wine list and old-fashioned parlor atmosphere are hard to resist.

ATTRACTIONS

Wildling Art Museum
(SY) 2329 Jonata Street, Los Olivos, (805) 688-1082, www.wildlingmuseum.org; Fee: Y; Open: Wed–Sun (during exhibitions only); Key: SF
Preservation, nature appreciation, and art education are the prevailing themes at this small but highly regarded American wilderness art museum. Four different exhibitions per year, plus a calendar of lectures, talks, workshops, and film screenings. A serene

throwback to the days when Los Olivos was known primarily as an artistic retreat.

The Chef's Touch
(SR) 1555 Mission Drive, Solvang, (805) 686-1040, www.thechefstouch.com; $$; Open: Classes every second Wed, restaurant L Wed–Mon, brunch Sun, D Thu–Sat
A one-stop shop for all things foodie: cookbooks, catering, kitchenware, and more. Cooking classes are only held every second Wednesday and typically sell out, but the bistro is open six days a week. There are four tables in a courtyard, which is shared with next-door tasting room Trio.

Wheel Fun Rentals
(SR) 475 First Street, Solvang, (805) 688-0091, www.wheelfunrentals.com; $$; Open: Daily; Key: CHEESE, TH
Rentals for convenience and novelty's sake. The four-seater surrey is a definite photo op.

MUSINGS ON *SIDEWAYS*

Sam Marmorstein, Owner, Los Olivos Wine Merchant & Cafe

Whether you loved or hated *Sideways* (I personally hated it), it definitely changed the game for the Santa Barbara businesses featured in it. Below, first-person perspective from the man who owned Los Olivos' only pre-*Sideways* hot spot.

"The cafe was busy before, but it's been crazy-busy since. However, our focus really hasn't changed," says Los Olivos Wine Merchant & Café owner Sam Marmorstein. "*Sideways* did a good job showcasing some of the beauty of the area—that it's a place to relax with great local wines and food. However, the movie is a skewed story of two imperfect people going on a wine binge. I don't think anyone should emulate what those two guys did. That's not the way people act."

Marmorstein adds, "Nobody who knows anything about wine believes [the anti-Merlot rant]. It seems like half the people who saw that movie came out of that thinking Pinot was the only way to go. But that does a huge disservice to Merlot. Here, in Santa Barbara, we do great Chards, great Merlots, plus Sangioveses and Syrahs that are really good as well."

RESTAURANTS

Los Olivos Café
(SY) 2879 Grand Avenue, Los Olivos, (888) 946-3748, (805) 688-7265, www.losolivoscafe.com; $$$; Open: L and D daily; Key: DS, TH, RR (weekends)

As we've discussed, it's the restaurant you saw in *that* movie. Moving along to the important stuff: The California-Mediterranean cuisine is simply prepared to showcase its fresh and flavorful ingredients. Local organic produce, grass-fed beef, and free-range chicken have been standards since the restaurant opened. Almost everything's made in house, from pastas and pizzas to ice cream. Sam refers to the atmosphere as "casual but elegant." Others refer to it as "super-fun to look at . . . but you'll never get a table on a weekend."(Unless, presumably, you are wise and reserve in advance.)

In addition to the dining room and patio, an adjacent tasting bar can seat up to twenty people. There, it's first-come, first-served, and customers are encouraged to order spontaneously: a glass of wine or a bottle, a tasting flight with a cheese plate . . . or perhaps baked Brie or some rustic spreads. The wine shop pours five to six wines from different producers in the area, changing its selections weekly. It sells 500 different wines, most of them local. It also has its own label, Bernat Wines, made at an organic Los Olivos vineyard.

Panino
(SY, 101) 2900 Grand Avenue, Los Olivos, (805) 688-9304, www.paninorestaurants.com; $; Open: L daily

Gourmet sandwiches and salads in a quaint pretty sidewalk setting. Unexpectedly, this family-owned business seems to have aspirations to take over California—six locations are open to the public as of summer 2008.

Brothers' Restaurant at Mattei's Tavern
(SY) 2350 Railway Avenue, Los Olivos, (805) 688-4820, www.matteistavern.com; $$$; Open: D daily; Key: DS

A steakhouse for the wine country: mouthwatering cuisine and convivial vibes in a former 1880s stagecoach stop. The landmark building sits just apart from the main Los Olivos drag. This is probably the only restaurant in town spacious enough to afford diners a little privacy, even when it's at max capacity.

Mattei's Tavern: old-fashioned folksy, with great Cal regional fare.

Los Olivos Grocery
(SY) 2621 Highway 154, Santa Ynez, (805) 688-5115, www.losolivosgrocery.com; $; Open: B, L, D daily; Key: VEG
Sandwiches, great cheeses, and salads you can take with you on a jaunt to the wine country or a stagger back to your hotel.

Café Angelica
(SR) 490 First Street, Solvang, (805) 686-9970; $$; Open: L and D daily; Key: LN, DS
Downtown Solvang's most popular patio cafe, with a pretty indoor dining room that's only for rare overcast days and service that's just as sunny as the average summer forecast. It features an Italian menu with a few California influences.

Olsen's Danish Village Bakery
(SY) 1529 Mission Drive, Solvang, (800) 621-8238, (805) 688-6314, www.olsensdanishbakery.com; $; Open: Daily
Of all the Danish bakeries, sweet shops, and cafes in Solvang, this is the insider pick for quality and authenticity. Family owned and presided over by a Danish master baker, the Scandinavian import is famous for its pastry and cakes. Butter is the secret ingredient to success.

SHOPPING

Global Gardens
(SY) 2477 Alamo Pintado Avenue, Los Olivos, (800) 307-0447, (805) 693-1600, www.globalgardensgifts.com; Fee: Y; Open: Daily; Key: RR (for groups of eight or more), VEG

Tastings of olive oil, fruit vinegars, and gourmet spreads make for a nice change from wine. Mixed nuts, fruit chews, and other nibbles are also available, as are some non-munchable gift items.

ACCOMMODATIONS

Fess Parker Wine Country Inn and Spa
(SY) 2860 Grand Avenue, Los Olivos, (800) 446-2455, (805) 688-7788, www.fessparker.com; $$$$ (free wine tasting included); KEY: TH, DS, LN

These über-twee village digs are owned by a former Disney star who played Davy Crockett and Daniel Boone in the 1960s through the 1980s. The self-consciously country chic theme demands khakis, not coonskin. The rooms are located across the street from the lobby, so not only *can* you walk off-property and explore the surrounding village, you actually *must*. The master of the house often makes an appearance during Thursday night sing-alongs.

Hadsten House
(SR) 1450 Mission Drive, Solvang, (800) 457-5373, (805) 688-3210, www.hadstenhouse.com; $$; Key: KIDS

This surprisingly stylish downtown lodging provides tangible evidence of Solvang's ongoing transformation from smorgasbord heaven to hipster hangout: Formerly a motor lodge, it underwent a $5 million renovation in 2007, reopening as a modern, Euro-styled hotel/day spa. The exterior underpromises while the interior overdelivers, with a sparkling indoor pool, the biggest commercial outdoor Jacuzzi in Santa Barbara County, and an elegant leather-furnished dining room. The sumptuous complimentary breakfast features fresh pastries from Olsens, and the in-room amenities include makeup remover and bath crystals. Everything in the restaurant is made from scratch, and local publications have already tapped it as the best in town. The specialty is the burger done "all the way," with standard fixings plus spinach, avocado, fried egg, sauteed onions, roasted peppers, and four cheeses.

Royal Scandinavian Inn
(SR) 400 Alisal Road, Solvang, (800) 624-5572, www.royalscandinavianinn.com; $$; KEY: TH

Recently acquired by the Chumash, this hotel has meeting space for 400 people, plus one of only two full bars in town (the other one is a dive, not recommended to tourists). It's large for a wine country inn, with 133 rooms. The Danish theme is kept to a minimum, and weekend shuttles go to Chumash Casino.

Spurs and Syrah

You're a hundred times more likely to spot a cowboy than a celebrity in the rural canyons and surviving Spanish land grants of Santa Barbara County. The wineries, attractions, and characters in this section are part of the colorful cultural fabric and generation-spanning history that give the region real depth. Sip your way to a greater understanding of the land and its stories, from the early Spanish land grants to the 1980s Syrah influx to the latest breakaway boutique labels.

WINERIES

Bridlewood Estate Winery
(SY) 3555 Roblar Avenue, Santa Ynez, (800) 467-4100, (805) 688-9000, www.bridlewoodwinery.com; Fee: Y; Open: Daily; Key: DS
Though it's a relative newcomer in the game, this winery's on its way up, in terms of production and public profile, thanks to a recent Gallo acquisition. Veteran winemaker David Hopkins is one of the most outspoken proponents of the "blending is better" school of thought. His sole standalone wine is also a signature: the Estate Syrah, made from what Hopkins calls his "Vintage Vineyard." Bridlewood's various Syrahs and Viogniers rack up

Santa Barbara Syrah Basics

Jill Tweedie, Owner and Chief Executive Officer, Breakaway Tours

Possibly the predominant grape on the world wine scene, Syrah has yet to break big with the American consumer—but it's on the way. Get the 411 on what many think is going to be the "next big thing" in California wines.

- Syrah (or in Australia, Shiraz) is probably the best-known Rhône grape—"the new red darling" among wine aficionados.
- Syrah is not the same as Petit Sirah.
- Syrah is one of the few grapes that can grow successfully in warm or cool climates.
- Warm-climate Syrah and cool-climate Syrah make two entirely different wines.
- In Santa Barbara County's sub-appellations, you have some warm-climate vineyards and some cool-climate vineyards.
- Warm-climate Syrah is darker in color, heavier on the palate, and more opaque, with jammier "stewed fruit" flavors.
- Cool-climate Syrah has higher acid, is more fruit forward, and has more bright, black-pepper notes.
- Like all Rhône grapes, Syrah is often blended—traditionally with other Rhône grapes, but these days also with Cabernet, Malbec, and so on.
- In Santa Barbara, winemakers can do crazy kitchen-sink blends (i.e., Syrah/Sangiovese) without being thought odd, because that's just how we roll.

international awards steadily; other standouts include an estate Pinot Noir and the reserve Arabesque. The tasting room pours a few flights and luncheon foods and gifts are also available for purchase.

Brander Vineyard
(SY) 2401 Refugio Road, Los Olivos, (800) 970-9979, (805) 688-2455, www.brander.com; Fee: Y; Open: Daily; Key: RR (for groups of eight or more)
This winery has numerous single-vineyard Bordeaux wines, including must-try Merlot. There's a welcoming staff and a pretty front picnic area.

Ian Blackburn says: "Fred Brander was a pioneer in Santa Barbara wine country—as a grape grower and a vineyard owner as well as a winemaker. He helped a lot of brands get started, but for the past ten years he has focused on his own winery. Known as the specialist for Sauvignon Blanc."

Beckmen Vineyards
(SY) 2670 Ontiveros Road, Los Olivos, (805) 688-8664, www.beckmenvineyards.com; Fee: Y; Open: Daily
Together with nearby Brander and Bridlewood, this winery is part of what insiders nickname the "killer bee" triumvirate and produces some Bordeaux and Burgundy varietals, as well as a whole portfolio of Rhônes. It's known for its numerous hillside estate vineyards.

Kenneth Volk Vineyards
(FC) 5230 Tepusquet Road, Santa Maria, (805) 938-7896, www.volkwines.com; Fee: Y; Open: Daily; Key: FO
Head to the top of Foxen Canyon Wine Trail, on the Santa Maria border, and discover the latest boutique start-up by a legendary Santa Barbara winemaker. In addition to the standbys—Cabernet, Chardonnay, Merlot, Pinot—Volk produces an "Heirloom Collection" comprised of rare varieties like Negrette and Malvasia. Nominal tasting fee waived with purchase.

Jill Tweedie says: "At the old Byron tasting room location. Ken Volk was the former winemaker at Wild Horse. He got big, sold off, and started his own little place here to get back to the basics of making wine."

Koehler Winery
(FC) 5360 Foxen Canyon Road, Los Olivos, (805) 693-8384, www.koehlerwinery.com; Fee: Y; Open: Daily; Key: FO
A world apart from its famous neighbors, this little winery has a funny, offbeat tasting room staff, an on-site menagerie,

and off-the-grid appeal. Small-production estate wines include a Chardonnay and a Syrah. The specialty blend is a delicious Cab-Sangiovese "super-Tuscan."

Jill Tweedie says: "An unknown on the south end of Foxen Canyon, with a beautiful, quaint little picnic spot. There are huge trees on the property, and goats cruising around on the hill. A very user-friendly, approachable presentation."

Foxen Winery

(FC) 7200 Foxen Canyon Road, Santa Maria, (805) 937-4251, www.foxenvineyard.com; Fee: Y; Open: Daily; Key: FO

History meets funky at this small but highly regarded winery located on Rancho Tinaquaic, a land grant acquired by William Benjamin Foxen, ancestor of co-owner Dick Doré. Other co-owner/winemaker Bill Wathen studied vineyard management

For the Love of Syrah

Bob Lindquist, Founder of Qupé

I was an employee of Zaca Mesa in 1979, along with Jim Clenenden and Adam Tolmach (founders of Au Bon Climat), when the decision was made to plant Syrah. Ken Brown was the winemaker, and he ultimately gets the most credit. Zaca Mesa was looking to plant something new and unique. The owners were going to plant Petit Sirah, but we as a group convinced them otherwise.

I started Qupé in 1982 and 1983, while still working at Zaca Mesa. I rented space in their cellar and bought the grapes for the 1982 Syrah vintage from Estrella River. The original budwood came over from Hermitage in the northern Rhône, and was first planted in the University of California at Davis (UC Davis) test block. Gary Eberle got hold of some of that budwood from UC Davis and planted it in Paso Robles. That grape is now planted throughout the Central Coast. It's primarily what I grow. It's still referred to as the Estrella River clone, though the vineyard is no longer around.

I love French Syrah. I felt the variety had a lot of potential, and there was little being done with it here, so I saw it as a niche. I also made Chardonnay from the beginning, because I wasn't sure how Syrah would sell. Luckily, it caught on . . . in increments. When I first took it out, I only had about 300 cases, and I was able to sell it pretty quickly to forward-thinking people who said, "Hey, this is new and different." But I'll tell you, for every restaurateur and retailer who bought it, there were probably ten who said, "Nah, I can't sell that!"

at Cal Poly in the early 1970s and has been in the business ever since. He gets grapes from the choicest blocks of Santa Barbara's fabled Bien Nacido and Seasmoke vineyards, as well as from various Santa Ynez vineyards.

Jill Tweedie says: "One of my favorite wineries, housed in an old blacksmith's shop from the 1800s. If they're closed and you drive by, you could miss it. Bill and Dick are the owners. They're a bit twisted, lots of fun, and brave with their big red wines."

Jim Fiolek says: "A portion of Tinaquaic is the only Mexican Land Grant that has stayed in the family since it was granted."

Lafond
(SR) 6855 Santa Rosa Road, Buellton, (877) 708-9463, (805) 688-7921, www.lafondwinery.com; Fee: Y; Open: Daily; Key: TH
The vineyards for Pierre Lafond's latest winery and his iconic original (Santa Barbara Winery) are located here, and so is the kitchen garden for Pierre Lafond Bistro. Winemaker Bruce McGuire has overseen the vineyards since 1981.

Alma Rosa
(SR) 7250 Santa Rosa Road, Buellton, (805) 688-9090, www.almarosawinery.com; Fee: Y; Open: Daily

Santa Barbara Pinot pioneer Richard Sanford left his eponymous label after selling out to a big company. And, in what is becoming a common refrain for the region, he opened this new boutique winery and returned to making wine according to his own philosophies. These hinge around organic farming, wildlife protection, and sustainable agricultural and business practices. Though the winery's first release year was 2006, there's already an interesting white portfolio, plus two vineyard-designated Pinot Noirs. The tasting room offers two tasting flights, one of which is a pricey all-Pinot grouping.

Mosby Winery
(SR) 9496 Santa Rosa Road, Buellton, (805) 688-2415, www.mosbywines.com; Fee: Y; Open: Daily
This is a tiny family-run winery specializing in Italian varietals like Sangiovese. Beautiful painted labels look like Italian stained glass. The owner goes back to Italy every few years to study Italian wine-making techniques and to bring back equipment.

Blending Debunked

David Hopkins, Winemaker, Bridlewood Estate Winery

Chatty, charismatic, and ever so into his work, David Hopkins should probably be named California's official wine-blending ambassador. He fulfills the function already, title or no. Nobody ever agrees on anything in the wine business, so I'm not going to say David's words are the gospel . . . but they're as close as anything could be. *Blending* is an old-world European technique involving the synergistic mixing of multiple lots of wine to maximize the attributes of those lots.

Myth: Some grape varieties shouldn't be mixed.
Fact: There are very few stand-alone wines that are 100 percent of one varietal—especially if you're talking about expensive red wine.

Myth: *Blending* refers only to mixing wines made from different grape varieties—i.e., Syrah and Cabernet.
Fact: Blends can be made from different grape varieties, different lots of the same variety, the same variety grown in different areas, or different varieties grown in different areas.

Myth: Blends are made from a bunch of different grape varieties thrown together in the fermenter.
Fact: Most winemakers ferment separately to understand the wine that a particular block can make. If you have three lots of Syrah, each should have an individual flavor profile at the end of fermentation. If you experiment with blending them, sometimes you find that two lots taste better together. Sometimes, you say, "You know, these two wines fight with each other. So I think we need to bottle them separately and have two separate labels."

Myth: Blending is déclassé.
Fact: Most California winemakers feel that the wine is inferior if they blend wine, and they're embarrassed. That's just because we have been predisposed by our unique history to think of monovarietal wines as somehow better. However, most of Europe understands blends. For example, in France's Chateauneuf-du-Pape, it has been discovered over time that certain grapes blended (for example Grenache, Mourvedre, and Syrah) create a sum that's greater than the parts. Because of tra-

dition, the French usually label by the château, without placing emphasis on the varietal(s) or the vineyard(s).

Myth: If wine is good, you don't need to blend it.
Fact: It's not necessarily that a lot isn't good as a stand-alone; it's that it could be better. Every winemaker's dream is to make a great stand-alone wine from a vintage vineyard, but in reality, only a small percentage of vineyards are noteworthy and possess a noble *terroir*. At the same time as you experiment with and refine vineyard techniques, in hopes of discovering a potential "vintage vineyard," you continue to blend. The goal is always to create the *best possible wine.*

Myth: If it's a blend, it'll say so on the label.
Fact: Wineries are not required by law to put variety percentages on the label. Even when you specify the variety of the wine (i.e., Cabernet), the wine only has to be 85 percent of the specified variety. It doesn't matter what the other 15 percent is!

ATTRACTIONS

San Ramon Chapel
(FC) 6600 Foxen Canyon Road, Santa Maria, (805) 934-4332, www.ranchosisquoc.com, www.sanramonchapel.org; Fee: N; Open: Daily; Key: FO
Built as a burial ground for Benjamin Foxen by his grandchildren, the chapel is on the road outside Rancho Sisquoc winery. The phone number above reaches the winery, which is really the main tourist attraction for all but serious history buffs.

Mount Figueroa
(SY) Figueroa Mountain Road and Catway Road, Santa Barbara; Fee: N; Open: Daily; Key: FO
Hike and/or bike to Mount Figueroa, Santa Barbara's highest summit. The drive-in access point is the Figueroa Mountain Ranger Station.

David Hopkins says: "A great place to go up and watch the stars. It's the tallest mountain in the area."

SHOPPING

Rancho Olivos
(SY) 2390 N. Refugio Road, Santa Ynez, (805) 686-9653, www.ranchoolivos.com; Open: Mid-afternoons Fri–Sun or by appt.

Taste several kinds of award-winning olive oils at a working olive orchard and press. Rancho Olivos proudly carries arbequina, Italian, and garlic-flavored extra-virgin olive oils, among others.

RESTAURANTS

Andersen's Pea Soup
(SR) 376 Avenue of Flags, Buellton, (805) 688-5581, www.peasoupandersens.net; $; Open: B, L, D daily; KEY: TH, KIDS, CHEESE
The best pea soup ever—no joke, and no exaggeration. Often filled with families, and so touristy it's hilarious, this landmark nonetheless will soothe your soul with good, healthy yumminess straight out of the soup pot—and bread to go along with it.

LENA STAMP: I've eaten here at least fifty times since I was a tot; the place never fails me. And I don't even like pea soup.

Trattoria Grappolo
(SY) 3687 Sagunto Street, Santa Ynez, (805) 688-6899, www.trattoriagrappolo.com; $$; Open: L Tues–Sun, D Mon–Sun; Key: DS, PU, SCENE

This is a small, warm dining room packed to the nooks and crannies with cowboys, winemakers, West Hollywood weekenders, and the occasional Santa Barbara cougar. The front has no real wall, just semi-opaque screens that lend an indoor/outdoor feel but still keep out the elements. Handsome, charming, quintessentially Mediterranean staff and owners offer a medium-size wine list full of Central Coast discoveries. Food is rich but stops just short of being too heavy. Handmade pastas are outstanding.

Cold Spring Tavern
(FAR OUT) 5995 Stagecoach Road, Santa Barbara, (805) 967-0066, www.coldspringtavern.com; $ (B/ L), $$$ (D); Open: Daily; Key: FO, DS
Far out on the old Wells Fargo stagecoach trail, but worth a drive.

An afternoon jam at Cold Spring Tavern.

David Hopkins says: "Music, motorcycles, and barbecue. Grilled everything, over a hot oak flame, with hand-rubbed cayenne, salt, and pepper."

ENTERTAINMENT AND NIGHTLIFE

Maverick Saloon
(SY) 3687 Sagunto Street, Santa Ynez, (805) 686-4785, www.mavericksaloon.org; $; Open: PM/OWL, On-site BBQ open AM/PM except Thur; Key: CHEESE, PU, SF, SCENE, SKETCH

A divey watering hole frequented by ranchers, surfers, college kids, winemakers, tourists, and everyone else imaginable. Drinks are cheap, and the entertainment ranges from two-step lessons in the early evening to DJ-spun hip-hop until 2 a.m.

ACCOMMODATIONS

Ballard Inn & Restaurant
(SR) 2436 Baseline Avenue, Ballard, (800) 638-2466, (805) 688-7770, www.ballardinn.com; $$ (inn), $$$ (restaurant); Open: D Wed–Sun; Key: RR (for restaurant)
This is a cozy fifteen-room country inn with a surprisingly outstanding restaurant that gets a lot of local traffic. Old-fashioned wallpaper, swagged curtains, and checked quilts lend a farmhouse feel.

Jim Fiolek says: "The chef is phenomenal. Make reservations—they only seat thirty-six."

The Victorian Mansion
(101) 326 Bell Street, Los Alamos, (805) 344-1300, www.thevick.com; $$$; Key: CHEESE, DS
The pet project of an LA escapee with a wildly creative streak and a substantial decorating budget, this six-room luxury B&B is an upmarket, grown-ups-only version of San Luis Obispo's famous Madonna Inn. Not only do suites look like television set stages, they also have background music and movie choices to fit each individual theme. For example, the Fifties Suite pipes in 1950s rock and shows *American Graffiti* and *Rebel without A Cause.*

1880 Union Hotel
(101) 362 Bell Street Los Alamos (805) 344-2744, www.unionhotelvictmansion.com; $$
Not to be confused with the Victorian Mansion down the street—though it's extremely easy to confuse the two, which have almost identical addresses and were owned by the same person up until a few years ago—this property is now under new ownership, as is its neighbor, and is done up (as its landmark status befits) in refurbished past-century style. Very nice service.

Skyview Motel
(101) 9150 Highway 101, Los Alamos, (805) 344-3770, www.theskyviewmotel.com; $; Key: SKETCH
You've got to love a venue the locals describe as "a little Bates Motel, but totally fine and very clean." Or maybe not love it, but trust their word and dig the just-right room rates. Newly renovated, with a pool and in-room refrigerators.

TOUR PROVIDERS

Breakaway Tours
(ALL) 3463 State Street, Suite 141, Santa Barbara, (800) 799-7657, www.breakaway-tours.com; Fee: Y; Open: By appt.
This touring company offers all custom itineraries, serving three regions on the Central Coast, and specializing in wine education tours. Vehicle size ranges from vans to motor coaches. A typical one-day itinerary will visit three wineries, though a fourth winery can be added upon request. Los Olivos Café caters their picnic luncheons. Note: Offices located in Paso Robles and Pismo Beach, too.

Jill Tweedie (owner/chief executive officer) says: "It's all up to the palate and the choice of the customer. If they want to visit boutiques, we're happy to do that. Whether they want single-varietal wines or all Syrahs, we'll do it."

LearnAboutWine.com
(MULTIPLE) 2118 Wilshire Boulevard, #462, Santa Monica, (310) 451-7600, www.learnaboutwine.com; Fee: Y; Open: By appt.
Based in Los Angeles, this organization makes wine appreciation fun and approachable. Founder/chief educator Ian Blackburn holds weekly classes in Los Angeles and does wine events all over Southern California—including the annual Stars of Santa Barbara tasting. His customized small-group tours of Santa Barbara combine grape education, history, and a smattering of insider gossip.

Sustainable Vine
(ALL) P.O. Box 40814, (805) 698-3911, www.sustainablevine.com; Fee: Y; Open: By appt.
A ten-passenger bio-diesel van with a well-stocked iPod takes small groups on behind-the-scenes tours of little-known boutique wineries, two-thirds of which are not open to the public. A local pick!

SUGGESTED TWO-DAY ITINERARIES

{WINE (ON THE) 101}

DAY ONE

From Santa Barbara

Morning: Taste at Jaffurs *and/or* Santa Barbara Winery

Late morning: Stop by C'est Cheese *or* Metropolous for picnic supplies.

Afternoon: Have lunch at Dine C'est Cheese *or* Metropolous *or* drive to Summerland Winery for a tasting followed by a picnic on the beach.

Mid-afternoon: Sunbathe on Summerland Beach *or* visit your choice of wineries on the Santa Barbara Urban Wine Trail.

Late afternoon: Have a glass of wine at Wine Cask *or* at the adjacent wine bar Intermezzo.

Evening: Dinner at Wine Cask *or* at Intermezzo *or* Olio e Limone.

DAY TWO

From Santa Barbara

Morning: Take Highway 154 into Santa Ynez and taste/tour Gainey and Roblar.

Afternoon: Have a picnic lunch *or* do a cooking activity at Roblar.

Mid-afternoon: Taste in the "studio" at Artiste *and/or* visit Firestone for wine and beer tasting.

Evening: Have dinner at Hitching Post II.

{THE TIPSY PEDESTRIAN}

DAY ONE

From Solvang

Early morning: Have pastries at Olsen's Danish Village Bakery.

Mid-morning: Taste at Honeywood/ Old Mission, then follow the road to smaller tasting rooms.

Afternoon: Visit Wandering Dog *or* the Chef's Touch.

Mid-afternoon: Explore the historic town center on a surrey bike *or* visit Tastes of the Valley (both are great photo ops).

Late afternoon: Have a caffeinated pick-me-up at Bulldog.

Evening: Have dinner at Café Angelica.

Late evening: Taste at Alisal Cellars *or* Wandering Dog.

DAY TWO

From Los Olivos

Morning (or night before): Make reservations at Los Olivos Café *or* Mattei's.

Mid-morning: Taste at Los Olivos Tasting Room, Carhartt, Consilience, Qupé, Longoria, and/or Epiphany until exhausted.

Afternoon: Have lunch at Panino *or* pick up sandwiches at Los Olivos Grocery.

Mid-afternoon: Hit the recommended venues above, followed by all others, until 5 p.m.

Late afternoon: Visit Los Olivos Café *or* Mattei's.

Evening: Have dinner at Los Olivos Café *or* Mattei's.

{SPURS AND SYRAH}

DAY ONE

From Los Alamos

Morning: Take a customized tour of Foxen Canyon vineyards (see list of recommended providers).

Afternoon: Have lunch, included with tour.

Mid-afternoon: Stop by historic San Ramon Chapel for a photo op.

Evening: Have dinner at Cold Springs Tavern *or* Ballard Inn.

Overnight: Stay at Ballard Inn.

DAY TWO

From Ballard

Morning: Cut over to Santa Rita wineries: Alma Rosa and La Fond *or* Mosby.

Afternoon: Have Andersen's split pea for lunch.

Mid-afternoon: Visit two or three of the "Killer Bees" in Santa Ynez: Brander, Beckmen, and Bridlewood.

Evening: Have dinner at Grappolo.

Late evening: Enjoy dancing and drinking at Maverick.

CALENDAR OF EVENTS

MARCH

- Taste of Solvang
  www.solvangusa.com

APRIL

- Santa Barbara County Vintners Festival
  www.sbcountywines.com/events/festival.html

JUNE

- Santa Barbara Wine Festival
  www.sbnature.org/winefestival

JULY

- Stars, Stripes & Syrah
  www.santaynezwinecountry.com

OCTOBER

- Celebration of Harvest
  www.sbcountywines.com

DECEMBER

- Holiday in Wine Country
  www.santaynezwinecountry.com/events.html

RESOURCES

www.foxentrail.com
www.santaynezwinecountry.com
www.sbcountywines.com
www.staritahills.com
www.solvangusa.com

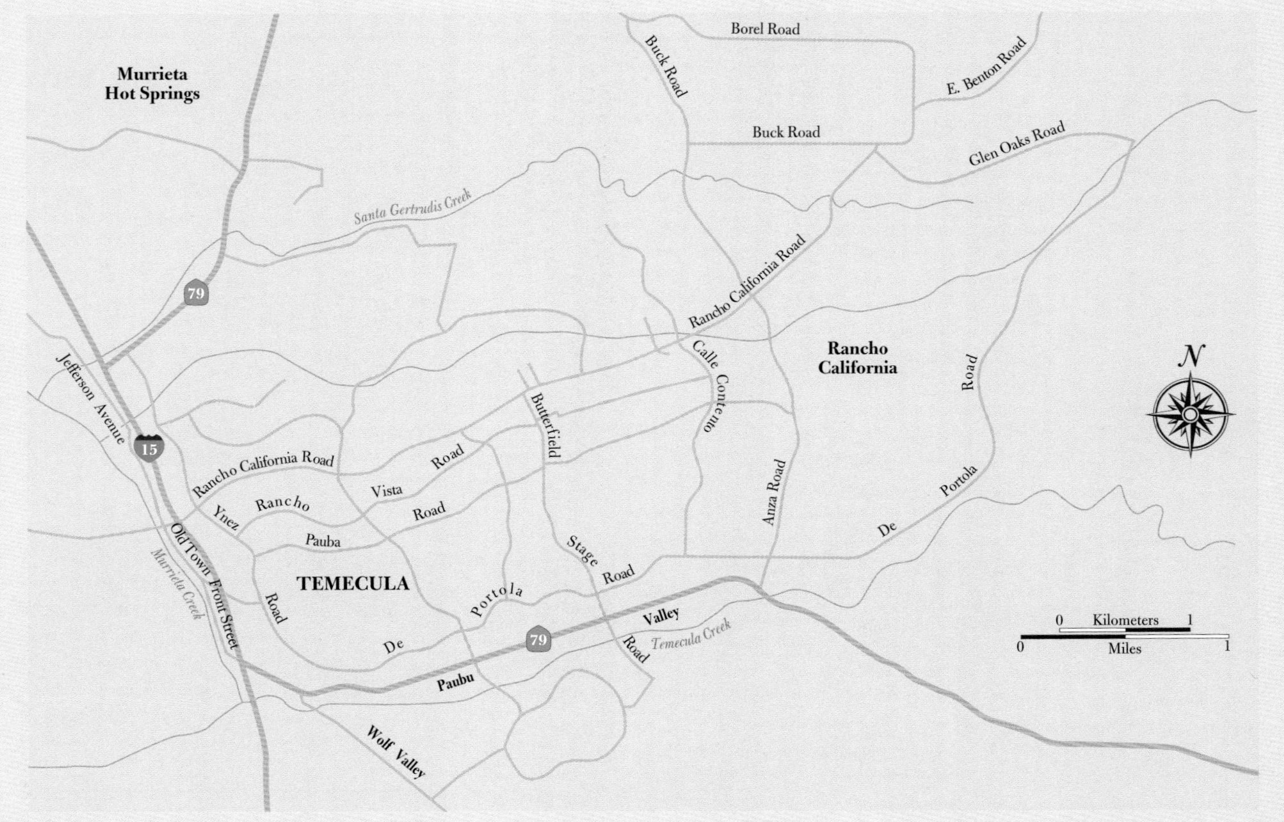
Murrieta Hot Springs
Borel Road
Buck Road
Buck Road
E. Benton Road
Glen Oaks Road
Santa Gertrudis Creek
79
Rancho California Road
Rancho California
N
Jefferson Avenue
15
Calle Contento
Butterfield
Rancho California Road
Road
Vista
Rancho
Road
Ynez
Pauba
Anza Road
Road
De
Portola
Stage
Road
TEMECULA
Murrieta Creek
Old Town Front Street
Road
Portola
De
79
Valley
Road
Temecula Creek
Paubu
Wolf Valley
0 Kilometers 1
0 Miles 1

TEMECULA

Welcome to Southern California's little slice of wine country.

Just "up the hill" from four major So Cal metropolitan areas, this itty-bitty region specializes in the two-day getaway. It is unpretentious and easily navigable, with wineries that range from family-owned boutiques to self-contained luxe resorts. Temecula's strengths are its year-round events calendar and its mixed-use wineries. While every other region's wineries stay separate from restaurants, hotels, etc., Temecula wineries almost all have an on-site restaurant or music program—and in some cases, a hotel or a spa. With its straight-shot geography, pioneer-styled "Old Town," and group-friendly focus, this town draws everyone from corporate groups to wedding parties to golfers. (And yes, the wine is a bit of an afterthought, but for many people, that's okay.)

Getting Here

Nearby airports are San Diego, Los Angeles International, Ontario, and Orange County (John Wayne). All are within one to two hours' driving distance, although rush hour traffic could double that time. Temecula is just off Highway 15.

Weather

The local literature would have you believe that average summer temperatures are in the mid-80s Fahrenheit, but that oh-so-modest prediction should get bumped up to mid-90s from June through September. The great thing about that is that winter weather rarely drops below the mid-70s.

Recommended Transportation

Ironically, this place has more shuttle and car hire services than most of the big regions. Either hitch a ride on one, or book something of your own—a limo? A van? A trolley? All are readily available. And all are preferable to being tailgated by a local redneck going 90 mph in a 4 x 4 truck.

Style

Casual dress, but nothing so sloppy you wouldn't be comfort-

The Balloon and Wine Festival is a perennial crowd-pleaser.

able in the evening. You'll probably segue from wine tasting to dinner or an event. When in doubt, golf attire/resort casual always works.

Fees

Tastings from $5 to $15.

Bird's-eye View

Most of Temecula's big wineries are located along Rancho California Road, with a number of smaller ones cropping up along De Portola and Monte de Oro.

Right where Jefferson intersects Rancho California, it turns into Old Town Front Street, Temecula's historic downtown area. With over six hundred antique stores, boutiques, and galleries arranged around a wooden boardwalk replete with "mountain man" monuments, the only thing this California West throwback is missing is the grizzled, toothless miners—and they appear on holidays and special occasions, for a fee. Speaking of special occasions, Temecula has an endless supply of them. The town's event calendar is specifically designed to draw bored LA and San Diego day-trippers back repeatedly, for small-town events like car shows, Perry Mason murder mystery weekends, an annual bluegrass festival, and a Dickensian Christmas.

The residential part of Temecula doesn't have wineries or gold miners or other tourist-beguiling features, but it does have a few upscale hotels and restaurants that are all the more appealing for being off the well-trodden wine track.

Area Key:
WT = De Portola, Rancho California wine trails
OT = Old Town
NT = Newer parts of Temecula

The Panel

John Kelliher, owner, Grapeline

Jim Lilly, owner, Temecula Valley Wine Shop

Karen Lindstrom, GM, the Castle

Barrie Lynn, the Cheese Impresario

Jennifer and Bill Wilson, owners Wilson Creek Winery

Un-Geekified, De-Mystified, Kick-Back

Whether they've been here five years or twenty, Temecula's winery owners are a down-to-earth bunch. Those who have been around longer—and we're only talking a couple of decades, tops—get patriarch status in the region, and any newcomers (even incoming companies) are watched with interest. Running a winery out here is almost always a family affair: You see husband-and-wife teams, brothers and father-and-son duos, and so on. One of Temecula's most respected wine merchants, Jim Lilly, fills us in on the best local wineries for un-geeks who still appreciate good wine.

WINERIES

Palumbo Family Vineyards
(WT) 40150 Barksdale Circle, Temecula, (951) 676-7900, www.palumbofamilyvineyards.com; Fee: Y; Open: Fri–Sun or by appt., limos/shuttles by appt.; Key: LN
This vineyard offers limited-production, estate-grown wines made with passion and plenty of expertise. Locals have huge respect for this family-owned operation, which does red wines only. Their wines are available at a few select stores in town.

Jim Lilly says: "A little mom-and-pop operation with small production—only 900 to 1,300 cases per year. I totally respect this guy because he basically told me about three years ago that he was going to start a wine club and cap membership at 500 members because he was interested in producing quality, not getting more people. He's capped it, he's stayed with it, and he has people on a waiting list."

Hart Family Winery
(WT) 41300 Avenida Biona, Temecula, (951) 676-6300, www.thehartfamilywinery.com; Fee: Y; Open: Daily
It's fitting that this is the first winery most people see when driving in from the freeway, because it's a pioneer of Temecula wineries. The wine portfolio is diverse, but the production is very small—only 5,000 cases total per year.

Jim Lilly says: "When I first moved to this town seventeen years ago, Joe Hart was one of my favorite winemakers, and he continues to produce great wines. I'm not going to tell you every single wine is great, but I wouldn't say that in Napa either. Hart has been consistent year after year, and he's one of my top picks."

Leonesse
(WT) 38311 De Portola Road, Temecula, (951) 302-7601, www.leonessecellars.com; Fee: Y; Open: Daily
Though it seems to be cast in the typical Temecula mold—a broad wine portfolio, no particular specialty, and an emphasis on the hospitality program—wine enthusiasts contend that this glossy newcomer has made quality wine production a priority.

Jim Lilly says: "This is the most commercial of the group. However, they are striving to produce quality wines. They do good reds, decent whites, great port. They have an amazing tasting room with a great feel to it and

Southwest Vintners and the Law of the Land

Whenever a region establishes a reputation for anything, suddenly there's an "establishment" to go along with it—the power players, heavy hitters, and dues takers. And then there are the little guys . . .

For the young boutique Temecula wineries that can't afford to buy into the established Temecula Valley Winegrowers Association, there's now Southwest California Vintners (SWCV), which was created to promote the little guys and keep them on the right side of Riverside and San Diego county officials. The SWCV member wineries—which you usually won't see on an official Temecula map—include Longshadow Ranch, Oak Mountain, and Briar Rose, plus many others, most of which only produce a few hundred cases a year. A couple tour companies, in particular Going Grape, will bring guests out to these wineries, and area wine aficionados like Karen Lindstrom (who gave us this heads-up—thanks, Karen!) can recommend the best producers of the bunch. For ongoing membership and event info, check www.swcv.org.

a great view, particularly from the patio. They're very friendly; staff greets you when you walk in the door, and make you feel comfortable.

Robert Renzoni Vineyard
(WT) 37350 De Portola Road, Temecula, (951) 302-VINO (8466), www.robertrenzoni vineyards.com; Open: Daily

Much buzz accompanies the opening of this winery, which is owned by an East Coast importer family. Los Angeles wine aficionados in particular expect great things of the Renzonis, who only planted their own estate grapes in 2006, but are already pouring some of their first releases in their tasting room on De Portola Road.

ATTRACTIONS

Old Town Front Street
(OT) Front Street, Temecula, www.oldtowntemecula.com; Fee: N; Open: Varied; Key: TH,

CHEESE

Aesthetically and spiritually this historic town center falls somewhere between Tombstone and

Main Street, Disneyland (probably a lot closer to Disneyland, if we're being honest). Although there may have been shootouts at the corral more than a century ago, these days it's much more likely to host a sock hop. Nonetheless, the picturesque wooden buildings and chalk-muraled sidewalks have a lot of charm, particularly during festival days or summer weekends, when weekly live concerts and farmers' markets anchor the busy event calendar (check Web site for details).

Lake Perris
(FAR OUT) 17801 Lake Perris Drive, Perris, (951) 940-5600, www.parks.ca.gov; Fee: To camp; Open: Daily; Key: FO
All kinds of warm-weather activities take place at this state recreation area: water skiing, Jet Skiing, boating, biking, horseback trail riding, and fishing. Campsites with or without electrical hookups are available, as are group campsites and horse-friendly ones.

Palomar Observatory
(FAR OUT) 35899 Canfield Road, Palomar Mountain, (760) 742-2119, www.astro.caltech.edu/palomarnew; Fee: N; Open: Daily; Key: FO
This is one of the most important and best-known observatories in the country, located on a mountain peak with an elevation of 5,500 feet. The main attraction is the 200-inch Hale Telescope. This is a CalTech research facility, and as such, is closed to the public at night. It has a small gift shop that's open on the weekends or daily in summer.

RESTAURANTS

Allie's Tapas au Vin
(NT) 41653 Margarita Road, Temecula, (951) 695-8620, www.alliestapas.com; $$; Open: D daily; Key: PU
The warm colors and vibrant flavors of the Mediterranean inspired this California bistro, which is a newcomer with a well-known duo behind it. Terra-cotta walls, high ceilings, and an exhibition kitchen provide a framework for a small plate experience that starts with chutneys and tapenades paired with top-shelf fruit martinis. The cocktail list has a few surprises, including an elderflower/sparkling wine dazzler. Banquette seating occupies one wall, while a twelve-foot

wine wall is built in across from it. Locals discovered the place mere months after its opening—it's a much-needed upscale dining destination in a busy residential neighborhood.

Penfold's Cattle Company
(OT) 42072 Fifth Street, Temecula, (951) 699-2895, www.penfoldscattlecompany.com; $$; Open: D daily; Key: DS
Keep an eye on this unassuming gourmet meatery, for it may very well morph into the gourmet room you were never expecting. A New York managing partner/chef/level 2 sommelier brings all kinds of fine dining inspirations to bear in this classic third-floor space in Old Town Temecula. Founded by local entrepreneur Ladd Penfold, the restaurant specializes in the very best cuts of prime Angus beef. That much will stay the same; and it's likely that the booth seating, exposed-beam ceiling, and etched-glass windows will continue to define the architecture.

ENTERTAINMENT AND NIGHTLIFE

Killarney's Irish Pub & Grill
(NT) 32475 State Highway 79 South G101, Temecula, (951) 302-8338, www.killarneysirishpubandgrill.com; $; Open: L and D, OWL, Daily; Key: CHEESE, PU
What better to balance out a day of Syrah and Chardonnay than a night at the pub? Irish stout, Irish cheer, and heavy-as-a-stone Irish food bring good feelings to the fore—unless you overindulge. The kitchen specializes in two things: deep-fried (shrimp, calamari, chicken strips, fish) and regular-fried (burgers, flatiron steak). Service is friendly, the crowd enthusiastic, and even though some of the events are a little, ahem, not super-highbrow (i.e., the Baby Dollz Lingerie–sponsored Ladies' Night), they're unpretentious and therefore fun.

SHOPPING

Temecula Valley Wine Shop
(NT) 29073 Overland Drive, Temecula, (877) 4TV-WINE (9463), www.tvwineco.com; Open: Daily, PM Thu-Sat
The newer, bigger, better incarnation of a longtime Temecula wine retailer, this shop/wine bar carries wines from about twelve different countries worldwide. Nothing hits the shelves unless owner Jim Lilly tastes it first. However, he doesn't try to talk his customers into buying based on his picks. "We all have personal tastes and preferences. I spend a lot of time talking to my customers and finding out what they like, plus a significant amount of time taking them through tastings, educating them about wine," Lilly says.

Not surprisingly, the majority of the shop's business is repeat. Not only do they buy retail, but they sample extensively from the bar's rotating selection of twenty-five wines by the glass. The focus goes more on fun in the evenings, with live entertainment three nights weekly. The monthly wine club event features a different world wine region every time—Lilly claims you could be a member for years and never see the same wine twice. There are themed tastings every Saturday evening and wine classes every other week. Centrally located near the mall in the residential part of Temecula.

ACCOMMODATIONS

Temecula Creek Inn
(NT) 44501 Rainbow Canyon Road, Temecula, (951) 694-1000; $$; Key: DS
A winding driveway takes you past golf fairways and low-rise bungalows before ending up at a surprisingly cozy little lobby snuggled between flower beds and willow trees. Low-rise buildings house the spacious guest rooms, which have recently been revamped with plasma TVs, iPods, and other modern accoutrements. A central plaza underlines this hotel's large-group capabilities: With a beautiful rock waterfall and other features, it's obviously intended to host outdoor cocktail parties

and other corporate mixers. Wall-to-wall windows in the restaurant afford views of the course and the patio pond. The gem of the place, though, is the Stonehouse, a once-upon-a-time mining quarters dating back to the 1800s. This fully restored little nook hosts countless weddings and other occasions, with overflow diverted to the back by the resourceful staff.

Loma Vista B&B
(WT) 33340 La Serena Way, Temecula, (877) 676-7047, (951) 676-7047, www.lomavistabb.com; $
Pretty, friendly, and with only ten rooms, this is the quintessential wine country B&B. The outdoor gardens are ideal for early morning breakfast. Rooms are somewhat themed, with names to match the wine motif. Wilson Creek almond champagne is served complimentary.

Wine and . . .

When we think of Temecula, we think of . . . jazz, bluegrass, golf, balloons, street festivals, and wine. That's right: Wine shares the spotlight every time. Old Town event planners are eager to incorporate wine into the many festivals on the calendar, while winery owners prove equally eager to add live entertainment to their offerings. In other regions an afternoon concert at a winery is a rare treat; here it happens most days of the week in summer and during harvest. Approximately half of Temecula's wineries have on-site restaurants, and a few have spas or hotels on their property as well.

WINERIES

Thornton
(WT) 32575 Rancho California Road, Temecula, (951) 699-0099; Fee: Y; Open: Daily; Key: DS
This is probably the loveliest of the area wineries. The entry path leads past a charming kitchen garden, which each Thornton chef has contributed to over the years. The expansive courtyard boasts sweeping vineyard views, while the multilevel architecture perfectly lends itself to live concerts and large events. Even when it's empty, the sun-drenched area feels inviting. Thornton was the first winery to do live concerts, and it's really got the organization down pat, from the elevated VIP seating to the casual outdoor grills serving inexpensive fare for general-admission guests. The venue also holds other interesting events, including blending parties and wine and herb tastings. As far as wine goes, it's most famous for its sparkling wine, but it also releases a well-regarded estate Syrah.

Wine, Charity, and Celebration

Jennifer and Bill Wilson, Wilson Creek Winery

Every year that Wilson Creek Winery has been eligible for the Business of the Year Award, it has won—and its owners have high hopes for a repeat victory next time around. Just about every big event the winery hosts, including its annual summer Sunset Jazz in the Vines series, is a fund-raiser for a local cause.

"We work with all kinds of local charities," says Jennifer Wilson, who keeps an open-door policy toward local organizations. "Typically Friday is our evening for charity events."

In summer that switches over to Saturday for Jazz in the Vines, a four-concert series that benefits children with autism. This series is among Temecula's more popular winery events, incorporating alfresco dining and copious quantities of signature almond champagne.

"It's upbeat and lively; everyone's dancing and there's a good crowd. We drink wine and champagne, and we have fun," says Jennifer. The series is definitely her pet project; it was born of a love of jazz. "My husband and I have gone to many jazz concerts and jazz cruises. We got to know a lot of jazz musicians, and they

(continued)

Hot air balloon tours depart from Wilson Creek.

became our friends. Wine and jazz go perfectly, and having the venue here, we wanted to use it," she explains.

For all the other events, she lets the charity organization dictate the entertainment program. The YMCA throws a formal ball, Hospice of the Valley selected the popular Day of Wine & Chocolate, and Rotary International recently switched its live entertainment from a philharmonic orchestra to Superdiamond (the Neil Diamond cover band extraordinaire).

Whether for charity or not, local events are always popular with city dwellers. "It's unique and special for them. They can have a wonderful vineyard experience, with music and dining under the stars, and then they can go home," says Bill Wilson. His favorite event, the Barrel Tasting, happens twice yearly, and more than twenty local wineries participate.

"It's like a progressive dinner . . . only it's an entire weekend based around wine, food, and all the winemakers getting together." And yes, it benefits the local wine association. In wine country there's no better cause than that.

Callaway
(WT) 32720 Rancho California Road, Temecula, (800) 472-2377, (951) 676-4001, www.callawaywinery.com; Fee: Y; Open: Daily; Key: TH, DS
One of the oldest and most famous wineries in the region, this place is known for its sparkling wines and its many weddings and private events. Guests enter through the wine shop/gourmet food shop. The tasting room is stand-up, with floor-to-ceiling vineyard views. A large grassy lawn outside affords similar views. The barrel room—which is the largest in town—often hosts larger groups. In keeping with the Temecula way, this winery just opened an on-site Cal-Med restaurant.

Wilson Creek
(WT) 35960 Rancho California Road, Temecula, (951) 699-9463, www.wilsoncreekwinery.com; Fee: Y; Open: Daily; Key: DS
Almond sparkling wine and "Decadencia" chocolate port in a Dutch chocolate cup are the signatures, but Wilson Creek does a wide range of wines—and that's just to start. Grape Escape Balloon Adventure launches here almost every morning year-round (weather permitting). The Creekside Grill opened in the summer of 2008, as did a 2000-person-capacity performance space.

Must-Try Temecula Pairings

Behold a creative list of recommended Temecula wine-and-experience pairings—some you may have seen before and some are completely unique to the region.

Wine and Concerts: It started with jazz and classical. When that proved successful, winery owners experimented with bringing in country, rock, and even indie.
Where: Thornton, Wilson Creek, Wiens, Churon

Wine and Spas: Perhaps it's not strictly health-conscious in the greenie granola sense, but this relatively new concept offers the ultimate in relaxation by some people's standards.
Where: South Coast Wine Resort

Wine and Helicopters: Three Temecula properties have heliports—impressive, considering its tiny size.
Where: South Coast Wine Resort, Thornton, the Castle

Wine and Balloons: Temecula's weather is perfectly suited to year-round hot air ballooning. The Temecula Valley Balloon & Wine Fest is one of the biggest events of the year.
Where: Lake Skinner

Wine & "Rods": You can look, but you can't drive. The annual Rod Run brings hundreds of classic cars and tens of thousands of fans to Old Town twice a year.
Where: Old Town Temecula

Wine and Film: In addition to an annual film festival, the local film commission sponsors a youth film camp and "sneak preview nights," where locals give their candid feedback on potential selections.
Where: Tower Plaza, Pechanga

Wine and the Bard: Shakespeare would definitely approve of this new but promising summertime pairing, which thus far has not found a permanent winery home.
Where: Leonesse

Wine and Condos: No one's done it yet, but a few places are thinking about building condos on winery grounds.
Where: Mount Palomar

There's always something on the calendar, whether it be a cigar dinner, a bridal show, or a holiday brunch. In spite of all that, the venue counts weddings as its real niche. The setting is perfect for romance: acres of vineyards, beautiful gardens, a gazebo, and the namesake creek.

ATTRACTIONS

Pechanga Resort & Casino
(NT) 45000 Pechanga Parkway, Temecula, (888) PECHANGA (732-2642), www.pechanga.com; $$; Open: Daily extended hours; Key: TH, LN
This big, busy Native American-operated casino has more than slots and blackjack to recommend it—namely, an amazingly diverse high-end wine list with about 970 labels on it. Self-contained resort property with restaurants, entertainment, and a hotel.

Temeku Hills
(WT) 41687 Temeku Drive, Temecula, (951) 694-9998, www.temekuhills.com; Fee: Y; Open: Daily, weather permitting; Key: RR
While it's not connected to any winery, the location just off Rancho California makes this Ted Robinson-designed course ideal for a morning tee time.

RESTAURANTS

Smokehouse Restaurant
(WT) 35053 Rancho California Road (at Ponte Family Estate), Temecula, (877) 314-9463, (951) 694-8855, www.pontewinery.com; $$; Open: L daily, B Sun; Key: SCENE, DS, RR (weekends)
The fare and social scene are equally big draws at Ponte's on-site restaurant, which serves up California cuisine, innovative pizzas, and grilled meats. The service gets consistently high marks. Reservations recommended on weekends. The brunch spot in town.

John Kelliher says: "Hip, up-to-date—a fan favorite."

Café Champagne
(WT) 32575 Rancho California Road, Temecula, (951) 699-0099, www.thorntonwine.com; $$$; Open: L and D daily; Key: DS
The restaurant at Thornton has as much of a reputation as the namesake bubbly itself. The seasonal, contemporary menu has French flair and many California ingredients. It's great for special occasions.

John Kelliher says: "Very high end and elegant. A birthday and anniversary tradition."

Cheese and Wine, Anytime

Barrie Lynn, Cheese Impresario

Cheese is the new chocolate—only better, 'cause it's a real food instead of a dessert. You can eat it all day if you want. Barrie Lynn, the Cheese Impresario, takes us through a day of decadent wine and cheese pairings and then recommends her fave places to buy.

10 a.m. Bubbly pairs with anything. And it's fun to have a soft, mushy cheese in the morning. Perhaps a beautiful Brie d' Maux AOC from France, with a French baguette and a little fruit.

Noon Sauvignon Blanc is great for daytime drinking. The classic *terroir* pairing is a Sauv Blanc and a fresh goat cheese from the Loire Valley. Drizzle it with honey and a little lemon zest, or alternatively, with olive oil and some fresh pepper.

2 p.m. Pinot Noir. It depends on the style of Pinot, but I love Gruyère with most of them. I've served it with duck sausage and pâtes. Garnish with cornichons for a fun little luncheon.

5 p.m. Merlot is beyond delicious with a beautiful Gouda—but not a superaged one. I would recommend the vintage Van Gogh.

7:30 p.m. Syrah. With the jamminess of the wine, I love a big aged cheddar. It's one of those classic sweet-savory combinations. Try to get an older cheddar.

9 p.m. Sangiovese. The classic pairing is a Parmigiano Reggiano. Or there are some great American ones like the SarVecchio Parmesan. It's fabulously nutty and sweet, but it's very parmesan-y, with flavor crystals.

11 p.m. Port. Enjoy a beautiful bleu cheese with one of the local ports, out on the patio looking at the stars, and then go to sleep like a baby.

ACCOMMODATIONS

South Coast Winery Resort & Spa
(WT) 34843 Rancho California Road, Temecula, (951) 587-9463, www.wineresort.com; $$$; Key: CHEESE, SCENE, TH, PU, DS

It's a toss-up where this property should be categorized, because it offers so many experiences. It's a resort, with seventy-six guest villas situated on the vineyards, so close that guests can slide open their French doors and walk right up to the vines. It's a winery, with a tremendously busy tasting room that doubles as a hangout spot for wine club members and their friends. It has a restaurant and a separate bar. And perhaps most distinctively, it has its own full-service Grape Seed Spa. With a saltwater pool, eleven treatment rooms, water massage, and specialty classes like the

signature Vino Vinyasa, the spa acts like a magnet for the bub-and-scrub crowd. And, in a move that other spas might disapprove of, but that lots of clientele absolutely love, each treatment comes with a complimentary bottle of wine. At sunset the Grape Seed's second-story balcony is filled with mellow, spa-glowing women sipping and chattering away in their bathrobes and slippers.

The Castle

(WT) 35925 Rancho California Road, Temecula, (951) 699-3940, www.thecastlebandb.com; $$; Key: VEG, CHEESE

One man's whimsy is another's wine country weekend. This property was originally conceived by a wealthy local businessman who'd always wanted to own a castle. Once he'd constructed it and lived the dream for a few years, he and his wife got tired of rattling around the ten-bedroom structure like two lonely peas in an oversize pod, and let his sisters turn it into an inn. The change took place in phases, with no accompanying fanfare, so few people are aware that a castle awaits them in Temecula.

Visually the place is a cross between a McMansion and a movie set: There's a heliport in the driveway, a vast hand-painted Italian mural on one wall, and a dining room table that seats twenty-four. The rooms are individually decorated—quite beautifully and with excellent attention to detail. There's the Venetian, with masks and Carnival art and a bronze gilt four-poster; the Celtic, with tartan fabrics and an oak armoire; and the Medieval (aka the "naughty room"), featuring leather appointments, stained glass, and a whip on the wall. The innkeeper is a wine buff and one of the proprietresses a chef, which gives the place some unexpected foodie cache.

Inn at Churon Winery

(WT) 33233 Rancho California Road, Temecula, (951) 694-9070, www.innatchuronwinery.com; $; Key: DS

Lots of buzz about this Provençal-inspired boutique winery hotel. The vineyard setting is picturesque, and the service is friendly and down-to-earth.

TOUR PROVIDERS

The Grapeline
(ALL) 27464 Commerce Center Drive, #f209, (888) 894-6379, www.gogrape.com; Fee: Y; Open: Daily; Key: TH
This company organizes public and customized private tours (ten passengers minimum). The typical schedule includes four winery visits, the first of which incorporates a full behind-the-scenes tour. Lunch is usually a picnic at the second. Private passengers can change this up however they want. Passengers on a public tour can't make special itinerary requests, but they can peel off at the end for a vineyard dinner or a private chat with a winemaker.

It's worth noting that, although it operates in four regions, this company is actually based in Temecula—and the owners know absolutely everything that's going on in the area. "We get regular updates from all the wineries. If they have a specific event they'll call us, because they know we'll pass the info along to our guests," says owner John Kelliher.

Going Grape
(WT) Temecula, (951) 852-1923, www.goinggrape.com; Fee: Y; Open: Daily by appt.
A small group tour provider, owned and operated by a woman who knows the local wine business well and makes a point of visiting new boutique wineries, particularly Southwest Vintners members, in addition to more-established tasting rooms.

SUGGESTED TWO-DAY ITINERARIES

{UN-GEEKIFIED, DE-MYSTIFED, KICK-BACK}

DAY ONE

From Temecula

Morning: Taste at Hart and Palumbo (call first to make sure they're open).

Afternoon: Have lunch at Leonesse restaurant, followed by tasting.

Mid-afternoon: Stop by Temecula Valley Wine Shop for a flight or a glass.

Evening: Have dinner at Penfold's.

DAY TWO

From Temecula

Morning: Taste at Renzoni and other South Coast–affiliated wineries.

Afternoon: Cool off at Lake Perris.

Evening: Have dinner at Allie's Tapas.

Late evening: Have drinks at Killarney's.

{WINE AND . . .}

DAY ONE

From Temecula

Morning: Take a balloon ride at Wilson Creek, followed by tasting.

Afternoon: Taste at Thornton, with food pairings.

Mid-afternoon: Spa treatment at South Coast.

Late afternoon: Drink a complimentary bottle of wine on the patio of South Coast spa. Have appetizers or dinner at the on-site restaurant.

DAY TWO

From Temecula

Morning: Have breakfast and tasting at Churon.

Afternoon: Have lunch at Smokehouse, followed by tasting at Ponte.

Late afternoon: Pechanga for gambling.

Evening: Have dinner at Pechanga.

CALENDAR OF EVENTS

JANUARY AND OCTOBER

- Barrel Tastings

JUNE

- Temecula Valley Balloon and Wine Festival

  www.tvbwf.com

SEPTEMBER

- Day of Wine and Chocolate
- Temecula Valley Food and Wine Classic

RESOURCES

www.temeculawines.org

PHOTO CREDITS

Photos on pages v, xii, xvi, 2, 5, 10, 14, 24, 32, 33, 36, 48, 54, 61, 67, 73, 74, 82, 83, 94, 100, 101, 102, 113, 118, 121, 123, 126, 128, 132, 136, 138, 142, 143, 146, 156, 159, 163, 167, 169, 170, 181, 185, 186, 188, 192, 194, 203, 204, 212, 215, 218, 220, 225, 228, 237, 247, 252, 253, 254, 260, 261, 262, 268 © Shutterstock

Page 3: Calistoga Chamber of Commerce

Page 9: Courtesy of Quintessa

Page 26: Castello di Amorosa, Jim Sullivan

Page 29: Indian Springs Resort, Calistoga, CA

Page 58: Jo Diaz, Diaz Communications

Page 64: J Vineyards & Winery

Page 76: Gloria Ferrer Caves and Vineyards

Page 81: Dan Ham Photography

Page 85: Jo Diaz, Diaz Communications

Page 87: Gundlach Bundschu Winery Caves, Photo by Rocco Ceselin

Page 106: Goldeneye Winery, Duckhorn Wine Company

Page 114: Sarah Cohn Bennett, co-owner of Navarro Vineyards with Baby Doll sheep; Photo by Terrence McCarthy.

Page 130: Courtesy of Concannon

Page 148: Courtesy of Ironstone Vineyards

Page 173: Courtesy of the Highlands Inn Pacific Edge

Page 198: Brittany App, courtesy of Paso Robles Wine Country Alliance

Page 205: Front View of Lone Madrone Tasting Room, Paso Robles, CA. Courtesy of Lone Madrone

Page 222: Jaffurs Wine Cellars

Page 234: Courtesy of G. DIAMOND

Page 245: Courtesy of Cold Spring Tavern

Page 263: Photograph supplied courtesy of Wilson Creek Winery & Vineyards.

INDEX

ABOUT THE AUTHOR

Lena Katz is the California, Hawaii, and Mexico travel blogger for Orbitz; the creator of the Playboy Scout; and founding editor of *LAX Magazine,* the official in-terminal publication of Los Angeles International Airport. She has been quoted as a travel expert by the *Wall Street Journal* and *Entertainment Tonight,* and regularly contributes to *Brides,* MSNBC, AOL, and the *Los Angeles Times*. She lives in Los Angeles, California.